Polling and the Public

Polling and the Public

What Every Citizen Should Know

Eighth Edition

Herbert Asher
The Ohio State University

CQ PRESS

A Division of SAGE
Washington, D.C.

CQ Press
2300 N Street, NW, Suite 800
Washington, DC 20037

Phone: 202-729-1900; toll-free, 1-866-4CQ-PRESS (1-866-427-7737)

Web: www.cqpress.com

Cover design: Anne C. Kerns, Anne Likes Red, Inc.
Composition: C&M Digitals (P) Ltd.

⊛ The paper used in this publication exceeds the requirements of the American National Standard for Information Sciences—Permanence of Paper for Printed Library Materials, ANSI Z39.48-1992.

Printed and bound in the United States of America

18   17   16   15   3   4   5   6

Library of Congress Cataloging-in-Publication Data

Asher, Herbert.
    Polling and the public: what every citizen should know / Herbert Asher. — 8th ed.
       p. cm.
    Includes bibliographical references and index.
    ISBN 978-1-60426-606-1 (alk. paper)
    1. Public opinion polls. 2. Public opinion—United States. I. Title.

HM1236.A75 2012
303.3'80973—dc22

2010052870

To the memory of my parents,
Joseph and Betty Asher

Contents

Preface

Since the last edition of this book was published, the prominence and pervasiveness of public opinion polling in the United States and throughout the world have continued to grow. Americans have been routinely queried about their views on the war in Afghanistan, the war against terrorism, the state of the American economy, health care reform, and the performance of the president. In response to unfolding events, other issues—gun control, offshore drilling, global warming, immigration, gay marriage, and many others—also became popular topics for public opinion polling.

Not only could Americans learn from the polls what their fellow citizens thought about various topics, but they could also learn what citizens of other nations thought about the United States, American culture, and the policies of the American government. For example, Americans learned that the citizenry of many Middle East nations strongly disapproved of aspects of American foreign policy. Indeed, the democratization of many previously authoritarian nations and the internationalization of public opinion polling have meant that people all over the world can now express their views through polls and also learn what people in other nations are thinking.

In the past decade polling has faced new technical and methodological challenges. Traditional telephone polling has become more difficult with the increased reliance on cell phones, the decrease in landline usage, and the wider use of call-screening devices. The huge growth in Internet use has resulted in a dramatic increase in Web surveys, some done with care and sensitivity to good polling standards, and others simply contemporary versions of the pseudopolls often conducted by news media and other organizations, in which respondents select themselves to participate. Thus, we are witnessing major developments in polling with respect to the substantive topics amenable to polling, the geographical reach of the polling enterprise, and the methodological challenges facing pollsters.

Despite their prominence, polls are still not well understood by many Americans. My central objective when I first wrote this book was to help readers become wiser consumers of public opinion polls. In preparing this eighth edition, I still have that same objective. The prevalence of public opinion polls and their frequent misuse make it imperative that citizens be able to evaluate critically the assertions that people, organizations, and governments make on the basis of polls. Candidates for public office, office-holders, and many different public, private, and nonprofit groups sponsor public opinion surveys to advance their own objectives. As polling data become more central to political and civic discourse, it is more important that citizens understand the factors that can influence poll results.

As I have tried to help readers become better consumers of polls, I have also had to establish boundaries and limits for this book. Most of my focus is on consumers of polls on public issues; I give scant attention to research that focuses on consumer preferences in the marketplace. I have also tended to use as major sources the academic journals and books that focus on public opinion and devote little attention to the huge volume of publications on market research. Finally, in covering various topics and controversies, I often provide only a small sampling of the relevant literature and research, lest this book become overly detailed, technical, inaccessible, and incredibly long.

Chapter 1 explains the types of polls, their importance, and Americans' mixed attitudes toward public opinion research. Chapters 2 through 5 address the methodological aspects of polling, such as nonattitude assessment; the wording and order of questions; sampling techniques; and interviewing procedures. These topics are treated in a nontechnical fashion with numerous examples that illustrate the major points. Chapters 6 through 8 are more analytical and more substantive, focusing on how the news media cover polls, the uses of polls in campaigns and elections, and the interpretation of polls. The last chapter considers the role of polls in a democratic polity. At the end of each chapter is a set of exercises designed to help the reader become a more skillful judge of public opinion polls.

This book should be readily understandable to a diverse audience—college students taking courses in politics, public opinion, communications, and journalism, as well as practitioners in the fields of journalism and campaign management. In addition, the general public should find it a helpful guide to evaluating the methods and merits of public opinion polls. As with earlier editions, no statistical expertise is assumed or required.

Two Ohio State University graduate students, Christopher Devine and Nicholas Felts, were superb research assistants in the preparation of this eighth edition. And I am very grateful to the reviewers who offered outstanding suggestions for this revision: David F. Damore (University of

Nevada, Las Vegas), Jonathan Morris (East Carolina University), Monica Schneider (Miami University), and Carole J. Wilson (Southern Methodist University). The staff of CQ Press once again did a fine job of editing the manuscript and getting the book into print in a timely fashion. In particular, I would like to acknowledge the contributions of Charisse Kiino, Nancy Loh, and Laura Stewart. I also express my deep appreciation to the various polling organizations and newspapers that are so generous in sharing their surveys with the broader public. They provided many of the substantive examples I used here. In particular, the CBS News/*New York Times* polls, the ABC News/*Washington Post* surveys, the Gallup Organization, the Program on International Policy Attitudes (PIPA) at the University of Maryland, and the Pew Research Center for the People and the Press have been invaluable resources in the preparation of this edition. Finally, organizations such as the American Association for Public Opinion Research (AAPOR) and the National Council on Public Polls (NCPP) have played a key role in enhancing the integrity and quality of public opinion polling.

—Herb Asher

1 Polling and the Public

Americans today are inundated with the results of public opinion polls sponsored by the news media, by political campaigns, and by many public, private, and nonprofit organizations. Some of the polling is on matters of immediate national importance, such as the wars in Iraq and Afghanistan, the performance of the American economy, health care reform, immigration, or the war on terror. But polls are conducted on almost any conceivable topic, be it a genuine public policy issue such as abortion, education reform, deficit spending, the environment, or offshore drilling for oil or something more frivolous such as the guilt or innocence of a celebrity accused of a crime or which alcoholic beverage is the preferred choice of Americans or who should win American Idol. As a result, Americans are learning more and more about the attitudes of their fellow citizens.

Public opinion polling has increasingly become an international phenomenon because of the demise of totalitarian regimes in many parts of the world and because of the widespread dissemination of polling methods and techniques and the rise of polling organizations throughout the world. Whereas polling was once largely concentrated in North America and Europe, today in many nations in Latin America, the Middle East, Asia, and Africa, polling has become almost routine. These international polls enable Americans to learn about the attitudes of people in other nations, including what they think about American popular culture and foreign policy. In 2002 and 2003, during the lead-up to the war in Iraq, many Americans were surprised by the widespread hostility that polls in other countries revealed and by street demonstrations by citizens of traditional allies such as Germany and France against the proposed U.S. action. Polls conducted in Lebanon in 2006 showed that huge majorities of Lebanese citizens did not believe that the United States was playing the role of an honest mediator in the conflict between Hezbollah and Israel. In 2010, results from the

Pew Global Attitudes Project showed that President Obama was more popular in many other nations than he was in the United States. The Pew data also showed that in twenty nations surveyed in 2007 and 2010, favorable views of the United States rose substantially and that confidence in the American president rose dramatically, although in a subset of nations with whom the United States had major foreign policy challenges and differences, attitudes toward the United States remained wary and skeptical (Stokes 2009). The internationalization of polling is also evidenced by the growing use of polls (and American-style campaign techniques in general) in national elections throughout the world. Not only have preelection polls become commonplace, but so also has the use of exit polls in areas as disparate as Palestine, Mexico, and Russia.

It is fascinating to learn about the opinions of people in other countries, but it may be difficult at times to evaluate the quality of the polling done in those nations, particularly those without a tradition of public opinion research conducted by reputable survey research organizations. Moreover, American media reports of international polls often focus much more on the substantive results and much less on the methodological and technical aspects of the research. In 2003, the National Council on Public Polls (NCPP) issued a cautionary statement urging that reporting on international polls give special attention to how they were conducted. NCPP observed a number of instances in which claims were made that a poll was representative of an entire country when, in fact, the sample might have been selected from only a few parts of the country or from only a few segments of its citizenry. Although our focus in this book will be mainly on polling in the United States, many of the lessons of the book will apply to evaluating international polls.

In the United States, polls are increasingly being used not only to inform but also to convince and even manipulate Americans in ways advantageous to the polls' sponsors. Public opinion polls have become integral to political debates and arguments, with all sides trying to advance their cases by citing supportive poll results. The aim of this book is to help citizens become more astute judges of polls, so that they will not be misled by assertions made on the basis of polling data. I will accomplish this objective by explaining in nontechnical language the factors that can affect poll results—such as question wording, sampling techniques, and interviewing procedures—and by critiquing various types and uses of polls.

The Importance of Polls

Why should citizens become more astute consumers of polls? One reason is simply to avoid being manipulated by those who use polls inappropriately to promote their own ends. Other reasons are more positive. Some people make major economic and career decisions on the basis of public opinion polling. For example, the businessperson who commissions a survey on customer preferences or the television station manager who underwrites a survey on audience demographics will use the information obtained to make important business decisions. Potential candidates for public office may commission a poll to assess their electoral prospects before deciding whether to run. Governmental entities such as school boards and library boards that receive funding from tax levies voted on by the electorate will often conduct polls prior to placing a tax issue on the ballot. In these cases a commercial polling organization is likely to conduct the polling. But the more knowledgeable the businessperson, the would-be candidate, and the board member are about polls, the better able they are to communicate their objectives and requirements to the survey organization and to apply the results of the survey to their own decision making.

Polls also are important for the average citizen. Through the substantial coverage the news media give to polls, citizens can compare their own beliefs with their compatriots'. As citizens use the polls in this manner, they need to be aware of the factors that affect the poll results so that they do not accept or reject them too quickly or uncritically.

Polling plays an integral role in political events at the national, state, and local levels. In any major event or decision, poll results are sure to be a part of the news media's coverage and the decision makers' deliberations. How should an international crisis, such as North Korea's or Iran's nuclear threat, be resolved? How should the United States respond to events in Afghanistan or the Middle East or the Gulf of Mexico? Should a Supreme Court nominee be confirmed by the Senate? What is the best location for a new recreational center in the community? Should state taxes be raised? Because polls may influence how politicians respond to such public issues, citizens need to understand the essentials of public opinion polling.

Finally, public opinion polls are playing an ever-larger role in political discourse in the United States because of the improved technology of polling, the introduction of courses in polling methodology in journalism curricula, the widespread assumption (challenged by Benjamin Ginsberg—see chapter 9) that polls are the best way to measure public opinion, and the belief that public opinion polls are instruments of democracy because they allow everyone's views to be represented. More worrisome is the huge growth in the use of pseudopolls—nonscientific and often biased polls that private and public groups conduct through a variety of mechanisms, including the print and electronic media and the Internet, and that are often confused with legitimate public opinion polling. All of these factors ensure that even greater reliance on the polls will characterize future political debate. To participate in that debate in an informed and analytical fashion, Americans will have to come to grips with public opinion polls—a valuable source of information to citizens and leaders alike.

The Pervasiveness of Polls

That public opinion polling is a growth industry in the United States is undeniable. The polls most familiar to Americans are those conducted for and reported by the major communications media. For example, major television networks often sponsor polls in collaboration with a print news organization: CBS News with the *New York Times,* ABC News with the *Washington Post,* and NBC News with the *Wall Street Journal.* Other collaborations exist between print media and electronic media with particular polling organizations: Fox News and Opinion Dynamics, *USA Today* and the Gallup Organization, and CNN and Opinion Research Corporation. These media-sponsored polls often become an integral part of the print or electronic news story that the media outlet produces. Likewise, the major newsmagazines often incorporate polling information in their news stories. An examination of the stories featured on the covers of the three leading U.S. newsmagazines—*Time, Newsweek,* and *U.S. News and World Report*—between 1995 and mid-2003 reveals that about 30 percent of them cited public opinion polls. Other stories also used polling data. Readers of these magazines, then, will be more astute judges of the reporting if they are knowledgeable about the strengths and weaknesses of public opinion polls.

The proliferation of polls also is evident in newspaper and television news coverage. Typically the polls the stories cite have surveyed citizens about their views on political issues, candidates, and incumbents (especially the president); their preferences about possible courses of government action; their general attitudes toward politics and the political process; and countless other political and nonpolitical matters. More specifically, polls in 2010 have regularly queried Americans about such topics as immigration, health care reform, the economy, the federal budget deficit, terrorism, wars, the Gulf of Mexico disaster, financial institution regulation, the performance of the president and the Congress, and the Tea Party movement.

Polling is conducted on nonpolitical topics, some of them frivolous, as well as on issues of national importance. Indeed, it seems that almost any topic can show up in public opinion polling. For example, the January 31, 2000, issue of *U.S. News and World Report* featured a story on "Hell" that described a public opinion poll in which a sample of Americans were asked whether there was a Hell (64 percent said yes) and what they thought it was like. As the final episode of the television show *Cheers* neared in

1993, the *Times Mirror* Center for the People and the Press queried Americans about such weighty topics as whether Sam should have stayed single, married Diane, or married Rebecca. That survey also asked Americans who their favorite *Cheers* character was and which character they would like to see continue in his or her own series (Mills 1993). In 2006, as various Hollywood superstars such as Jennifer Aniston, George Clooney, Tom Cruise, Angelina Jolie, and Brad Pitt were prominent in the news for both professional and personal reasons, a Gallup Poll of a representative sample of Americans found that only Tom Cruise had a net unfavorable rating and indeed had lost substantial popularity in the previous year. Clearly, polling is everywhere.

The prominent national polls are complemented by visible and reputable state and local polls that focus on state and local matters as well as national affairs. For example, the New York *Daily News* and the television program *Eyewitness News* (produced by the ABC affiliate in New York City) have polled people in the city over the years on their views of the New York police, New York mayors, the likelihood of the Yankees and Mets baseball teams' making the World Series, and other matters of local concern. Likewise, the *New York Times,* in conjunction with WCBS-TV, has conducted extensive studies of race relations in New York City. Many states have first-rate polling organizations, often affiliated with a university or a major news organization. For example, the Eagleton Institute at Rutgers University, working with the *Newark Star-Ledger,* surveys New Jersey residents about their state government and about New Jersey as a place to live. Similarly, the Ohio Poll from the University of Cincinnati regularly surveys Ohioans about their views on elections and political matters. Publications such as *Public Opinion Quarterly* have provided summaries of state and local (as well as national) poll results.

The polls I have mentioned thus far are the most prominent and probably the most credible to the American public. Their prominence stems from the often substantial media coverage their results receive; their credibility derives from the public's perception that they are conducted scientifically and that the news organizations and other entities that sponsor them are themselves legitimate and objective. The most critical factor in making these polls scientific (and thus valid) is a carefully selected sample of respondents; after all, no polling organization can interview the entire adult American population of more than 220 million. From such a sample, the public and the media can generalize (within certain limits to be discussed later) to the larger population from which the sample was drawn. In later chapters I will detail what makes for a "good" sample. For now, two observations are appropriate. First, reputable public opinion polling also requires valid measurement strategies, effective data collection techniques, and skillful analysis of the collected data. Second, there may be circumstances in which useful conclusions can be reached even when the selected sample does not meet all the characteristics of being scientific (see the discussion of Internet polling in chapter 5).

Commissioned Polls

Although polls by the big news organizations seem the most prominent, they are only a tiny fraction of the public opinion polling done in the United States. Many other organizations commission polls for purposes other than informing citizens. For example, companies may hire a polling firm to gauge the public response to their products, and academic investigators may use surveys in their research. The results of those polls may not attract much public notice, but they still can affect the lives of citizens. An excellent example of a commissioned poll was the one that the Internal Revenue Service (IRS) paid for in 1984 to study the problem of tax cheating. Among the items in the survey were these statements, with which the respondent was supposed to agree or disagree:

Q: It's not so wrong to hold back a little bit on taxes since the government spends too much anyway.
Q: The present tax system benefits the rich and is unfair to the ordinary working man or woman.
Q: Since a lot of rich people pay no taxes at all, if someone like me underpays a little, it's no big deal (Sussman 1984).

Of the survey respondents, 19 percent admitted cheating on their returns; young, upwardly mobile professionals were the most likely to cheat. The IRS study also investigated ways to reduce cheating and found that Americans strongly rejected the use of paid informants to catch cheaters (Sussman 1985b). Although the honesty of tax cheaters' responses to questions about tax cheating is questionable, the IRS probably gained some useful insights into the magnitude of the cheating problem and the feasibility of alternative solutions.

The IRS study is typical of thousands that public and private bodies commission to address specific concerns. Indeed, the federal government sponsors many surveys measuring a wide variety of attitudes and behaviors. Often these surveys are longitudinal; that is, they are repeated over time, which allows the government to observe trends and changes. Some of the surveys are based on national samples, others on specialized samples that are more appropriate to the research questions being addressed. Government-sponsored surveys might study the purchasing practices of Americans, or assess the frequency of different types of high-risk sexual behavior, or monitor the use of illegal drugs, or follow the employment history of citizens. Commissioned surveys of this type, whether sponsored by the government or by private or nonprofit entities, are likely to be high-quality enterprises mainly because the sponsors have a genuine need for accurate information to address some organizational goal or problem. To that end they employ a reputable firm to design and conduct the survey and perhaps to analyze the data and interpret the results.

One complaint that Americans often express about the polls is the fact they have not been selected to participate in a survey. But as more and more businesses, organizations, and governmental agencies have become concerned with customer satisfaction and quality control, the opportunities to take part in a poll have grown dramatically. For example, the United States Postal Service mails out customer satisfaction surveys to business customers. The recipient of the survey can either fill out the hard copy version of the survey and mail it back or complete the survey on the Web. The Postal Service goes further in soliciting customers' opinions about the performance of the USPS. When I made a purchase at a branch post office in July 2010, I was given a receipt that at the bottom read:

HELP US SERVE YOU BETTER

Go to: https://postalexperience.com/Pos

TELL US ABOUT YOUR RECENT

POSTAL EXPERIENCE

YOUR OPINION COUNTS

After a visit to the Ohio State University Medical Center, I received a patient satisfaction survey. What has been more intriguing is the number of businesses that on the cash register receipt invite me to participate in a survey. For example, Giant Eagle supermarket wrote:

YOUR OPINION COUNTS!

Complete a survey at gianteaglesurvey.com

Macy's department store wrote:

Questions or Comments?

Please contact us at www.macys.com/tellus

One important feature of all these examples is that the percentage of people who reply and the representativeness of those who do reply may not be particularly important, in contrast with polls attempting to gauge American public opinion on key issues or trying to predict election outcomes. On these customer satisfaction surveys, it may be more helpful to the organization to hear mainly from disgruntled customers and therefore gain valuable insight how to improve service delivery. It may be the case that response rates are simply not as central a concern in this kind of survey as they would be in polls where one is trying to generalize to broader populations.

FRUGging, SUGging, and Pseudopolls

Some groups that sponsor surveys are not interested in measuring public opinion in a reliable and valid way. Instead, they want to promote a certain position and to convince the public of the rightness of that stand. The sponsors design those surveys to yield the desired results, most often through highly loaded questions, although subtler methods also are used. Sometimes in such surveys the people interviewed are chosen to ensure a predetermined outcome. In many cases, the poll itself is secondary to the real aim of the group: to raise money to support its objectives.

With the advent of computerized mailings and later the Internet, many organizations have enjoyed success raising money through direct mail and Web-based solicitations. Polling then becomes a device to generate donations—that is, the sponsoring organization encourages recipients of the mailings and e-mails to make their views known *and* to contribute to a good cause. Many of these appeals come from political groups, ranging from the Democratic and Republican Parties to various issue-based and ideologically oriented groups and organizations. And they have become very sophisticated in both the messaging and the technology of their appeals. Pages 9 and 10 show parts of the mailings from two distinct organizations—the American Civil Liberties Union and the Ronald Reagan Presidential Foundation. The kinds of questions included in each survey reveal the agenda of each organization. For example, the American Civil Liberties Union asked respondents to indicate their level of agreement with the following two highly loaded statements:

Q: I believe that it is wrong for states like Arizona to pass unconstitutional racial profile laws that require the police to stop people on the street and demand that they "show their papers" based on how they dress, what language they speak or how they look.

5. To help the ACLU sustain its all-out efforts to restore our lost liberties and advance freedom, will you send a contribution today?

☐ **Yes**　　　　☐ **No**

Mr. Asher, the ACLU is working hard to protect the things you believe in. We hope you will choose this moment to support the ACLU.

Contribution Form

☐ YES, I'm acting on my beliefs. To help secure the future of civil liberties in this country and to aid the ACLU in its efforts to restore and advance our most fundamental and personal freedoms, I am enclosing a special contribution in the amount of:

☐ $100　　　☐ $150　　　☐ $200　　　☐ Other $_____

To keep you up-to-date and reach you quickly when our civil liberties face new threats, please provide your email address: _____@_____

☐ I am enclosing a check payable to the ACLU.

☐ Please charge my contribution to my credit card:

☐ Mastercard　☐ VISA　☐ AMERICAN EXPRESS　☐ DISCOVER CARD

Gift amount

Account number

Expiration date

Signature

2588424　　UNS100701004

Mr. Herbert B. Asher
34 W Poplar Ave Apt 501
Columbus, OH 43215-1690

Make checks payable to the ACLU, and return in the enclosed envelope or send to
125 Broad St., 18th Floor, New York, New York 10004-2400. Thank you.

Mailing from American Civil Liberties Union

≡ Reagan Legacy Survey ≡

PROTECTING THE REAGAN LEGACY

Can we count on you to stand with The Ronald Reagan Presidential Foundation – the only organization created by Ronald Reagan himself and specifically charged with protecting his legacy and sharing it with future generations?

Will you help overcome the distortions directed at Ronald Reagan and the principles that define his legacy?

☐ No. I do not want to preserve President Reagan's legacy of peace, liberty, and economic strength for future generations.

☐ **YES!** You can count on me to defend President Ronald Reagan's legacy and help current and future generations discover the powerful example of this great American leader!

To do this, I have enclosed a special gift of:

☐ $25   ☐ $50   ☐ $75   ☐ $100   ☐ $_____ (other)

☐ $2,740 Please contact me to arrange a VIP guided tour of The Reagan Library (including an exclusive visit of President and Mrs. Reagan's personal offices). In addition, please send me the Air Force One replica.

☐ I can't give a gift right now, but have enclosed $5 to help cover the costs of processing my Reagan Legacy Survey form.

> ☐ I have enclosed a gift of $50 or more. Please send me my beautiful Air Force One replica model for display in my home or office.

☐ I wish to donate by credit card. My information is below.

Herb Asher
34 W. Poplar Ave: Apt. 501
Columbus, OH 43215-1690

Thank you! Your gift is tax-deductible to the fullest extent of the law. Please return this survey with your check made payable to The Reagan Foundation in the enclosed envelope.

⑨0049543367 A10DWIL062SC

Credit Card Giving Information	
Amount: $☐☐,☐☐☐.☐☐	Card Number
☐ Visa ☐ Discover ☐ MasterCard ☐ American Express	Phone Number
Expiration Date: ____/____	Cardholder's Name *(please print)*
	Cardholder's Signature *(required)*

Mailing from The Ronald Reagan Presidential Foundation

Q. I believe that it is wrong to use taxpayer dollars to fund abstinence-only education programs that promote a particular religious doctrine, deny young people access to reliable information about contraception and make it harder for them to avoid unintended pregnancies and sexually transmitted diseases.

The Ronald Reagan Presidential Foundation asked the following two biased questions:

Q: President Reagan also believed that churches, charities, and other voluntary organizations had a vital role to play in our communities, and that government could not—and should not try to—solve all social problems. The Left wants all social services to be provided by a European-style welfare state. **Do you agree that we should not look to government to fix everything that's "wrong" with America?**

Q: When confronting a serious economic downturn early in his presidency, Ronald Reagan cut taxes and government spending, unleashing the economic boom of the late 1980s. Today, government printing presses are working overtime to pay for federal bailouts and takeovers. **Do you believe fiscal conservatism, hard work, enterprise, and faith in the free market are still the best way out of economic hard times?**

The American Association for Public Opinion Research (AAPOR), the major professional association of public opinion researchers, part of whose mission is to protect the integrity and reputation of the polling enterprise, has condemned the practices of "FRUGging"—fund-raising under the guise of surveying—and "SUGging"—selling under the guise of research. Part of AAPOR's concern about these practices is enlightened self-interest: Sound public opinion research needs respondents who are willing to participate in the polling enterprise. In recent years, respondent participation rates have declined. There are many reasons for it, but an important factor is the behavior of aggressive and sometimes unethical telemarketers, who disturb and disrupt citizens through intrusive telephone calls. Many Americans had gotten so fed up with telemarketers, some of whom pretended they were conducting a public opinion survey when in fact they were trying either to raise money or to sell a product, that they became hostile to legitimate telephone requests to participate in a public opinion poll. In response to growing citizen anger about excessive telemarketing, the federal government established a "do not call" registry. Citizens who registered their telephone numbers would be protected from unwanted telemarketing calls. The "do not call" registry fortunately provided an exemption for legitimate survey research and public opinion polling, and subsequent court decisions have upheld the important distinction between intrusive telemarketing and genuine public opinion research. Today, the "do not call" registry, as well as a federal provision that requires that charitable fund-raisers state at the very beginning of their telephone call that their purpose is to seek a charitable contribution, should dramatically lessen the problems of "frugging" and "sugging."

But groups can choose to raise money through direct-mail solicitation and Web-based surveys, and here the use of a public opinion poll as a ploy to raise money is still widespread. Many groups involved in fund-raising, and/or generating survey responses that support their own agendas, construct extremely biased surveys and then ask respondents for their opinions. Consider these examples: The Committee Against Government Waste has asked, "Before you received this letter, were you aware of the gross mismanagement and waste of funds in the U.S. Department of Defense's purchase of parts?" The American Farmland Trust has asked, "Were you aware of the gravity of the problem of our vanishing farmland before receiving this mailing?" In case the literature accompanying the poll does not convince respondents of the correctness of the group's position, a carefully constructed question or statement may achieve the same end, as illustrated by the following questionnaire items and their sponsoring organizations:

Q: Are you in favor of allowing construction union czars the power to shut down an entire construction site because of a dispute with a single contractor, thus forcing even more workers to knuckle under to union agents?
National Right to Work Committee

Q: Despite a volatile stock market and public opposition, Republicans remain determined to privatize Social Security. Do you support privatization?
Democratic Congressional Campaign Committee

Q: Do you feel that all of the TV networks are in serious danger of losing the public's confidence and trust because they hire so many liberal Democratic activists as top corporate executives who formerly worked for Ted Kennedy, Walter Mondale, Gary Hart, George McGovern, Mario Cuomo, Jimmy Carter and the National Democratic Party?
Fairness in Media

Q: Did you know that the United States continues to embrace lousy trade deals with countries that use prison labor, slave labor, and child labor?
Fight Back America

Q: Speaker Nancy Pelosi and the liberals who now control Congress have talked about reinstating the Death Tax—a leading cause of the termination of successful small businesses in America. Reinstating the Death Tax would increase taxes by an estimated $91 billion. *Do you support or oppose the Death Tax?*
The Heritage Foundation

Q: Do you believe that American business and industry will be able to compete in the world economy if the Obama Administration bends to pressure from radical environmentalists and implements draconian regulations on emissions, energy consumption and transportation beyond what is required in other industrialized countries?

Republican National Committee

All the preceding items were carefully constructed to generate responses sympathetic to the sponsors' objectives. In fact, for several reasons these enterprises should not be called "polling." First, in most cases the sample is not scientifically selected; instead, the surveys and fund-raising requests are mailed out to lists of citizens who are thought to be likely supporters. Whether the people who actually respond are at all representative of a larger population is of little concern. Second, the questions are often poorly formulated and fundamentally flawed (deliberately so). Third, if the survey data collected are tabulated at all (and many times they are not), little analysis can be conducted because the original survey was very short and omitted key questions about the demographic and political characteristics of the respondents. In other words, collecting opinions is not necessarily valid polling.

Orton (1982) has identified similar examples of what he calls *pseudopolls*. For example, media of all types often encourage their audiences to express their views. But even with hundreds or thousands of replies, these so-called polls are usually not representative simply because the people who opt to participate are likely to differ in important ways from the overall population. They may be more interested, informed, and concerned about the topic at hand and thus hold views different from those of the overall population.

Radio talk shows and call-in polls became a prominent source of pseudopolls in the 1990s. A 1993 *Times Mirror* poll revealed that citizens who listened to and called radio talk shows were not representative of the overall citizenry; instead, they tended to be more Republican, more conservative, more male, and slightly more wealthy and educated. It is thus not surprising that radio phone-in polls often generate results more conservative and pro-Republican than the outcomes obtained through scientific polling.

Other examples of pseudopolls are the questionnaires that members of Congress send to households in their congressional districts. Typically, these are addressed to "Postal Customer," and there is no sure way of knowing just who in the household actually completed the survey. Although thousands of these questionnaires may be returned to a congressional office, it is difficult to ascertain whether the respondents' demographic

Jeff Stahler: © The Columbus Dispatch/Dist. by United Feature Syndicate, Inc.

characteristics and opinions are truly representative of the broader constituency. In some instances the questions are loaded to guarantee responses
compatible with a legislator's predispositions and record. This is not to say
that completed questionnaires are ignored or discarded; in most cases the
results are tabulated and later reported to the constituency in a newsletter.
But the major purpose of these questionnaires is to convince voters that
members of Congress care about their opinions.

The highly publicized surveys on marital relations once conducted by
feminist author Shere Hite and by newspaper columnist Abigail Van Buren,
otherwise known as "Dear Abby," are also pseudopolls (Squires and Morin
1987; Smith 1988). Hite distributed 100,000 extensive, open-ended questionnaires to women's groups and to individual women who requested one.
She received about 4,500 replies, a response rate of only 4.5 percent. In
one of her columns, Abby wrote, "Readers, I need your cooperation for an
important survey. Questions: Have you ever cheated on your mate? How
long have you been together? You need not sign your name, but please
state your age and indicate whether you are male or female." She received
more than 200,000 responses (Smith 1988).

In both the Hite and "Dear Abby" surveys, the sampling method and the questions generated unrepresentative and misleading results, despite the large number of respondents to Abby's poll. (Reputable, scientific national polls typically have a sample of about 1,000 to 1,500 respondents.) Hite found that 70 percent of women married five or more years were having extramarital affairs; 15 percent of Abby's married female respondents claimed to have been unfaithful. As Smith (1988) argues, both surveys could not be correct, and indeed both were overwhelmingly likely to be wrong because of the shortcomings in the sample selection and the actual questionnaires. Allowing citizens to select themselves into a survey guarantees biased results because of the motivations that lead people to participate in such surveys in the first place.

Since the 1970s magazines have regularly published the results of sex surveys of their readers; the magazines know that sex increases readership. In the past, they typically conducted the surveys by including the questionnaire in the magazine and encouraging readers to complete it and mail it back, although today online responses are encouraged. *Redbook* and *Cosmopolitan* in the 1970s, *Playboy* in the 1980s, and *The Advocate* in the 1990s are among the magazines that have sponsored such surveys. In some cases the response rate was low, but the number of completed questionnaires very large, simply because of the size of the magazine's readership. For example, the *Playboy* response rate was about 2 percent, but that translated into 100,000 replies. *The Advocate* response rate was 18 percent, with almost 13,000 questionnaires returned (Lever 1994, 18). Despite the large number of replies to a typical magazine survey, one must be very careful when generalizing the results to any broader population, whether it be to straight males based on the *Playboy* survey or to gay males based on the *Advocate* poll. The reason is that self-selection presents a double problem. First, the readers and subscribers to a particular magazine may not be representative of the broader population of which they are members. Second, the people who actually complete the questionnaires may not be representative of the magazine's total readers and subscribers. Nevertheless, the results of these surveys typically receive a lot of news media coverage (that probably enhances magazine sales).

The latest development in pseudopolls is the online survey on the Internet. Many businesses, media outlets, and other organizations invite visitors to their Web sites to participate in online surveys. Magazines that formerly included hard copy questionnaires in their issues are today more likely to invite their readers to participate in an online survey. For example, in its September 2006 issue, *Baby Talk* magazine published a story on the views of younger versus older moms based on the responses of more than 15,000 readers to an online survey. Like other pseudopolls, the online survey often generates many thousands of responses, but it is not a valid survey because the respondents selected themselves to participate rather than being part of a scientifically selected sample. They are unlikely to be a representative sample because only those people who are interested in the topic are likely to participate. Moreover, many citizens do not have access to the Internet in the first place—although this is becoming much less of a problem.

Online surveys have become commonplace on the Web sites of numerous media organizations. For example, citizens who went to the CNN Web site and to the Fox News Web site on July 28, 2010, could have participated in Web surveys. The CNN Quick Vote asked, "Are video games bad for kids?" while the Fox News question was more elaborate:

> A federal judge on Wednesday blocked some of the toughest provisions in the Arizona illegal immigration law, putting on hold the state's attempt to enforce federal immigration policy. Though the rest of the law is still set to go into effect Thursday, the partial injunction on SB 1070 means Arizona, for the time being, will not be able to require police officers to determine the immigration status of anyone they stop or arrest. Should Arizona fight the judge's ruling?

When I entered each Web site, the number of responses was large: 15,091 on CNN and 56,528 on Fox. The CNN respondents by a 56 percent to 44 percent margin thought video games were bad for kids, while more than 96 percent of the Fox respondents thought that Arizona should fight the judge's ruling.

Both the CNN and the Fox questions seem to me to be reasonably worded. Yet even though thousands of people responded to these questions, there is no guarantee that they are representative of any larger group of Americans. Fortunately, both Web sites cautioned readers, "This is not a scientific poll." But four years earlier, CNN users were provided a more detailed cautionary note about the results; it read: "This Quick Vote is not scientific and reflects the opinions of only those Internet users who have chosen to participate. The results cannot be assumed to represent the opinion of Internet users in general, nor the public as a whole. The Quick Vote is not responsible for content, functionality or the opinions expressed therein." Online surveys and conditions under which they might provide useful information are discussed in greater detail in chapter 5.

The key point, of course, is that pseudopolls are highly flawed and may give misleading portraits of public opinion because of loaded and unfair question wording, self-selection bias in the respondents, outright efforts to stack the results, or other deficiencies. Despite their deficiencies, however, these unscientific enterprises must be discussed and criticized because they are becoming more prevalent in the United States. At times, Americans hear the results of a pseudopoll and pass them along to colleagues as if they were legitimate public opinion research findings, thereby giving the pseudopoll greater credibility and dissemination than it merits. For example, in July 2010, I had the experience of discussing the recently enacted federal health care reform act with a friend who did not like the legislation. As part of his argument, he cited a Columbus-area survey of doctors that indicated that 74 percent of respondents thought that health care delivery would be somewhat worse or much worse with the passage of the bill. I challenged his data and he referred me to a story (Crane 2010) in the *Columbus Dispatch* newspaper. I checked out the story, and in the second paragraph the reporter indicated that the results of the survey were not scientific. Indeed, 5,500 doctors in the seven-county Columbus metropolitan area had the opportunity to participate in the online survey and 78 did, a response rate of 1.4 percent. Thus, the 74 percent figure was 58 doctors out of the 78 responding, clearly a dismal response rate and a very small number in absolute terms. What if the doctors who did participate in the survey were those most angry about the health care reform measure? The point of this example is that the results of an unscientific online survey became part of the argument against health care reform, despite the cautions of the reporter who wrote the original story.

There is some evidence that a substantial number of Americans give credence to various kinds of pseudopolls. Brodie et al. (2001, 13) report that 26 percent of Americans believe that a survey in which readers fill out a questionnaire printed in a magazine almost always or most of the time accurately reflects what the public thinks. Twenty-seven percent believe that Internet surveys almost always reflect what the public thinks, and 35 percent give high marks to surveys in which people are mailed a questionnaire and asked to complete it. According to Brodie and her colleagues, fewer than 40 percent of Americans realize that selecting survey respondents at random produces a better, more accurate result than the self-selected samples such as radio call-in or magazine write-in polls rely on. The importance of these unscientific Internet polls was also brought home to me when I received an e-mail in August 2006 from a friend urging me to support Israel on the CNN Web site, which was asking whether Israel's actions in Lebanon were justified. My friend argued that "this survey is shown all over the world, and will have a strong impact on world public opinion."

All of this suggests that bad polling practices and results can mislead many Americans. Citizens are subjected to many different kinds of polls, all of which may later affect them in some way through decisions made on the basis of poll results. That is why it is important that citizens be aware of the gamut of polls and be able to evaluate them. If they are able to recognize unscientific polls and their associated deficiencies (as well as the shortcomings of scientific polls), then people are less likely to be misled by them. This leads to the central concern of this book—the citizen as a potential consumer of public opinion polls.

The Citizen as a Consumer of Polls

Whatever the quality of the polls, they can affect the attitudes and behavior of citizens. Even media-sponsored polls designed simply to report citizens' attitudes (and perhaps to keep up with the competition and improve ratings) also may help to *shape* preferences, particularly during a presidential primary season. At such times polling is frequent, and the links among a candidate's poll standing, news media coverage, and primary election fate are pronounced. (The role of polls in elections is considered in chapter 7.)

Americans are major consumers of public opinion research on a wide variety of topics. But are they smart consumers? Americans should be aware of the problems and limitations of polls before they "buy" anything from them. Often someone is actively promoting the poll results to generate support for his or her objectives. It might be the president, citing polls to argue that the American people support administration policies. It might be a local builder, waving the results of a neighborhood poll purporting to show local support for a rezoning ordinance to permit his commercial construction project to go through. It might be a regional transportation commission, citing poll results to justify the establishment of bus lanes on freeways. Or it might be a friend or neighbor selectively using poll results to win an argument.

Citizens need not become experts at drawing samples, constructing questionnaires, or analyzing data to be better consumers of public opinion research. Instead they can become aware of the steps involved in conducting a survey and the possible consequences of the steps, so that they are better able to reject bad "merchandise" and appreciate good buys.

Readers should not construe this book as a condemnation of public opinion research; in fact, most of the highly publicized polls, as well as many private polls, reflect high standards of polling. Indeed, public opinion polling has improved dramatically over the past sixty years in areas such as sample design, question wording and format, interviewing techniques, and methods of data analysis. Interested readers may consult the fiftieth anniversary issue of *Public Opinion Quarterly* (1987) for discussions of how polling practices have changed over time. A very concise history of polling can be found in *Public Opinion: Measuring the American Mind* (Bardes and Oldendick 2003, chapter 2); Weisberg (2005, chapter 1) provides an informative overview of the development of survey research as a scientific discipline. Fortunately, there are many Web sites that citizens can go to for the latest poll results as well as information about polling procedures and methodology. These are listed at the end of the book, but let me just highlight a few here. The Web site of AAPOR contains information about a wide variety of polling topics, including best practices and ethical standards (www.aapor.org). Many polling and survey research organizations provide information about the results of their polls as well the methods and procedures that were utilized in their polling. Four prominent examples are the Gallup Organization (www.gallup.com), the American National Election Studies (www.electionstudies.org), the Pew Research Center for the People and the Press (www.people-press.org), and the National Opinion Research Center (www.norc.uchicago.edu). For political junkies who want to keep up with latest election polls and issue surveys, there are many media outlets as well as the Web sites of state-based polling organizations. These media and the state organizations tend to cover only those polls that were conducted under their auspices. For extensive coverage of political polls (and often information about polling practices and procedures), the following four Web sites are particularly helpful: www.fivethirtyeight.com, www.politico.com, www.pollster.com, and www.pollingreport.com. Polling practices, of course, continue to change with the advent of the Internet and the increased challenges faced by traditional telephone polling, topics addressed in chapters 4 and 5. An appreciation of the art of conducting and analyzing surveys will leave citizens less susceptible to the intellectual tyranny that can occur when a public opinion poll is deemed by its sponsor to be scientific and its results are presented as therefore beyond question or challenge.

Citizens' Views of Polls

Historically, ordinary citizens' reactions to public opinion polling have often been positive, although their views of pollsters themselves are much more skeptical. One study rated the credibility of forty-four different professional groups that speak out on public issues; pollsters finished thirty-forth in the ranking (Morin 1999b). But 25 percent of the respondents in a 1996 Gallup survey said they regularly followed the results of a public opinion poll in a newspaper or magazine, and an additional 16 percent said they did so occasionally (Morin 1996b). Fifty-nine percent of the respondents said they did not follow a poll regularly in a print medium; of course, they might sporadically read about polls, or they might be aware of the polls through the electronic media. That Gallup Poll and others like it have indicated that

Americans held fairly positive views about the accuracy of polls. More than two-thirds of the Gallup sample said the polls were right most of the time. Eighty-seven percent supported polls as "a good thing."

In 2001 the Henry J. Kaiser Family Foundation, in conjunction with *Public Perspective* magazine, conducted an extensive survey on the role of polling in a democracy and on the views of the public, policy leaders, and the media toward polling (Brodie et al. 2001; Witt 2001). The opinions of the public were mixed. Twenty-eight percent of the respondents said that conducting a public opinion poll was a very good way to learn what a majority of people in the country think, and an additional 56 percent said it was a somewhat good way. But when they were asked to choose among town hall meetings, polling, talking to people on the street and at shopping malls, or talking to people who call, write, or e-mail public officials as the best way for officials to learn what the public is thinking, 43 percent opted for town hall meetings and only 25 percent for polling.

The same study also asked how useful people thought polls are for enabling officials in Washington to understand how the public feels on issues. Twenty-two percent of the respondents said that polls were very useful; 54 percent said somewhat useful; 13 percent, not too useful; and 8 percent, not useful at all. The 75 percent (54 + 13 + 8) who rated polls as somewhat useful or lower were then presented the following question:

Q. For each of the following statements, please tell me if you think it is a major reason polls are only somewhat useful or not useful for officials to understand how the public feels about important issues, a minor reason, or not a reason:

Statement	Percentage rating it a major reason
Polls don't accurately reflect what the public wants.	43
Polls don't ask for the public's opinion on the right issues.	39
The results of polls can be twisted to say whatever you want them to say.	58

In the same survey, only 50 percent of the respondents strongly agreed or somewhat agreed that "public opinion polling is based on sound scientific principles," whereas 80 percent strongly or somewhat agreed that "the questions asked in polls often don't give people the opportunity to say what they really think about an issue" (Brodie et al. 2001, 22–23). All of these results suggest that Americans have some genuine reservations about the polling enterprise itself and about politicians' use of polls.

Other, anecdotal evidence also supports that finding. Most teachers and practitioners of public opinion polling have encountered citizens who have expressed utter distrust of polling. Some complain that they have

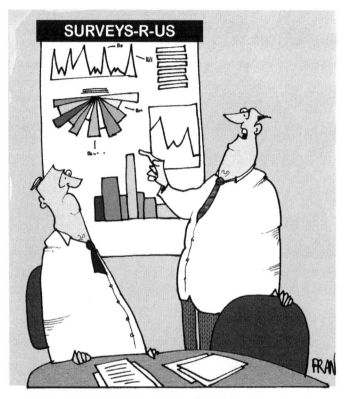

87% OF THE 56% WHO COMPLETED MORE THAN 23% OF THE SURVEY THOUGHT IT WAS A WASTE OF TIME

www.CartoonStock.com

never been interviewed and don't know anyone who has, and they therefore wonder just how representative samples can be. Koch (1985) found that people who have never participated in a poll are dubious about the accuracy of survey results.

Others base their doubts on the size of the samples. In talking about polling with diverse audiences, I repeatedly hear people ask how a sample of 1,500 respondents can possibly represent 220 million adult Americans. And despite my brilliant answer by analogy—a doctor takes only a sample of a person's blood (fortunately), and a chef need taste only a spoonful of soup (assuming the soup is stirred properly) to test its seasoning—much skepticism about polls remains. Indeed, a 1985 Roper survey produced an estimate that only 28 percent of Americans believed that national polls with sample sizes of 1,500–2,000 could be accurate, while 56 percent said they could not be (Sussman 1985c). (And many national polls today have sample sizes closer to 1,000 respondents.) The 1996 Gallup survey discussed above obtained similar results. Another study found that citizens who questioned the accuracy of polls attributed their skepticism to characteristics of the respondents as well as aspects of the polling enterprise itself (Dran and Hildreth 1995). Skeptics worried whether pollsters talked to the right people, as well as whether sample sizes were adequate. (I will discuss sampling and what makes a poll scientific in chapter 4.) Other concerns focused on pollster manipulation of surveys and media misuse of polls.

Polls have received much criticism pertaining to their growing role in elections and in election coverage by the news media. The argument is often made that polls have contributed to the packaging of candidates: Aspiring leaders are accused of first consulting the polls and then staking out their positions, thereby abdicating their leadership responsibilities on vital public issues. Polls are seen as encouraging a horse-race mentality among the news media, which concentrate on who's ahead and who's behind, who's gaining and who's falling back, as measured by the polls, instead of focusing on issues and the candidates' qualifications. Candidates themselves have complained about the role of polls. Indeed, the most common reaction from candidates who are shown to be losing in the preelection polls is the assertion that the only poll that counts is the one on Election Day. In the presidential nominating process, when multiple candidates are seeking a party's nomination, the media cannot and do not cover all candidates equally. Instead they give greater coverage to the viable candidates, and viability is most often determined by how much money candidates have raised and how well they are doing in the polls. Clearly, the polls do more than reflect how well candidates are doing; they may also affect how well candidates will do (see chapter 7 for a more detailed discussion of this phenomenon).

Exit polls—interviews with citizens just after they have voted—enable the television networks to project election outcomes even before the voting is finished. This practice has angered many citizens as well as political elites. Newspaper columnist Mike Royko encouraged voters to lie to exit pollsters, and others (such as Munro and Gans 1988) have simply encouraged a public boycott of exit polls. Congress has conducted hearings to try to get the networks to alter voluntarily the ways they report exit polls and election projections. The election night debacle in Florida in 2000 was a major black eye for exit polls, pollsters, and the broadcast media. When television networks prematurely called Florida for Gore early on election night and later, again prematurely, called it for Bush, the excesses and frailties of media election coverage, with its reliance on exit polls, were fully exposed. The premature leaking of exit poll results on Election Day in 2004 helped generate postelection controversy about the fairness of the election, especially in states such as Ohio and Florida, when early exit poll reports did not correspond with the actual election outcomes. In 2008, there was much less controversy about the exit polls, in part because the election outcome was not as close as in the two previous presidential races and also because there was no one single state that determined the election outcome. Exit polls are discussed in depth in chapter 7.

Other observers have condemned the impact of polls on American politics, none more harshly than Daniel Greenberg (1980), who wrote:

> Given the devastation that opinion surveys have brought to the American political process, we shouldn't be asking how polls can be sharpened but rather why they are endured and how they can be banished.
>
> Polls are the life-support system for the finger-to-the-wind, quick-change politics of our time and, as such, are the indispensable tools for the ideologically hollow men who work politics like a soap-marketing campaign. . . .
>
> The effect of this—on campaigns, as well as on administrations between campaigns—is an obsession with salesmanship rather than with governance.

The nation's political cartoonists, many of whom are syndicated in newspapers that themselves conduct polls, have had a field day attacking the polls, particularly their frequency, duration, and intrusiveness in the presidential selection process. Smith (1987, 209) found that polls were treated negatively in 61 percent of the comics and cartoons he analyzed and worried how this would affect citizens' reactions to polls. Several years ago, political commentator and writer Arianna Huffington established the Web site Partnership for a Poll-Free America. Huffington has been particularly critical of the polling enterprise because of low response rates (a topic discussed in chapter 4).

Various practitioners of polling and survey research have become concerned about what they see as increased skepticism, cynicism, lack of interest, and even hostility toward polls. Prominent pollsters such as Harry O'Neill, of the Roper organization, and Kathy Frankovic, director of polling at CBS News, have called on their industry colleagues to be more reflective about their enterprise and more sensitive to its shortcomings (O'Neill 1997; Morin 1998a). Black (1991) advocates greater sensitivity to the needs of respondents by (1) making the interview itself a more interesting and rewarding experience for respondents; (2) keeping promises made to respondents in such areas as the length of the interview and the provision of final reports if requested; and (3) maintaining high quality throughout the polling enterprise.

In many ways, it has become easier to conduct public opinion surveys today, in part because there are so many vendors who can sell samples or conduct the interviews or perform the data analyses. And as the technology of online surveys has become more available and cheaper, this has resulted in more Web-based polling. This proliferation of polling leads one to worry whether recent entrants into the polling business may have weaker ties to the profession and a lesser commitment to the high standards that should characterize public opinion polling. This suggests the need for careful self-policing by the polling industry to protect the profession and its reputation among the public. And, as I argue throughout this book, citizens need to become more educated consumers of the polls. The point is that there is growing unease among many practitioners of polling because the lofty status that public opinion assessment has enjoyed may be in some jeopardy.

In May 1997 the American Association for Public Opinion Research (AAPOR 1997a) issued a publication detailing the "best practices" that should characterize public opinion research. The last recommendation called for the disclosure of "all methods of the survey to permit evaluation and replication" and presented a comprehensive list of items that exceeded the standards for minimum disclosure laid out in the AAPOR code (see chapter 6 for a fuller discussion of disclosure standards). AAPOR also condemned a number of survey practices, such as presenting the results of any self-selected poll as if they were the product of genuine scientific survey research. It also sharply criticized "push polling"—an election campaign tactic disguised as legitimate polling. In a push poll, a campaign contacts a large number of voters under the guise of conducting a public opinion poll, presents some negative information about another candidate, and then asks some questions about that candidate. Indeed, one of the major warning signs of a push poll is the large number of respondents contacted, a number substantially larger than would be needed for a valid and representative public opinion poll. The aim of push polls is not to acquire legitimate information about the election contest but to push potential voters away from a particular candidate. (Push polling is discussed in greater detail in chapter 7.)

The Luntz case illustrates the role of AAPOR in helping to police the polling profession. In April 1997 the executive council of AAPOR formally chastised pollster Frank Luntz for violating AAPOR's Code of Professional Ethics and Practices. Prior to the 1994 congressional elections, Luntz claimed that his research showed that sizable majorities of Americans supported all parts of the GOP's "Contract with America." But when asked to

Speed Bump

make public the wording of his poll and other information, Luntz refused. AAPOR rebuked him for failing to meet the standards of disclosure (AAPOR 1997b). Later it turned out that Luntz's evidence of support for the Contract with America was highly suspect and misleading. Nevertheless, the House Republican leadership used the alleged poll results to build legislative support for the items in the program. In general, political leaders who use the polls to "prove" that the public supports their positions have an advantage in the public discussion of issues.

Although they are sometimes angry or skeptical about poll results, Americans often think polls are accurate and fair. They often resent the intrusiveness and presumed power of the polls, but they eagerly consume the latest public opinion findings about myriad topics. This love-hate relationship is probably inevitable in the U.S. political system. Americans want their voices to be heard, and therefore they attack the polls when they think such devices are undermining genuine citizen involvement and influence. Yet in a large and heterogeneous nation such as the United States, the polls may be the best mechanism for reflecting the diversity of public opinion. The simple fact that polls generally count all respondents equally bestows on polls a democratic character that enhances their appeal in a democratic society.

Polling and Democracy

Different theories and opinions compete concerning the role of polling in a democratic society. Advocates of polls emphasize that polling is an opportunity for citizens to participate in democracy and that it permits quick and repeated assessments of public opinion. Polling is particularly valued by those who prefer a democracy in which the people govern directly rather than through elected representatives. Some advocate polling citizens on their policy preferences and enacting those preferences, thereby circumventing the "middleman"—the elected representative—although such a system would ignore many important features of the governing process, such as dialogue, deliberation, bargaining, and compromise. Many in this group are fascinated with the possibility that technological innovations might facilitate direct governance by the citizenry. The huge advances in communications in recent years have rendered the virtues and feasibility of direct democracy through technology even more tantalizing.

Some proponents of the more traditional theory of representative democracy also welcome public opinion polls, because they provide systematic information on the preferences of the citizenry. They argue that citizens' opinions should influence the behavior of their elected representatives and that any mechanism that can provide information on citizens' opinions is bound to foster democracy. But the empirical evidence is mixed on the extent to which popular preferences are actually translated into public policy. On the one hand, examples of the government's seeming unresponsiveness to public opinion are numerous. For example, in 2006, polls repeatedly showed majorities of Americans in support of expanded embryonic stem cell research, yet Congress was unable to override the president's veto of legislation that would accomplish that. Likewise, polls in summer 2006 showed Americans increasingly critical of the war in Iraq and increasingly favorable to some kind of timetable for reducing American involvement, yet the mantra from the Bush administration going into the 2006 elections was, "Stay the course." One could, of course, argue that stem cell research and especially Iraq are such complex issues that it would be naïve and even misguided to expect that preferences revealed in public opinion polls should automatically be translated into public policy. But the fact remains that the polls revealed a disjunction between popular opinion and government policy. Polls regularly showed an overwhelming majority of Americans favoring some form of gun control, such as handgun registration or waiting periods, for years before Congress finally passed the so-called Brady law in 1993. That measure had first been introduced in 1987. Moreover, the Brady law was the first major federal gun control legislation since 1968. A 2009 Ohio Poll showed that 73 percent of Ohioans favored allowing medical use of marijuana, but the state legislature and governor were adamantly opposed to such a measure (Marshall 2010). Multiple polls in 2009 showed that majorities of Americans opposed taxpayer-funded bailouts for American automobile companies, but the Congress nevertheless approved it. On the other hand, some empirical studies have found substantial congruence between the attitudes of the public and the actions of government on certain issues (Erikson 1976; Page and Shapiro 1983, 1992). Although these studies are careful not to hastily attribute government decisions to popular preferences, they suggest conditions under which citizen influence is likely to be significant.

Another benefit of polls, according to polling proponents, is the opportunity for citizens to learn about their compatriots and to dispel myths and stereotypes that might otherwise mislead public discourse. For example, Morin reported poll results that challenged the stereotype of evangelical and fundamentalist Christians as monolithic, homogeneous supporters of the religious right (Morin 1993a, 1993c). A *USA Today*/CNN/Gallup poll conducted in December 1993 showed that stereotypes of the opponents in the gun control debate were misleading. For example, the attitudes of gun owners on various aspects of gun control did not differ substantially from the attitudes of nonowners, particularly concerning less-sweeping forms of gun regulation. Other public opinion polls have provided insights, sometimes surprising ones, on race and prejudice in the United States. A Louis Harris poll conducted in 1993 showed that the traditional victims of bigotry—blacks, Asians, and Latinos—often expressed intolerant views of other minority groups. And a study by Sniderman et al. (1993) debunked the simplistic notion that conservatives were prejudiced toward blacks and liberals were not. Although on many items conservatives were less tolerant than liberals toward blacks, the key point for Sniderman and his colleagues was that the differences were often very small.

DOONESBURY © (2002) G. B. Trudeau. Reprinted with permission of UNIVERSAL UCLICK. All rights reserved.

Polls at times reveal how unaware or ill-informed Americans are. For example, a Gallup Poll conducted in October 2004 found that 42 percent of Americans believed that Saddam Hussein was personally involved in the September 11, 2001, terrorist attacks, when there was no evidence of any such involvement. A Harris poll conducted in July 2006 showed that 64 percent of the respondents believed that Saddam Hussein had strong links to Al Qaeda, and 50 percent thought that Iraq had weapons of mass destruction when the United States went to war with Iraq. One has to wonder about the sources of such opinions, a topic we return to in chapter 9.

Even more surprising were some of the opinions uncovered in a national Scripps Howard/Ohio University poll conducted in July 2006. That poll found that more than a third of Americans believed that federal officials either assisted in the September 11 terrorist attacks or took no steps to prevent them, so that the United States could justify going to war in the Middle East (Hargrove and Stempel 2006). Sixteen percent speculated that secretly planted explosives, and not airplanes, were the real causes of the World Trade Center towers' collapse. And 12 percent suspected that the Pentagon was struck by a military cruise missile on September 11, rather than by a plane. One partial explanation for these results was based on where people got their information: Citizens who regularly used the Internet, but did not rely on "mainstream" media, were much more likely to believe in September 11 conspiracy theories, whereas people who read daily newspapers or listened to radio newscasts were much less likely to do so (Hargrove and Stempel 2006). As information sources become more numerous, diverse, and specialized, and as citizens themselves become much more selective in their sources of information, it will not be surprising if public opinion polls increasingly uncover surprising pockets of opinion on particular topics.

Perhaps this selective use of information sources along with ideological and cultural predispositions help account for some of the polling on beliefs about President Obama. A Pew Research Center survey in 2010 found that almost 20 percent of Americans thought that the president was a Muslim, with more than a third of conservative Republicans sharing that view. A *Washington Post*/ABC News poll that asked an open-ended question about where Obama was born found that 68 percent said he was born in the United States, 14 percent in another country, and 19 percent did not know. When the 19 percent who did not know were asked their best guess as to where the president was born, the totals became 77 percent who said the United States and 20 percent another country. When broken down by partisanship and ideology, there were some substantial differences. Fifteen percent of Democrats vs. 31 percent of Republicans believed that Obama was born elsewhere. Likewise 12 percent of liberals versus

36 percent of strong conservatives thought the president was born in another country. And a Harris poll found that 14 percent of the sample (and 24 percent of the Republicans) thought that Obama might be the Antichrist (Brynaert 2010). As upsetting and disturbing as these results might be to some, they help provide insight and context into the often rancorous atmosphere of contemporary American politics.

In contrast to the favorable arguments of proponents, many critics of polling worry about the harmful consequences of polls for a democratic political system. They agree that citizen influence is a key component of a democracy and that public opinion, properly measured, can be useful in governing. But they argue that polls give a misleading impression of how a democracy actually operates. Public opinion is not synonymous with the results of public opinion polls, yet today the two are treated as though they were identical. A focus solely on poll results ignores the dynamics of how opinions are formed and how they change and often overlooks factors that may shape (and manipulate) public opinion, such as the behavior of leaders and interest groups. Polls may present an overall picture of the distribution of opinion, but the reporting and use of polls often ignore important differences in preferences among subgroups. The result is a misleading picture of similar attitudes across different segments of the American population. Margolis (1984) claims that polls may not be the optimal way to measure public opinion on politically and socially sensitive topics. He argues that in some instances actual behavior provides a more valid expression of public opinion than verbal responses to survey questions.

A more radical criticism of polls is that they are simply a sop to the citizenry, that they give people a false sense of being influential, when in reality political power is held and exercised by elites who may or may not act in the public interest. Social scientist Johan Galtung (1969) makes the point most effectively when he argues that surveys are too democratic: they generally count all respondents equally, whereas people are tremendously disparate in the resources and skills they bring to bear on political decisions. To the extent that a survey is seen as a quasi referendum on an issue, it is misleading because the participants in the referendum have different degrees of opportunity to shape government outcomes.

Weissberg (2001) argues that polls should not shape public policies and that policymakers should ignore the polls. He provides an elaborate rationale for this position but essentially argues that poll respondents do not and cannot incorporate all the factors that policymakers have to consider when adopting specific policies. Weissberg claims that although polls measure what citizens want, those wishes do not in most instances take into account the costs or risks of the stated preference. That is, it is easy for respondents in a poll to say that they prefer more spending on education or health care, but such responses do not reflect the costs or the potential problems associated with that increased spending. Only the policymaker has that information, and it is the policymaker who must make the ultimate decision based on much more than citizen preferences.

A related criticism of polls concerns their consequences for leadership in the United States. The simplistic version of this argument says that officeholders blindly follow the polls rather than work to educate and persuade the public. That argument is exemplified by an editorial in the *Akron Beacon Journal* (May 8, 1994) entitled "Foreign Poll-icy." It begins by asserting, "The name of Stanley Greenberg may not be familiar to most Americans. It should be. He is Bill Clinton's pollster, and for all intents and purposes, he conducts the country's foreign policy." Other observers, such as Barnes (1993), have also described the critical role Greenberg played in the Clinton administration, just as he did in the presidential campaign. Polling results in 1998 and 1999 on health care, patients' rights, and prescription drugs showed that Americans cared about those issues, and the findings prompted the GOP congressional leadership to offer its own health care proposals to head off any political backlash from its opposition to the Clinton administration's proposals (Alvarez 1998).

Other critics of polling argue that the widespread awareness of public preferences that polls generate has limited the ability of leaders to make unpopular choices. Still others complain that leaders can easily manipulate the polls—for example, by giving a major, televised address that can influence opinions in polls taken right afterward, thereby generating poll results that paint an inaccurate picture of the extent of support for their policies. Some make the fundamental point that polls (and the news media) have altered the style and substance of governance by emphasizing the consequences of politicians' actions for the next election. The result is a shortsighted approach to problem solving. Compare this with poll proponents' defense of the impact of polls on leadership, which argues that officials should have information about citizens' attitudes before they make major decisions and that the polls, whatever their limitations, are the best way to acquire that information.

As stated earlier, citizens often have a love-hate relationship with polls, and this ambivalence holds for what role the polls should play in governing in a democratic polity. Citizens do not want leaders who slavishly and cynically follow the polls, and yet they do want leaders who follow the views of the public, and one of the ways to assess those views is through public opinion polling. A Gallup Poll conducted in October 2005 during the Bush administration found that 61 percent of Americans thought the nation would be better off and 33 percent thought it would be worse off if leaders followed the views of public opinion polls more closely. But when one breaks down these results by the partisanship of the respondents, a more complex picture about the role that polls should play emerges. The Republican division on better off/worse off was 49 percent to 44 percent, while the Democratic division was 76 percent to 17 percent, with the independents falling in between. Clearly the Democrats advocate following the polls since their party is not in power, and they believe the polls will show substantial opposition to Bush administration policies. In contrast, for the Republicans, their party is in power and the polls become a less necessary tool of governance.

The cartoon on page 28 is a jab at the Bush administration and the president himself for his reliance on public opinion polling. In the 2000 presidential election, candidate George W. Bush criticized the Clinton/ Gore administration for slavishly following the polls and claimed that in a Bush administration decisions would be made on the bases of principles and values and not because of polls. In hindsight, there were striking similarities between the Clinton and Bush administrations, and one marked difference, when it comes to polling and political research in general (Harris 2001a, 2001b). The similarities are simply that both administrations used polls, focus groups, and the like extensively to ascertain what Americans were thinking, how citizens would respond to various policy alternatives, and what were the best ways to package those alternatives. The major difference between the two was that Clinton himself was actively involved in reviewing the poll results in weekly meetings with key members of his administration (Harris 2001a), whereas Bush relied more on recommendations from his chief political operative, Karl Rove. Harris discussed how polling results affected Clinton administration policies. For example, a needle exchange program for drug addicts, to combat the spread of AIDS, was dropped when polls indicated substantial public opposition. In another example, when the Clinton administration enjoyed a federal budget surplus, it did not want the Republican Congress to spend that surplus on a tax cut. Public opinion polling helped the Clinton administration learn that the public overwhelmingly preferred devoting the surplus to Social Security rather than to tax cuts. Thus the president challenged Congress to "save Social Security first," a theme that put the Republicans on the defensive on tax cuts until George W. Bush became president.

These two examples raise important points. Surely the Clinton administration was using polls for political purposes, to build support (on how to use the surplus) and avoid voter anger and opposition (on the needle exchange proposal). Yet it was also the case that the polls were telling the administration what popular preferences were, and the administration then followed those preferences. Obviously the question for leadership is: To what extent does one follow the polls and public opinion, and to what extent does one lead and try to change citizens' opinions? Any presidential administration does both. Harris points out that the Clinton administration took major actions on trade policy, military intervention in the Balkans, and other matters that went against the grain of American public opinion at the time. Murray and Howard (2002) found that the Reagan and Clinton administrations polled extensively from their first days in office, whereas the Carter and first Bush administrations polled only sporadically in their first three years but became very active in polling in their fourth year. They conclude that the public opinion polling operation has become institutionalized in the White House but that there are differences in how each administration uses polls and political research in general.

The evidence from the George W. Bush presidency showed that polling, focus groups, and political research were as central as they were during the Clinton administration despite claims to the contrary (Harris 2001b; Tenpas 2003). For example, *Washington Post* reporters Peter Baker and Dan Balz (2005) analyzed how the tone of President Bush's prime-time address on Iraq was very much influenced by public opinion research. The Bush administration brought Christopher Gelpi, an academic expert on public opinion during wartime, onto the National Security Council staff as a special adviser for strategic planning. Gelpi and his colleague Peter Feaver had conducted research on the determinants of popular support for military missions. They found that one of the key factors in maintaining public support for military action was a perception that the war could and would be won. The costs of the war and the circumstances of how it began were less relevant in influencing public support than was belief that the war would have a positive conclusion. That finding influenced the president's speech and his subsequent messages on the war in Iraq: progress was being made and the war would be won.

In the first eighteen months of the Obama presidency, the role of administration polling was evident in the successful effort to pass health care reform and in the subsequent predictions that polling numbers would become more favorable to the reform once it was actually implemented. In April 2009 at a climate change meeting headed by Carol Browner, the White House coordinator of energy and climate policy, Obama administration personnel advised advocates of climate change legislation that the polling data showed that green jobs and energy independence were more helpful terms than climate change to describe the legislation (Wasserman 2010). As Republicans opposed the Obama administration agenda, polling played a major role in their strategy and tactics. Paul Ryan, a Republican U.S. representative from Wisconsin and a leader in his party on deficit reduction, was asked why more of his Republican colleagues were not supporting his budget plan (which included major changes in Medicare,

Medicaid, and Social Security). He responded: "They're talking to their pollsters and their pollsters are saying, 'Stay away from this. We're going to win an election'" (Bacon 2010).

What, then, is the verdict on opinion polls in the United States? They are now an integral part of the political and social landscape, and they are likely to become more prominent in the future, even as the technology of polling changes. Polls can provide citizens and leaders with useful information; they also can be highly misleading and inaccurate. Polls may enhance the opportunities for citizen influence; they also can serve to manipulate the public. In 1965 George Gallup wrote optimistically about the future of the polls:

> As students, scholars, and the general public gain a better understanding of polls, they will have a greater appreciation of the service polls can perform in a democracy. In my opinion, modern polls are the chief hope of lifting government to a higher level, by showing that the public supports the reforms that will make this possible, by providing a *modus operandi* for testing new ideas. . . . Polls can help make government more efficient and responsive; they can improve the quality of candidates for public office; they can make this a truer democracy. (Gallup 1965–1966, 549)

More than four decades have passed since Gallup made those claims, and discourse about the polls has become much more critical. Nevertheless, as citizens become wiser consumers of polls, Gallup's lofty aspirations are more likely to be realized.

The chapters that follow consider polls in detail and raise some methodological points, often in the context of important substantive examples. Chapter 2 addresses the problem of "nonattitudes"—they are what polltakers measure when citizens do not have genuine opinions on a topic and yet answer the poll questions anyway. Despite pollsters' best efforts, citizens often respond to questions on which they have no real opinions, so that the poll yields misleading results.

Chapter 3 discusses the wording of questions and their order and context. Examples of poorly worded questions likely to produce skewed results have already been cited, but the wording of a question is not the only important consideration. A survey is, after all, a series of questions, and their order and context can greatly affect the results.

Chapter 4 focuses on various sampling techniques and their advantages and disadvantages. It also deals with sample size and error. Chapter 5 explains in detail how different interviewing procedures can affect results.

Chapter 6 examines how the news media report the polls, and chapter 7 analyzes the role of polls in elections. Because Americans learn about polls primarily through the mass media, how they cover polls greatly influences public opinion. This influence is particularly interesting in the case of high-visibility national polls because the organization that reports the polls also is responsible for conducting them. Chapter 7 argues that the polls have come to play an intrusive role in elections and that their use by candidates and their reporting by the media often ill serve citizens and the electoral process. Elections are the most visible opportunity for citizens to influence their government, and to the extent that polls affect elections, citizens should be sensitive and wary.

Chapter 8 explains that the analysis of poll results is more an art than a science—and one that affords many opportunities for manipulative interpretation and dissemination of poll results to sway public opinion. Chapter 9 ties together the various themes, offers suggestions about better ways to use polls, and discusses the effects of polls on the American polity.

Exercises

1. Keep a one-week log of the public opinion poll results that appear in your local daily newspaper. Note the topic of the poll and the source. Also note how much information was provided about how the poll was conducted. What conclusions can you make based on these findings? Do you think adequate information was provided about how the poll was conducted?

2. Pick one of the weekly national newsmagazines (*Time* or *Newsweek)* and examine how it used and reported polls during one calendar month. Keep a record of the topics of the polls and how much information was provided about how they were conducted. Also note how the poll results were used. Were they incorporated into and discussed in the story, or did they appear as a sidebar?

3. For one week, go to Fox News and to the CNN Web site each day and record the daily poll questions that they ask their users. Also record the results of the poll questions. Then try to find genuine public opinion polls that have asked similar questions around the same time. Compare the results of the Internet and the scientific polls on similar topics. How similar or dissimilar are the results of the two? How would you explain this?

4. A number of survey items that the author claimed were biased are shown on pages 12-13. Do you agree that these are biased questions? If so, what do you think makes them biased? Be specific in your critique of the items.

2 The Problem of Nonattitudes

To produce an informative and accurate public opinion poll, a researcher must perform several tasks successfully. These include constructing a questionnaire with properly worded and ordered questions, selecting a representative sample, correctly interviewing the respondents in that sample, analyzing the data appropriately, and, finally, drawing the correct conclusions. But before any of these tasks can be performed, a researcher must ask a fundamental question: Is the proposed topic of the poll one on which citizens have genuine opinions? If it is, then the topic is suitable for a public opinion survey. But if the topic is so remote from citizens' concerns that they do not hold real views on it, then any poll on the topic will measure *nonattitudes* rather than attitudes. Any information obtained will be suspect—even if the questions are properly worded, the sample is scientifically selected, and the data are appropriately analyzed.

The presence of nonattitudes is one of the simplest yet most perplexing problems in public opinion polling. Too often in a survey context, people respond to questions about which they have no genuine attitudes or opinions.[1] Even worse, the analyst or the poll sponsor or the news organization treats the nonattitude responses as if they represented actual public opinions. Under these circumstances, a misleading portrait of public opinion can emerge because no distinction is made between people with real

---

1. The terms *attitude* and *opinion* are used interchangeably. Many social scientists differentiate between attitudes and opinions by treating opinions as more transitory, as verbal manifestations of some underlying attitude, words elicited by the public opinion survey. For the purposes of this chapter, this distinction is by no means critical, although the reader should recognize that public opinion data at times may simply be verbal responses (opinions) that pollsters hope accurately reflect some underlying attitudes.

views on an issue and those whose responses simply reflect their desire to appear in an interview as informed citizens or those whose responses are simply artifacts of being asked a question in the first place. Unfortunately, pollsters often find it difficult to differentiate between genuine attitude holders and persons merely expressing nonattitudes.

It is tempting to assume that citizens are interested in and informed about the issues that public officials and the media are widely discussing. Researchers often take for granted that citizens know the basic facts about their government and political system. But sometimes those assumptions lead pollsters to include questions on topics that people know very little about, even though the topics are prominent. For example, an obvious topic for public opinion polling is the state of the economy. Although citizens can certainly express valid opinions about their own and the nation's economic situation, an extended inquiry might be hindered by citizens' ignorance about key facts of economics. Morin (1993b) cites studies demonstrating the public's deficiencies in economic knowledge. In those studies only one in five respondents came reasonably close to knowing the national unemployment rate, and only about half could identify the correct definition of the federal budget deficit among four choices presented to them. The public also has major gaps in its knowledge of the American political system. A study that compared citizens' levels of knowledge in the 1940s and 1950s with contemporary ones found that, after controlling for educational levels, Americans today at each level of education are less informed about many aspects of politics than were their counterparts in the earlier decades (Delli Carpini and Keeter 1991). The study speculated that today people are simply less interested in politics. Because respondents with low interest are more likely to express nonattitudes, these results suggest that pollsters must exercise great care to avoid measuring nonattitudes.

The presence of nonattitudes in survey responses has been well documented (Converse 1970; Taylor 1983; Norpoth and Lodge 1985). A particularly intriguing study by Bishop, Oldendick, and Tuchfarber (1980) included a fictitious item in surveys conducted in the greater Cincinnati area. Respondents were presented with the following statement and question about a nonexistent Public Affairs Act: "Some people say that the 1975 Public Affairs Act should be repealed. Do you agree or disagree with this idea?" One-third of the respondents offered an opinion. After an effort to filter out nonattitude responses on this fictitious question, researchers found that 10 percent of the sample still offered an opinion. When the *Washington Post* included a question on the nonexistent Public Affairs Act in a 1995 national survey, 43 percent of the respondents offered an opinion: 24 percent supported repeal of the act and 19 percent were opposed (Morin 1995a). The *Post* also administered slightly modified versions of the question to two other samples of respondents. One sample was asked, "President Clinton said that the 1975 Public Affairs Act should be repealed. Do you agree or disagree?" The other sample was asked: "The Republicans in Congress said that the 1975 Public Affairs Act should be repealed. Do you agree or disagree?" The responses changed when references to Clinton and the Republicans were included; 53 percent of respondents now offered an opinion. And as expected, the Clinton version of the question found Democrats more favorable than Republicans to repeal of the act by a 36 percent to 18 percent margin. But in the Republican version of the question the results were reversed, with 36 percent of the Republicans favoring repeal compared with only 19 percent of the Democrats. Clearly, respondents were seeking cues and guidance from the wording of the question itself, something more likely to happen when people are confronted with topics that they have no meaningful attitudes about. A recently published book (Bishop 2005) makes a strong case that much of what passes as public opinion in media polls is "an illusion, an artifact of measurement created by the way in which survey questions are designed and administered to respondents, who often construct their opinions on the spot in response to the frequently vague and ambiguous questions presented to them" (xvi). Bishop demonstrates that when respondents have weak or no genuine opinions, their responses to polling questions are even more susceptible to influence by the format, wording, order, and response alternatives of the questions.

The existence of nonattitudes is not surprising; after all, an interview is a social situation in which a respondent interacts, in person or by telephone, with an interviewer the respondent does not know. Few people in such circumstances want to admit that they are uninformed, particularly on a popular or timely issue. So most people answer the questions, and the interviewer duly records their responses. Even on a self-administered mail questionnaire or on a Web-based survey, respondents may feel the need to show they are informed, and therefore they answer questions about which they have little information.

But ascertaining the cause and extent of nonattitudes is much more complicated than simply blaming citizens for their low level of information and scant regard for public affairs. For example, one potential sign of nonattitudes is response instability. That is, if the same citizens give different responses to identical survey questions asked at different times, it suggests that their responses are not deeply rooted in any underlying belief and instead reflect nonattitudes. An alternative explanation is that genuine attitude change may have occurred during the multiple administrations of the survey. Perhaps societal conditions were in flux; perhaps the news media or the actions and statements of political leaders have influenced citizens' responses. Or perhaps there were changes in the survey, such as slight modifications in question wording or different placement of survey items within the overall questionnaire (see chapter 3 for a discussion of the importance of question order and question context).

With all these possible influences at work, it would be difficult to assess how much of any response instability is due to nonattitudes rather than other factors. The problem is made more difficult when a survey measures a complex issue or phenomenon with only one or two items. At this point, an illustration of how a public opinion survey based on nonattitudes can go astray and mislead the public might be useful.

An Example of Nonattitudes

Some years ago I was part of a sample of Ohioans queried about their views on land use problems. The interview took place over the phone, and the sample was probably picked from the telephone book or voter registration list. (I surmised this because the interviewer knew my name.) After the interviewer identified herself and the sponsor of the poll, she asked, "Tell me, Mr. Asher, what comes to your mind when you hear the term *land use?*" As a social scientist familiar with public opinion polling, I recognized this as a screening question aimed at determining whether it was worthwhile for the interviewer to proceed with the interview. If I did not have the vaguest idea what *land use* meant, there would be little point in continuing the interview. In any event, I responded, "Hmmm. Land use. How you use the land!" This response must have been sufficiently brilliant for the interviewer to continue with the survey, for she then asked me, "Mr. Asher, what do you think is the most important land use problem facing Ohio?" I mentally squirmed and silently gave thanks that the telephone interviewer could not see my difficulty in thinking up a land use problem. After a delay of about ten seconds, I responded with something like, "Planned growth and development." She then asked, "Which level of government—state, county, or local—do you think should have primary responsibility for addressing the problem of planned growth?" I responded, although to this day I cannot recall which level of government I mentioned.

The interview continued, and about three minutes later the interviewer asked me, "Mr. Asher, what do you think is the second-most-important land use problem facing Ohio?" This time I really had to struggle for an answer. Finally I uttered triumphantly, "Sufficient parks and green space." And, of course, the interviewer then asked me which level of government— state, county, or local—should have primary responsibility for rectifying this problem. I gave an answer (which I cannot recall) and said to myself that if the interviewer asked me about the third-most-important land use problem facing Ohio, I was going to blast her and the entire research project on the grounds that it was measuring nonattitudes. Fortunately for the interviewer, she never asked that question, and the interview was concluded.

Some months later, a government report based on this survey described which land use problems Ohioans ranked as most important and which levels of government Ohioans wanted to take the lead in addressing them. The report also contained policy recommendations and cited scientific evidence to support its conclusions. As I read the report I grew angrier and angrier; it used survey results derived from what I assume were nonattitudes, opinions from respondents like me, who gave answers in response to the questions but had little information about or interest in land use.

As sponsors of public opinion polls should recognize, not every issue of central importance to them will be an appropriate topic of inquiry for the citizenry at large. Different people have different concerns, and those who conduct public opinion polls must incorporate that fact into their plans and proceed accordingly.

The Use of Screening Questions

Researchers can take steps in opinion polls to minimize the number of responses that are superficial reactions to the interview stimulus. The simplest strategy is to make it socially acceptable for respondents to say that they are unfamiliar with the topic of a question. This response would result in that question being skipped. Another strategy is to employ screening or filter questions to separate likely attitude holders from nonattitude respondents. The study by Bishop, Oldendick, and Tuchfarber (1980) on the fictitious Public Affairs Act employed a variety of screening questions to reduce the frequency of nonattitudes, for example, "Do you have an opinion on this or not?" "Have you thought much about this issue?" Respondents who could not pass the screening questions were not asked about the Public Affairs Act.

Over many election cycles, the American National Election Studies (ANES) has employed a variety of questions to lessen the problem of nonattitudes. For example, one item in the 2000 election survey asked respondents whether they thought the federal government had become too powerful. The exact wording of the question was, "Some people are afraid the government in Washington is getting too powerful for the good of the country and the individual person. Others feel that the government in Washington is not getting too strong. Do you have an opinion on this or not?" Sixty-two percent of the respondents said they had an opinion, and 38 percent said no. The sizable percentage saying no may seem surprising given that the appropriate size and power of the federal government is an enduring controversy of American politics and certainly was an issue in the 2000 presidential campaign. This example suggests that topics hotly discussed by political elites and the media may not be of great importance to the average citizen. In this case, asking people whether they had an opinion was an effective screening question that eliminated nearly two-fifths of the respondents. But how many of the eliminated respondents would have answered the question if they had simply been asked whether they thought the government was becoming too powerful or not? As it was, among the 62 percent with an opinion on the topic, 65 percent thought government had grown too powerful, 31 percent thought it had not, and the rest said that it depended or that they did not know (even though they had stated in response to the screening question that they had an opinion on the issue).

Another form of a screening question used in the ANES surveys over time allowed respondents to say that they had not thought much about the issue. Those who chose that response were not asked their opinions, thereby reducing the measurement of nonattitudes. As an example, the 2008 ANES survey (and earlier ANES surveys) included the following item:

> Some people think the government should provide fewer services, even in areas such as health and education, in order to reduce spending. Suppose these people are at one end of a scale, at point number 1. Other people feel it is important for the government to provide many more services even if it means an increase in spending. Suppose these people are at the other end, at point 7. And, of course, some other people have opinions somewhere in between, at points 2, 3, 4, 5, or 6. Where would you place yourself on this scale or haven't you thought much about this?

Over time when respondents are asked this question, typically about 15 percent say they had not thought much about the matter. This does not automatically mean, however, that the other 85 percent had thought about it and had genuine opinions. In many years when this question was administered to the sample, the responses tended to cluster in the middle, in category 4. This kind of distribution may reflect large numbers of citizens who are satisfied with the status quo or who genuinely take a neutral position on the issue. Or it may reflect the tendency of some citizens with genuine, nonneutral preferences on the issue to hide their preferences by opting for the safe middle category. Many such responses can be moved out of the middle category by using a branching format question, in which citizens who opt for the middle category are then asked whether they favor one side or the other more (Aldrich et al. 1982).

It is also possible that the presence of a large number of people in the middle category may signal problems of nonattitudes in the measurement.

Perhaps some proportion of people in the middle category place themselves there because they do not want to admit to the interviewer that they have not thought much about the issue or are unable to place themselves along the scale. For them, the middle category may appear to be a safe position that makes them seem informed without having to take sides on the issue. If so, then some of the category 4 responses may be nonattitudes rather than genuinely neutral opinions, and the portrait of American public opinion on this issue may be misleading.

The 2008 American National Election Study (and earlier ANES surveys) used so-called thermometer questions to assess citizens' feelings toward various political figures. But before the respondents answered, they were given the option of skipping over names that they did not recognize, to lessen the measurement of nonattitudes. This measurement tool is based on the ability of people to relate points on a thermometer to figurative degrees of warmth and coldness toward objects. Survey respondents were given the following instructions:

> I'd like to get your feelings toward some of our political leaders and other people who are in the news these days. I'll read the name of a person and I'd like you to rate that person using something we call the feeling thermometer. Ratings between 50 degrees and 100 degrees mean that you feel favorable and warm toward the person. Ratings between 0 degrees and 50 degrees mean that you don't feel favorable toward the person and that you don't care too much for that person. You would rate the person at the 50 degree mark if you don't feel particularly warm or cold toward the person. If we come to a person whose name you don't recognize, you don't need to rate that person. Just tell me and we'll move on to the next one.

Ideally, respondents who do not recognize a name or who feel they are unable to evaluate the person named would indicate that to the interviewer. However, the instructions may encourage some respondents to place the subjects of the survey at the 50-degree mark, including those whose names they do not recognize. Table 2-1 indicates how respondents rated various political figures in 2008. Keep in mind that George Bush was the outgoing Republican president, Barack Obama and John McCain were the major party candidates for president, Joe Biden and Sarah Palin were the major party candidates for vice president, Condoleezza Rice was a top level adviser to President Bush, and Rush Limbaugh a famous conservative commentator.

The percentage of respondents who did not recognize George Bush, Barack Obama, and John McCain or who could not evaluate them was very small; the comparable percentages for the other four political figures was much higher with Biden at 27 percent (4 + 23), Limbaugh at 25 percent

(3 + 22), Palin at 16 percent (3 + 13), and Rice at 15 percent (2 + 13). It appears, then, that the screening questions worked well because more of the respondents did not rate the less well-known political figures. However, it is disquieting that among the citizens who were able to rate these non-presidential political figures, a higher proportion gave a rating of 50 to Biden, Palin, Rice, and Limbaugh than to Bush, Obama, and McCain. (See the last column of Table 2-1.) For example, of those citizens evaluating Bush on the thermometer, only 11 percent (11/(11 + 88)) gave him a rating of 50. But of the proportion of respondents who could rate Limbaugh, 27 percent (20/(20 + 55)) gave him a rating of 50.

Since Limbaugh was not as well known as Bush, Obama, and McCain, it is not surprising that more respondents rated him at 50 on the thermometer scale. But the problem of measuring nonattitudes may also be at work here. Was a rating of 50 a genuine neutral point or simply a convenient

Table 2-1 Thermometer Ratings of Seven Political Figures (in percentages)

Figure	Rating other than 50	Rating of 50	Does not recognize	Cannot evaluate	Total % (N)	% of Ratings at 50
			Evaluation			
Bush	88	11	0	1	100 (2,323)	11
Obama	87	12	0	1	100 (2,323)	12
McCain	80	19	1	1	100 (2,323)	19
Biden	54	19	23	4	100 (2,323)	26
Palin	66	17	13	3	100 (2,323)	20
Rice	66	19	13	2	100 (2,323)	22
Limbaugh	55	20	22	3	100 (2,323)	27

Source: 2008 American National Election Study, Stanford University and the University of Michigan producers.

Note: Table entries are the percentage of respondents ranking each political figure in each category. The last column is the second column divided by the sum of the first two columns.

and safe home for the expression of nonattitudes that were not filtered out by the screening question? The latter interpretation is given greater credibility by Rush Limbaugh's issue stances. Limbaugh, as a strong conservative and an articulate and passionate advocate for his positions, is not likely to generate a lot of neutral responses—unless the respondent really knows little about his politics and is expressing nonattitudes rather than genuine opinions.

Another example of the effects of a screening question is provided by the measurement of self-professed ideology in the 2008 ANES survey. Respondents were asked the following question: "We hear a lot of talk these days about liberals and conservatives. Here is a seven point scale on which the political views that people might hold are arranged from extremely liberal to extremely conservative. Where would you place yourself on this scale, or haven't you thought much about this?" Despite the widespread use of liberal-conservative terminology in the discussion of politics and campaigns, almost one-fourth of Americans said they haven't thought much about it. Of those who could place themselves on this seven-point scale, 21 percent fell on the liberal side, 32 percent on the conservative side, and 22 percent in the moderate middle. When respondents who initially said moderate or hadn't thought much about it were pushed (If you had to choose, would you consider yourself a liberal or a conservative?), the conservative advantage in ideological self-definition grew: 54 percent conservative, 36 percent liberal, and 10 percent moderate (volunteered). Of course, one can question whether it is appropriate to force people out of the middle (in this case moderate) category, a topic we turn to in the next section.

A study by Benson (2001) provides a striking example of the consequences of including a screening question. In a study of citizens' attitudes about school vouchers and charter schools, half the respondents were simply asked whether they favored or opposed these initiatives, with no screening question or "undecided" category. The other half of the sample was asked the same questions with the added phrase, "or haven't you heard enough about that to have an opinion?" For the voucher question asked without the screening question, only 4 percent of the respondents volunteered "don't know" responses. But when provided the "haven't heard enough" option, 33 percent chose it. The charter school differences were even greater. Only 9 percent volunteered "don't know" to the first form of the question, but fully 63 percent said that they had not heard enough to have an opinion when asked the second form of the item. As Benson (2001, 40) noted, the percentage of respondents favoring charter schools plummeted from 62 percent to 25 percent because of the addition of the screening question. The level of popular support for charter schools looks very different depending on which form of the question one examines.

Finally, two examples from public opinion polling on current issues in 2009 demonstrate the impact on response patterns of including or excluding a screening question. The first example deals with the nomination of Sonia Sotomayor to the U.S. Supreme Court. An AP-GfK poll conducted on May 28–June 1, 2009, asked the following question of a national sample of adult Americans:

Q. "As you may know, Supreme Court Justice David Souter is retiring, and President Obama has nominated Sonia Sotomayor to replace him. Is your opinion of Supreme Court nominee Sonia Sotomayor favorable, unfavorable, or haven't you heard enough about Sonia Sotomayor yet to have an opinion?"

Favorable	34%
Unfavorable	18%
Haven't heard enough	39%
Unsure	9%

At almost the same time (May 26–June 1, 2009), a Quinnipiac University poll asked:

Q. "Do you approve or disapprove of President Obama's nomination of Sonia Sotomayor to the Supreme Court?"

Approve	55%
Disapprove	25%
Unsure	20%

The obvious difference between these two questions is the inclusion of the screening phrase "or haven't you heard enough . . ." in the first item. But look at the difference it makes in the pattern of responses. Imagine a newspaper story or a political argument that uses one question versus the other. The first item might result in a statement that about only one-third of Americans favor Sotomayor, while the second question might lead to the assertion that a clear majority of Americans approve of Sotomayor.

Polls conducted by different polling organizations in late 2009 on health care reform also demonstrate the consequences of including a screening component. An ABC News/*Washington Post* poll (November 12–15, 2009) asked, "Do you approve or disapprove of the way Obama is handling health care?" and found 47 percent of Americans approved, 49 percent disapproved, and 3 percent were unsure. A CBS News poll (November 13–16, 2009) asked the identical question and found 44 percent approval, 48 percent disapproval, and 8 percent unsure. A CNN/ Opinion Research Corporation poll (October 30–November 1, 2009) queried, "From everything you have heard or read so far, do you favor or oppose Barack Obama's plan to reform health care?" and found 45 percent in favor, 53 percent opposed, and 2 percent unsure. Finally, an NBC

News/*Wall Street Journal* poll (October 22–25, 2009) asked: "From what you have heard about Barack Obama's health care plan, do you think his plan is a good idea or a bad idea? If you do not have an opinion either way, please just say so." Here the results were 38 percent good idea, 42 percent bad idea, 16 percent no opinion, and 4 percent unsure. Clearly, the NBC/*Wall Street Journal* poll gives a somewhat different picture of American public opinion in suggesting that 20 percent (16 + 4) of Americans do not have a definite opinion on health care in contrast to the CNN poll, which indicates that only 2 percent of Americans are without a clear position.

Nonattitudes and the Middle Position in Survey Questions

The preceding examples illustrate how difficult it is to assess the magnitude of the nonattitude problem. They also raise another problem in attitude and opinion measurement: What does it mean when a person replies to a survey question, "I don't know" or "I can't decide" or "It depends"? Do these responses represent a genuinely neutral stance or something else? Should the responses of holders of nonattitudes be included at the neutral or middle point? Or should they be at a distinct point off the measurement scale, so as not to create a misleading image of large numbers of citizens thoughtfully adopting the middle position?

The response alternatives included in an item affect the extent of nonattitudes. For example, a CBS News/*New York Times* poll conducted in November 1985 asked a national sample of Americans, "Who should have the most say about what cuts should be made to balance the budget—the president or Congress?" Note that the question did not give respondents the option of stating that the president and Congress should have an equal say. About 4 percent of the sample volunteered that response, but what percentage of Americans would have opted for this alternative had it been explicitly presented? In marked contrast is the following question in a November 1985 ABC News/*Washington Post* poll: "As things presently stand, who do you think is ahead in military power, the United States or the Soviet Union, or do you think they are about the same in military strength?" Twenty-four percent said the United States was ahead, 26 percent said the Soviets were, 4 percent had no opinion, and 46 percent said that both nations were about the same in military strength. In fact, in the eight times that ABC News/*Washington Post* pollsters asked samples of Americans this question between 1979 and 1991, the percentage of respondents saying "the same" ranged from 34 to 55, with an average of 44. One can only speculate what the responses would have looked like if the middle choice had not been provided.

Research on the effects of including a middle choice in the response alternatives shows that such an option typically generates about 25 percent more noncommittal responses (Schuman and Presser 1977; Bishop, Oldendick, and Tuchfarber 1980; Presser and Schuman 1980). This finding suggests that the omission of such a choice will result in many substantive responses that are not very meaningful from citizens who have weak or nonexistent attitudes on a subject. In one study, Presser and Schuman (1980) administered survey items in two forms to random subsamples. The only difference between the two forms was that one offered a middle alternative and the other did not. For example, one item asked about the penalties for using marijuana: "In your opinion, should the penalties for using marijuana be more strict, less strict, or about the same as they are now?" The other version read, "In your opinion, should the penalties for using marijuana be more strict or less strict than they are now?" On average, about 23 percent of respondents answered "about the same as they are now" when that choice was included in the question. Only about 8 percent volunteered that response when it was not included.

Research by Bishop (1987) further demonstrates how the presence or absence of a middle response alternative can affect survey responses. Based on a series of experiments, Bishop's work confirmed earlier research in finding that citizens are much more likely to choose the middle alternative when it is included in the question than when it is omitted. Moreover, simply mentioning the middle category in the preface to a survey question will encourage respondents to select that option, even when it is not listed among the response alternatives. More important, Bishop presents evidence that suggests that "people who select a middle alternative when it is offered would not necessarily answer the question in the same way as other respondents if forced to choose between the polar alternatives" when the middle option is not provided (227).

The interpretation of a "don't know" response can be especially problematic because "don't know" can mean many different things (Coombs and Coombs 1976–1977; Faulkenberry and Mason 1978). For some people, "don't know" simply reflects the absence of a real attitude on the topic, but for others it may represent an inability to choose among contending positions. Smith (1984, 229) points out other ways in which "don't know" responses might arise. Respondents may be too insecure to take a stance, or they may decline to state their opinions out of a strong sense of privacy or because they do not want to offend anybody. Some respondents may want to hasten the completion of the interview by saying "don't know," thereby avoiding follow-up questions. Finally, just as respondents' nonattitudes may be disguised as attitudes, so too their middle responses (including "don't know") may mask genuine attitudes. Gilljam and Granberg (1993) found that poll respondents who were induced to respond to a survey item after they had initially given a "don't know" response to it expressed attitudes that were predictive of behavior. They concluded that indeed some poll respondents who had genuine attitudes kept them concealed by opting for the "don't know" response.

Berinsky (2004) has raised important normative questions about the reasons for and the consequences of "don't know" responses. He talks about two different paths through which a poll respondent might offer a "don't know" response. Certainly, for whatever reasons, citizens may not know abut the issue. But as Berinsky notes, there are some citizens who have opinions but fail to offer them in response to a polling question. Instead, these citizens may respond "don't know" because of perceived social pressures and the perceived costs of expressing a definite opinion on the topic at hand. If it turns out that the pressure not to offer an opinion on an issue is related to a particular stance on that issue, then the opinions that are expressed may not be fully representative of the actual range of opinions. For example, what if some citizens perceive that a particular response to a race-related question might be viewed as being anti-black? These citizens offer a "don't know" response, rather than their true opinion, because they do not want to appear prejudiced (see chapter 7 for a real-world example involving the election of David Dinkins as mayor of New York City). Berinsky's analysis showed that on a variety of issues, "don't know" responses may be masking some distinct policy preferences and that thus the responses of those who expressed a definite opinion were not fully representative of all the opinions in the sample. Berinsky's work raises a challenge to one of the major strengths of scientific public opinion polls—their representativeness. If distinct subsets of respondents have reasons to hide their true preference using the "don't know" category, then we have lost some valuable information about the opinions of the citizenry. The media and users of public opinion polls may need to be more sensitive to what "don't know" responses might actually mean.

Converse (1976–1977) investigated the characteristics of respondents, as well as the properties of survey questions, that might affect the frequency of "no opinion" and "don't know" answers. She found, as expected, that the higher the respondents' level of education, the less likely they were to give "no opinion" or "don't know" replies. For question characteristics, Converse found that the most important feature was the content of the item. As the subject matter of the question became more remote from the concerns and interests of citizens, the frequency of "no opinion" and "don't know" responses increased.

Other research sheds further light on how response alternatives and their ordering affect survey responses. Krosnick and Alwin (1987) found that respondents with less cognitive sophistication—less formal education and limited vocabularies—were more likely to be influenced by the order in which the responses were stated. Bishop (1990) also found that the effects on responses of using or not using a middle alternative are most pronounced among citizens who are less involved with the particular topic of the survey question. In general, the implications of the Converse, Bishop, and Krosnick and Alwin studies are that the consequences of response alternatives and their ordering are genuine but complex. Therefore pollsters must be sensitive to the potential distortion, and even manipulation, of responses that might occur because of how the response choices are presented.

Is it a good idea to force responses into polar categories and minimize middle or neutral answers? Or is it better to encourage people to choose the middle position? The answer, of course, is that it depends. If people

"I'm undecided, but that doesn't mean I'm apathetic or uninformed."

have genuine attitudes, then the public opinion researcher wants those attitudes clearly expressed. The inclusion of a middle category in such a situation might result in cautious citizens opting for the middle position, particularly on controversial issues about which they might not want to reveal their true opinions to the interviewer. Yet the omission of a middle category might lead people with weak or nonexistent opinions on an issue to choose one of the genuine response options, thereby creating false impressions of genuine attitudes. A similar dilemma occurs with screening questions. The researcher wants to screen out nonattitudes but does not want to make it too easy for people to avoid answering questions on which they have real views, or too difficult for them to answer questions when they have real, although weak, attitudes.

This is a problem without a simple solution. The public opinion pollster and the consumer of the research must simply be sensitive to whether and in what form screening questions are used on a survey. They must also be aware of the response alternatives provided to the respondents. Finally, the appropriateness of particular substantive questions to particular samples of citizens should always be a central concern of the political analyst and the public opinion consumer. In the political realm, issues of great concern to political elites may be of little interest to the rank and file.

Response Instability and Nonattitudes

If a survey is measuring genuine attitudes, the responses should show some degree of stability over time. Yet often survey responses fluctuate radically over a relatively short period. This type of fluctuation raises questions about how real the measured opinions were in the first place. Instability of responses to identical polling questions asked over time may be an indicator of nonattitudes. Zaller and Feldman (1992), however, offer a different explanation for unstable attitudes. They argue that citizens do not have highly specific, fixed attitudes about many topics; instead, people often have multiple and sometimes conflicting opinions on issues. How people respond to a particular survey question on a topic may be a function of what they happen to have on their minds at the time of the survey. And what is on their minds will be influenced both by their most recent life experiences and by the cues that the survey question provides. It is thus possible for citizens to respond differently on issues over a short period of time without that instability necessarily indicating nonattitudes: It may be that the real world or the survey context within which people respond to polling questions has changed. Assessment of the magnitude of the nonattitudes problem then becomes even more difficult.

The work of Zaller and Feldman has many implications. First, it serves as a reminder that the responses to survey questions can be affected by characteristics of the survey instrument, including question wording, question order, and response alternatives. Second, it also is a warning that opinions on complex topics should always be assessed using multiple survey items—not just one or two. Unfortunately, in many omnibus public opinion surveys, in which the investigators are trying to cover a wide variety of topics, it may be impossible to include multiple items on a single topic because of time and space considerations. The results one gets are then a function of which particular item was used. (This problem is discussed in greater depth in chapter 8.)

Finally, Zaller and Feldman's notion that the considerations that citizens bring to bear in the survey context affect their responses provides a rationale for giving respondents new information to find out whether their responses then change. For example, suppose one asked a sample of senior citizens about their views on Medicare-provided prescription drug benefits and received overwhelmingly supportive responses. Suppose that a follow-up question asking whether respondents would support such a program if it means higher Medicare premiums then produced much lower support for the program. Is this change in the distribution of opinions an indication of nonattitudes? The answer, of course, is no. The different distribution reflects the different considerations that come into play in the responses to the two questions. The first question evokes a health concern; the second introduces the cost factor and changes how respondents think about the issue. (This example of introducing new information to the respondent should not be confused with the illegitimate push polls discussed in chapter 7. Study of whether respondents' views on an issue change when new information is presented to them is appropriate.)

One strategy that uses multiple items to determine how genuine measured opinions really are is the "mushiness index" developed by the polling firm of Yankelovich, Skelly, and White. It was designed to assess the volatility of the public's views on issues, particularly the ones on which citizens provide answers even though they have little information or understanding about them. The mushiness index has four components in addition to a person's position on a particular issue: how much the issue affects the respondent personally, how well informed the respondent feels he or she is on the issue, how much the respondent discusses the issue with family and friends, and the respondent's own assessment of how likely it is that his or her views on the issue will change (Keene and Sackett 1981). On the basis of these criteria, Yankelovich, Skelly, and White placed issues into three categories, ranging from very volatile, or "mushy," to firm. They found that, in general, attitudes on domestic policy were less mushy than those on foreign policy.

The usefulness of the mushiness index is illustrated by the following example (Keene and Sackett 1981, 51). A sample of Americans was asked, "Do you favor or oppose restricting imports of foreign goods such as Japanese cars, textiles, and steel, which are less expensive than American products?" Fifty-four percent favored restricting imports, 41 percent opposed restrictions, and only 5 percent were unsure. But when the sample was broken down into three groups according to responses to the four mushiness criteria, the patterns of response were quite different. Among the mushiest group, 39 percent favored restrictions, 37 percent opposed them, and 24 percent were unsure; among the firmest group, 62 percent favored restrictions, 37 percent opposed them, and 1 percent were unsure.

How much respondents know about an issue (one component of the mushiness index) clearly affects their attitudes. When expansion of NATO became a prominent political issue in 1997, pollsters began asking questions about it. Because Americans are likely to have low levels of information and substantial nonattitudes about NATO and NATO expansion, a mushiness approach to ascertaining attitudes about the future of NATO would be appropriate. One poll conducted in early 1997 found that about 70 percent of the respondents had heard little about NATO expansion (Morin 1997b). Almost one-fourth incorrectly believed that Russia already was a member of NATO, and about 60 percent were predisposed toward NATO enlargement, a level of support that dropped substantially when NATO expansion was linked to the financial and other costs associated with bringing new members into the alliance. In general, surveys dealing with foreign affairs are more susceptible to the measurement of nonattitudes because such topics tend not to be as salient and interesting to many Americans.

Moore (2009) was very critical of pollsters for giving respondents information about a topic and then measuring their attitudes. He argued that pollsters should first ascertain whether people have information about the topic; if so, then measure their opinions. Moore cited two polls that contained questions designed to measure what Americans thought about one-party control of the national government that resulted from the 2008 election outcomes. A CNN poll (November 6–9, 2008) asked the following forced choice question:

Q. As you may know, the Democrats will control both the Senate and the House of Representatives, as well as the presidency. Do you think this will be good for the country or bad for the country?

Good	59%
Bad	38%
Unsure	3%

An Associated Press/GfK poll (November 6–10, 2008) asked the following question:

Q. As you may know, the Democrats will now control the House of Representatives, the Senate, and the presidency. Do you think it is good for the country, bad for the country, or does it not really make a difference that the Democrats now control the House, the Senate and the presidency?

Good	42%
Bad	34%
No difference	20%
Unsure	4%

Obviously, the inclusion of the "no difference" alternative in the second question has dramatically changed the distribution of the responses. In the first question, a sizable majority thought Democratic control was good for the country; in the second question, only a small plurality thought the same way. But Moore's main objection was that providing information to the respondents was creating opinion. He argued:

> . . . both polling organizations deliberately manipulated their respondents to come up with an opinion . . . by giving them information up front. Why did they need to tell the respondents that the Democrats controlled all three branches? Why not find out how many people knew that, and then—among those who knew it—ask whether it was good or bad, didn't make a difference, or didn't they have an opinion?
>
> But the major media pollsters are generally not interested in realistic measures of public opinion. . . . For CNN to say that 97 percent of Americans believe that Democratic control of the government is either "good" or "bad" . . . may fit journalistic needs but . . . is simply not true.

The mushiness index is not used widely in surveys, in part because it is too costly and time-consuming to ask all the questions needed to construct it, particularly when the survey covers a number of things. Nevertheless, the concept of mushiness is of interest analytically because it helps to explain a number of apparent anomalies in American public opinion. One puzzle is the rapid swings in public opinion often observed after the president of the United States delivers a speech devoted to a single issue, particularly a foreign policy issue. Public opinion is most volatile on issues that seem (a) distant in terms of their likely effects on people and (b) not especially susceptible to citizen influence. Americans often praise presidents for their ability to move public opinion, not recognizing that on some issues a somewhat mindless "follow the leader" mentality is at work, so that a president would be successful in moving public opinion in any direction, assuming the

White House is able to present the issue as beneficial to both the president's and citizens' objectives.

The rationale underlying the mushiness index did not originate with Yankelovich, Skelly, and White. More than fifty years ago George Gallup (1947) espoused survey designs that measured multiple aspects of a person's opinion. Indeed, Schuman and Presser (1981) and other investigators have emphasized the need to measure the importance of an issue to a person, as well as his or her opinion about it, to better understand the dynamics of attitude change. Yankelovich, Skelly, and White did, however, have the public relations acumen to coin a catchy phrase for their finding, which built on the results of earlier public opinion studies.

One suspects that many survey questions deserve high mushiness scores, but unfortunately those scores will not be calculated because, faced with insufficient time and space on the survey, researchers will not ask the necessary follow-up questions. Thus poll users need to ask themselves whether the topic of a survey is likely to be of concern to respondents or whether they will see it as an abstraction with little immediate and practical relevance. If the former, mushiness and nonattitudes are not likely to be a serious problem. A complicating factor is that the topic of a survey is likely to be of varying importance to different segments of the American population. Unemployed steelworkers and autoworkers are more likely to be concerned about foreign imports and thus to have more stable attitudes about them than, say, college students. Senior citizens are more likely to have well-developed views on Social Security and Medicare than a youthful population group. American public opinion on a particular issue includes the rather divergent views of various subgroups of the population, some of whom have genuine attitudes on the issue while others do not. Moreover, for those seeking to relate public opinion to the processes and decisions of government, the whole of public opinion may be less important than the opinion of a particular subset of people. On certain issues the views of a few people with genuine attitudes may have the greatest impact on government policy and policymakers.

Implications for Democracy and Public Policy

There is growing debate about how serious the problem of nonattitudes is in public opinion polling. Although there is widespread agreement that the American populace (or substantial portions of it) is poorly informed on many aspects of politics and public life (Delli Carpini and Keeter 1991, 1996; Alvarez and Brehm 2002), conclusions differ about what that ignorance about particular topics means for public opinion polling and for the functioning of a democracy. Some blame citizens for their disengagement and low information levels and wonder whether poll results can really tell us anything meaningful about citizens' policy preferences on some matters. Others say that part of the blame must be shared by the methods of polling, which do not provide citizens a full opportunity to elaborate on their preferences and opinions. Other scholars try to resolve this by partitioning the citizenry into separate groups defined by differing levels of political knowledge and then determining what impact those varying knowledge levels have on opinion formation and opinion stability. For example, Gilens (2001) distinguishes between general political knowledge and policy-specific information and examines their impact on the policy views of Americans. He observes that ignorance of policy-specific information leads many citizens to hold political views different from what they would profess had they acquired policy-specific knowledge. But he finds that the impact of policy-specific information is greatest for Americans with the highest levels of general knowledge; it is those citizens who are most likely to incorporate new information into their political judgments and perhaps change their views. In this situation, attitude change is not response instability and evidence of nonattitudes but instead is an indicator of "learning" upon receipt and incorporation of new information.

In a related vein, a study of the 1997 Canadian election took advantage of the fact that three of the political party leaders were new to the national scene, presenting the opportunity to study the impact of learning on public attitudes toward them (Blais et al. 2000). In a poll conducted prior to the election, respondents were asked whether they knew a lot, a little, or nothing at all about each of the leaders. In another survey conducted after the election, the same respondents (including those who earlier claimed they knew nothing about the leaders) were asked whether they liked or disliked each leader. One finding was that on average 74 percent of the Canadian respondents who indicated they were uninformed about a leader were willing and able to offer an opinion about that person, a reflection of the tendency of people to provide answers even when they have a meager knowledge base. The expressed likes and dislikes about the leaders did have a predictable impact on vote choice, more so for the most knowledgeable respondents but also for the least knowledgeable. The authors concluded that the least informed respondents were not answering randomly and expressing nonattitudes but instead were providing a meaningful rating of the leaders.

My own view (shared by Perlmutter [2002], Bishop [2005], and many others) is that Americans express opinions on many things, even when they have little information, and that the very act of polling and asking questions often creates opinions that might not otherwise be evident. The seriousness of the nonattitudes problem is partially a function of the purpose for which the polling results are being used. If one is merely describing the distribution of Americans' responses to some survey item, then the presence of some nonattitude responses in that distribution is not very worrisome. But if the poll results are being used to justify the adoption, continuation, modification, or elimination of some policy or program, then nonattitude responses are a more serious problem. And because descriptive polls are often exploited and distorted in policy arguments, the problem of nonattitudes must remain a concern. When we hear policy advocates cite reputable polls showing that Americans favor peacekeeping in Liberia, expanded free trade agreements, negotiations with North Korea, or greater engagement in various regions throughout the world, we must wonder how careful the investigators were to minimize the problem of nonattitudes during the data collection stage and how sensitive they were to the problem in publicly reporting their results. And lest readers believe that the problem of nonattitudes arises only in the context of foreign policy and international affairs, let me conclude this section with a discussion of a state-level poll. In 2001, a statewide poll was conducted in Ohio about citizens' support for passenger train service (Williams 2001). The two key items in the survey were the following:

Q: Ohio officials have considered promoting the development of passenger-train services. Do you strongly favor, favor, neither favor nor oppose, oppose, or strongly oppose passenger-train services in Ohio?

Strongly favor	30%
Favor	50%
Neither favor nor oppose	11%
Oppose	5%
Strongly oppose	1%
Refused to answer	0%
Don't know	3%

Q. If you were considering a trip to somewhere 75 to 300 miles away from home, and a fast, modern rail system was available in Ohio, how likely is it you would consider traveling by train?

Very likely	47%
Somewhat likely	37%
Somewhat unlikely	6%
Very unlikely	9%
Refused to answer	0%
Don't know	1%

Proponents of passenger rail service trumpeted the poll results. Bill Hutchison, president of the Ohio Association of Railroad Passengers, a sponsor of the study, said,

We had an idea that people were supportive [of rail] but had no way to back up that assertion. Mobility is being threatened by a transportation system that has all the balance of a two-legged stool. A third leg needs to be added, and that leg is rail passenger service. We hope public officials, community leaders and others will pay close attention to the results of this survey. (Williams 2001, C5)

Clearly the advocates of passenger rail wanted to use the poll results to help make the case for their cause. Why might citizens be wary of how the poll was used by advocates of passenger rail?

First, there was no screening question to try to weed out respondents who really had not thought about the issue. Second, the wording of the first question did not offer a "don't know" alternative but instead pushed respondents into one of the five mentioned categories. Third, the wording of the second question is somewhat suspect inasmuch as it asks respondents how likely it is that they would *consider* traveling by train and not the more direct question of how likely it is that they would travel by train. The question was also a bit leading and argumentative in its reference to a "fast, modern rail system." Fourth, there are probably insufficient items to measure the many aspects of passenger rail service, including how passenger rail would be funded. There was only one question in the survey about funding; it asked respondents which of four revenue sources they preferred: using state general revenue funds such as sales taxes (24 percent), borrowing money through a state bond issue (23 percent), raising the state gasoline tax by a penny per gallon (21 percent), or taking money from highway and transportation funds (19 percent). This is not a bad question, but it makes paying for passenger rail seem fairly easy to accomplish without much burden to the citizenry. The question does not truly tap how willing Ohioans are to spend more for passenger rail service or to take dollars from other programs to pay for it. Overall, the survey makes it easy for Ohioans to endorse passenger rail; after all, who would be against rail service if it could be established so easily? There are likely many nonattitudes in the responses; at minimum, the results seem to be a good candidate for a "mushiness" evaluation. The bottom line is that the poll results are being used to influence the outcome of a public policy debate on passenger rail.

Conclusion

The problem of nonattitudes remains one of the least considered aspects of public opinion polling. Other facets of public opinion research, such as question wording and sampling, receive much more attention, even to the point of being mentioned in television and newspaper reports of public opinion polls. But very few people raise the fundamental questions: Was the topic of the survey of interest to the respondents? Did the poll query people on topics about which they held genuine views? Did the survey questions adequately capture the complexity of the issue being studied?

Assessing the size of the problem of nonattitudes is a difficult task made even more so by the tendency of people to respond to questions not in terms of the questions' actual purpose and content but in terms of the cues that the questions provide and whatever meaning (often idiosyncratic) respondents read into them. For example, a person who is asked whether she favors selling military equipment to Saudi Arabia might answer the question not on the basis of any knowledge about Saudi Arabia but on the basis of a predisposition toward the weapons industry in general (she might be a stockholder in a firm that manufactures weapons). Citizens asked whether they favor joint U.S.-Russian space ventures might respond on the basis of their underlying view of Russia rather than on the basis of opinions about the best way to explore space.

Although nonattitudes can be a polling problem, Americans should not disregard polls, because on many issues the general public has genuine attitudes and is willing and able to express them. Only a small subset of the public may have real opinions on other issues, but even then events may transform such an issue into one that engages the serious attention of the mass public. Sometimes the public may even seem fickle on the issues it cares about and its positions on them. For example, Oreskes (1990) observed that in 1989, 64 percent of Americans said the drug problem was the most important one facing the nation. Yet a year later only 10 percent cited drugs as the most serious problem. Certainly it was not victory in the drug war that led citizens to downgrade the importance of the drug problem. Instead, it was more a matter of media and presidential emphasis. When the media and the president focused on the drug menace, then many Americans saw the issue as the critical one facing the nation. But as new issues arose and media and political attention shifted, Americans' views of which issues were critical also changed.

In conclusion, if pollsters are simply curious about what voters know and think about obscure issues, they can certainly ask questions, elicit a lot of nonattitudes, and report the results. No great harm is done, unless claims are made that the poll results demonstrate that citizens prefer one policy alternative over another. But when such claims are made, one should be skeptical, especially if the poll is about some issue remote from most people's lives. For example, while Americans may be informed and have genuine attitudes about Iraq, far fewer are aware of Darfur, yet pollsters ask about both. When the Gallup Poll queried Americans in February 2006 whether they could name six world leaders—the American secretary of state, the leader of Cuba, the presidents of Russia and Mexico, the prime minister of Great Britain, and the chancellor of Germany—18 percent of the respondents could name none, 17 percent one, and 14 percent two leaders. At the other end, only 2 percent could name all six and 15 percent five of the six. This suggests that a substantial number of Americans have major gaps in their knowledge about world affairs and world leaders. It may also suggest that we be alert to nonattitudes in measuring opinions about world affairs. When a *Washington Post* poll (April 21–24, 2009) asked Americans, "Do you approve or disapprove of the way Obama is handling U.S. relations with Cuba?" and then followed that up by a set of forced choice questions with no middle or unsure alternative dealing with diplomatic relations, trade embargo, and travel bans, perhaps one might worry that this approach is measuring nonattitudes or at least generating more definitive opinions than actually exist. Perhaps respondents should have been asked first what they know about American policy toward Cuba. Those respondents who had some knowledge on the topic could then be asked their opinions about aspects of U.S.-Cuban relations. (Similar examples and arguments can be made for many aspects of domestic affairs.) Pollsters and the media could help us better understand public opinion and the possible presence of nonattitudes if they would report citizens' opinions broken down by knowledge level, education level, or some other characteristic that measures their likely competence and awareness. If we observe that opinions and preferences differ dramatically according to the respondents' levels of information, that would certainly sensitize us to the potential problem of nonattitudes among some of them.

Nonattitudes are more a problem of the respondent than of the measuring instrument—that is, nonattitudes can arise even when a question is carefully constructed without any loaded words or implied alternatives. Nevertheless, deficiencies in the questions themselves can contribute to the problem of nonattitudes, as well as to many other difficulties encountered in public opinion polling. In the next chapter we take a closer look at how question wording, question order, and question context can affect the results of public opinion polls.

Exercises

1. In the first and second exercises in chapter 1, you were asked to keep a log of newspaper and newsmagazine polls. Now examine the subject matter of those polls and make your own judgment about whether nonattitudes are likely to be a problem. Then examine the actual wording of the questions (where available) to see whether screening questions were used and whether the "don't know" alternative was explicitly included.

2. Design a five-item survey on some aspect of popular culture that you believe would generate genuine attitudes among a sample of college students but would produce many nonattitudes among a sample of parents of college students.
3. Go to the Web site of any polling organization, such as Gallup, Harris Interactive, or Program on International Policy Attitudes (PIPA), and look for a summary report or press release on any poll dealing with foreign policy and international affairs other than Iraq, Afghanistan, and the war on terrorism. Examine that report or press release and draw your own conclusions about whether nonattitudes are likely to be a problem.

3 Wording and Context of Questions

Of all the pitfalls associated with public opinion polling, question wording is probably the one most familiar to consumers of public opinion research. The use of a loaded word or an inflammatory phrase can affect the pattern of responses to a survey question. For example, for a poll to show weak support for federal assistance to financially beleaguered entities (such as the savings and loan industry in the 1990s or the American automobile industry in 2009), the pollster need only ask Americans whether they favor a federal "bailout" of those entities. Few people favor a bailout, but many more support federal loans with proper safeguards that the moneys will be repaid. A poll likely to indicate scant support for providing foreign aid will ask an argumentative and leading question such as, Do you favor giving foreign aid to other nations when there are children in the United States who are suffering from hunger? To demonstrate support for foreign aid, a pollster could "load" the question differently: Do you favor giving foreign aid to other nations to help them resist terrorism and thereby enhance our own national security?

Individuals and groups with an ax to grind can easily construct questions that will generate the responses they want. The response alternatives they provide the interviewees also can help them achieve the intended result. As noted in chapter 2, if a middle alternative is not listed as one of the choices, fewer citizens will volunteer one, and that can alter the interpretation of a poll. For example, if a mayor wants a poll to indicate support for a city's spending policies on garbage collection, he or she might ask this question: Do you think the city is spending too much, too little, or about the right amount on garbage collection? Clearly, the response "about the right amount" is an endorsement of the mayor's current policies, and its inclusion as an explicit response alternative will provide a portrait of public opinion more supportive of the mayor's policies.

If an advocacy group wants to demonstrate through public opinion surveys that its issues are at the forefront of citizens' concerns, it might simply commission polls that ask citizens to select from a list of problems the most important one facing the nation and place the group's issue on the list among a group of relatively minor ones. For example, if an environmental group wanted to demonstrate the importance of the environment, it might ask Americans which of the following is the most important problem facing the nation: environmental quality, excessive telemarketing, traffic congestion, or ticket scalping at entertainment events. Undoubtedly, this survey would discover that environmental quality was the number-one issue cited. But what if the environmental group presented the results of this rather silly example without providing the actual question wording and response alternatives? Citizens might mistakenly assume that education, national defense, terrorism, immigration, Social Security, health care, and other prominent issues were on the list and that environmental quality came out on top in competition with all of those other major issues.

Even when the sponsor has no obvious ax to grind, question wording choices greatly influence the results obtained. In many instances highly reputable polling organizations have arrived at divergent conclusions simply because they employed different (although well-constructed) questions on a particular topic.

Less obvious than the impact of question wording is the effect on responses of the order and context in which specific questions are placed. A typical public opinion survey includes many questions, and the placement of a particular question can affect the responses to it. Yet most consumers of public opinion research know little about item order and therefore have little sense of how the context has helped to shape the responses.

Consider another hypothetical example—a survey assessing popular attitudes toward economic relations with China. The key question measuring support for most-favored-nation trade status for China is preceded by a battery of items about Chinese economic and trade policies that have cost American jobs. Obviously, the early questions on Chinese economic and trade policies will predispose respondents to be more hostile toward granting China favorable trade conditions. Or imagine a survey in which the popularity of the president is measured after a series of questions dealing with administration scandals and difficulties with the economy and Congress. Reactions to the president will be more negative when respondents are first reminded of these problems.

It will become clear that some "question effects" are obvious and therefore less likely to mislead people, whereas others are subtle and more problematic and may indeed manipulate and mislead unsuspecting consumers of public opinion research.

Question Wording

Six decades ago Stanley Payne wrote *The Art of Asking Questions,* a fundamental work on interviewing techniques. In the final chapter he presented a checklist of one hundred considerations, organized around themes such as the topic being studied, the structure of the question and the response alternatives, the treatment of the respondents, the words themselves, sources of bias, and the readability of the questions. Most of what Payne said then still holds true today and demonstrates that constructing good questions is largely a matter of common sense (Payne 1951).

Some problems with the wording of questions are obvious and may even be intentional, particularly in pseudopolls, whose sponsors are seeking specific results. Clearly, the use of loaded words will affect the results. For example, referring to labor union officials as union czars or union bosses, rather than union leaders, will certainly affect opinions about union officials. Questions also can be argumentative, pushing respondents in a particular direction. For example, the American Foundation for AIDS Research asked the following question in 1994:

> The AIDS epidemic is a national emergency. It has already claimed over 180,000 lives in the U.S. alone. Over one and a half million Americans now carry the AIDS virus. Do you think the majority of Americans realize how widespread this tragedy has become, and that the worst is still ahead?

Note that this is a compound question. It asks about two topics—the extent of the epidemic and its future—yet the respondent is not allowed to distinguish between the two. Sometimes compound questions are more disguised, so that the duality of the item is not evident until one interprets the responses. Classic examples are such questions as, Do you still beat your spouse? and Have you stopped using illegal drugs? Either a yes or a no answer to these questions leaves the impression that at some point respondents beat their spouses and used illegal drugs. Obviously, the solution here is to use two questions: Did you ever use illegal drugs in the past? Are you currently using illegal drugs?

A poll commissioned by General Motors in 2009 illustrates how one can predispose poll respondents to support an organization's preferred position (Bishop and Moore 2009). Before asking Americans directly whether the federal government should provide financial support to American automakers, the GM-commissioned poll first primed respondents to think about the economic importance of the auto industry and damage that would occur if the companies could no longer produce cars, as illustrated by the following questionnaire items:

FRANK AND ERNEST by Bob Thaves

FRANK & ERNEST: © Thaves/Dist. By United Feature Syndicate, Inc.

Q. Let me read you four facts about the auto industry's effect on the American economy.

  (1) The U.S. auto industry affects numerous other industries because it is the largest purchaser of steel, copper, plastics, electronics, and computer chips.
  (2) The U.S. auto industry provides pensions to seven hundred and seventy-five thousand Americans and health benefits to two million Americans.
  (3) The U.S. auto industry supports approximately five million U.S. jobs in all fifty states.
  (4) The U.S. auto industry has fourteen thousand dealers in nearly every town in America employing seven hundred thirty thousand people.

Q. Knowing this, if General Motors, Ford, and Chrysler were to go out of business in the next few months, how likely do you think this would be to trigger an economic depression in the U.S.—extremely likely, very likely, somewhat likely, not likely, or not at all likely?

More than three-fourths of the poll respondents replied extremely likely or very likely. Then the poll respondents were asked whether they were supportive of federal financial aid to the auto companies, and, unsurprisingly, they said yes by a 25 percent margin.

Problems with Wording in Straightforward, Factual Questions

Wording problems can arise on routine topics in legitimate surveys. Seemingly straightforward questions that employ relatively simple language can seem ambiguous to respondents. Even basic questions about the number of persons in a household or the number of children in a family can present difficulties. For example, in surveys in which the wife and husband were interviewed independently, their responses did not agree perfectly about such factual items as the number of children they had (Asher 1974b). Perhaps errors were made in transcribing their responses. Or perhaps the question was ambiguous. One spouse might have responded in terms of children living at home; the other in terms of the total number. Or one spouse might have included children from a previous marriage, and the other might not have. Martin (1999) found that respondents' reports of who lived in a household are generally accurate except when the household members are not continuously present, such as students, or are away periodically, perhaps for work-related reasons. Martin estimated that up to four million people nationally might be overlooked by surveys in general because of problems in reporting household members. Measurement of a respondent's age also has proved surprisingly problematic. Peterson (1984) showed that four different ways of measuring age in a survey yield substantially different refusal rates (that is, percentages of respondents refusing to answer the question), although the age data obtained were very similar across the four formats. Harker (1998) found that two different ways of measuring a person's income do not affect the response rates but do yield different reports of income levels. Finally, the simple way in which older surveys categorized race—white, black, and other—may no longer suffice as the United States becomes more racially and ethnically diverse and more citizens have multiracial backgrounds. The 2010 census allowed Americans to identify with more than one race.

Fowler (1992) argues that survey questions, even apparently straight-forward ones, must be adequately pretested before they are included in an actual poll. He discusses seven questions—used in national health surveys—that were subjected to extensive pretesting and found to have a number of ambiguous terms. For example, the very simple question "Do you exercise or play sports regularly?" was found to be ambiguous because different respondents had different views on what constituted exercise. The question was then modified to read, "Do you do any sports or hobbies involving physical activities, or any exercise, including walking, on a regular basis?"

Imagine the ambiguity that can arise from the simple question "Have you taken a vacation in the last few years?" Does "last few years" mean one or two years? Or could it mean three, four, or five years to some respondents? And what constitutes a vacation—going somewhere? Or does staying at home by the swimming pool count?

Sometimes survey respondents are asked to recall what are ostensibly factual matters, but it turns out often there is a substantial amount of mis-reporting. For example, Prior (2009) found that in many studies of media effects that examined how much exposure to the news people had, the way exposure was measured made a big difference in the estimated amount of exposure. When news exposure was measured by respondents' own self-report of how much news they watched on television, the obtained estimates were much higher than when measured by Nielson people meters, devices that are attached to television sets and activated by viewers pressing buttons indicating their viewing patterns. For scholars studying media effects, the choice of measurement strategies does make a difference: Survey respondents tend to overreport news watching. In a similar vein, Pascale et al. (2009) found that respondents to the U.S. Census Bureau's Current Population Survey tended to substantially underreport their enrollment in Medicaid when compared with the results obtained when directly examining Medicaid administrative records. The general point here is that survey reports of past actions and behaviors may not be as accurate as one might wish, for a whole variety of reasons including faulty memory and recall, social desirability effects, and many other factors that go beyond question wording and are inherent in weaknesses of the survey approach itself. We will return to this point in chapter 5 when we discuss alternative survey methods for measuring personally and socially sensitive topics.

If question wording can affect measurement of relatively objective matters such as a person's age, the number of children in a family, or the frequency of news watching, then how much might wording affect more subjective phenomena? The answer is that wording can make a great difference, as we will see throughout this chapter. One of my favorite historical examples occurred in 1982 when the Advisory Commission on Intergovernmental Relations sponsored three surveys asking Americans which services they would cut if funds were short (Herbers 1982). One question asked, "Suppose the budgets of your state and local governments have to be curtailed, which of these parts would you limit most severely?" About 8 percent of the respondents cited "aid to the needy" when that response was listed as one of the service areas that could be cut. But when the term "public welfare programs" was used in place of "aid to the needy" and the other choices remained the same, many more respondents (39 percent) opted to cut welfare. Obviously, "aid to the needy" is much more popular than "public welfare," and the program label used in the survey strongly influenced the results. In fact, Americans tend to complain about welfare in general but be highly supportive of specific programs that could justifiably be included under the rubric of welfare. As the federal and state governments in 2011 are facing major budget deficits and the need to cut programs, citizens should be attentive to how polls are used and misused by elected officials to justify their choices and, indeed, how these programs are labeled and described in the polls themselves.

Double Negative Questions

One general rule in constructing survey questions is to avoid double negatives. Yet such a mistake was made in a 1992 poll that the Roper organization conducted for the American Jewish Committee, on the Holocaust. The results of the poll and the subsequent media coverage generated controversy and consternation (Kifner 1994; Ladd 1994; Moore and Newport 1994; Morin 1994b, 1994c). The Roper question asked, "Does it seem possible or does it seem impossible to you that the Nazi extermination of the Jews never happened?" Fully 22 percent of the respondents said that it seemed possible that the Holocaust never occurred, and another 12 percent did not know. When these results became known, many people expressed shock and concern about American ignorance of the Holocaust and fears about the success of anti-Semitic revisionist historians. But it turned out that the convoluted question was largely responsible for these results. The Roper organization itself was so dismayed that such a poorly worded question had seen the light of day that it redid the survey for the American Jewish Committee. This time the question was: "Does it seem possible to you that the Nazi extermination of the Jews never happened, or do you feel certain that it happened?" With this wording, only 1 percent of respondents said it seemed possible that the Holocaust had never occurred. The Gallup Organization also tested the impact of alternative question wording and got results similar to Roper's (Ladd 1994). The pain and confusion caused by the first Roper question emphasize how careful one must be in wording questions.

Argumentative, Leading Questions

My favorite historical example of an argumentative question purporting to inform respondents comes from the 1982 Democratic primary race for governor in Ohio. Three major candidates were running: the former lieutenant governor, Richard Celeste; the incumbent attorney general, William Brown; and the former mayor of Cincinnati, Jerry Springer. The pollster for the attorney general included the following question in a statewide survey:

Q. As you may know, in 1974, Jerry Springer, who had gotten married six months earlier, was arrested on a morals charge with three women in a hotel room. He also used a bad check to pay for the women's services, and subsequently resigned as mayor of his city. Does this make you much more likely, somewhat more likely, somewhat less likely, or much less likely to support Jerry Springer for governor this year?

In addition to being factually incorrect on a number of points, this question was a blatant effort by the pollster to feed consumers information that would generate negative responses about a candidate and then use the replies for political purposes (see the discussion of push polling in chapter 7). In the context of the discussion of nonattitudes in chapter 2, this question was an attempt to create attitudes on the basis of the interview situation—something that can be done in a variety of ways. One technique is to present hypothetical situations to citizens and then ask them to react to those situations. Often the information obtained is of dubious use because the hypothetical situations have forced the respondents into a world that has little real meaning for them.

A more subtle example of a misleading question occurred in a 2010 survey of registered voters in Ohio conducted by Magellan Data and Mapping Strategies for The Buckeye Institute, a conservative policy organization. The offending question read:

Q. Thinking now about Ohio's $8 billion dollar budget deficit . . .

Q. Among the following three options, which do you think is the best solution to balance Ohio's $8 billion budget deficit? Increasing taxes, or cutting government services, or reducing the compensation packages of government workers?

The results were:

Reducing compensation packages of government workers	50%
Cutting government services	27%
Increasing taxes	16%
No opinion	7%

One should not be surprised that half of Ohioans opted for reducing the compensation of government employees. For most respondents (unless one is a government employee), it is the least painful option: One's taxes will not go up, and services will not be reduced. But it is a false choice in the context of the question, which refers to a "solution" to the $8 billion deficit. In no way does cutting the compensation of (presumably state) government workers "solve" the deficit problem; at best, it could make a small dent in the problem. One can only speculate how many Ohioans who opted for compensation reduction actually thought that this would solve the state's budget problems.

The Impact of Response Alternatives

Sometimes the response alternatives that a question provides can affect survey results. For example, Kagay and Elder (1992) examined attitudes toward Bill Clinton and George H. W. Bush as measured in two July 1992 polls, one conducted by Gallup and the other by CBS News/*New York Times*. The Gallup Poll asked voters if their opinions of a candidate were favorable or unfavorable; respondents could volunteer that they did not know enough to offer an opinion. By contrast, the CBS News/*New York Times* poll presented respondents four choices: favorable, not favorable, undecided, or "Haven't heard enough about the candidate to have an opinion." Needless to say, compared with the Gallup Poll, the CBS News/*New York Times* poll found fewer Americans offering an opinion because it provided two opportunities for respondents to refuse to rate the candidates, whereas the Gallup Poll provided no such opportunity. Thus the CBS News/*New York Times* poll found 36 percent of Americans favorable to Clinton, 24 percent unfavorable, 31 percent undecided, and 9 percent stating that they had not heard enough. The Gallup Poll, by contrast, found 63 percent favorable toward Clinton, 25 percent unfavorable, and only 12 percent volunteering "don't know."

Morin (1993d) has shown that slight modifications in the choices presented in the standard presidential approval question can alter the results. The standard question reads, "Do you approve or disapprove of the job ____ is doing as president?" Respondents are next asked whether they strongly or somewhat approve or disapprove. Another way of asking the question is to combine opinion and intensity in one item: "Do you strongly approve, somewhat approve, somewhat disapprove or strongly disapprove of the job ____ is doing as president?" In Morin's study, conducted during the Clinton administration, the half of the sample that received the first wording gave Clinton a 53 percent approval rating and a 38 percent disapproval rating. But the other half of the sample, responding to the second version of the question, gave Clinton a 62 percent approval rating (the two approval responses combined) and a 32 percent disapproval rating (the two disapproval responses combined). A *Time*/CNN poll conducted in August 1994 asked Americans, "Who is more responsible for today's gridlock in government?" Respondents were offered only two choices— "Clinton" or "Republicans in Congress." "Democrats in Congress" was not an option, yet it was a logical possibility. In the results 48 percent of respondents blamed the Republicans, 32 percent blamed Clinton, and 12 percent volunteered that both were equally at fault. Democrats in Congress might have been tempted to trumpet these results, but it was clear that the results were partially a product of the choices provided to respondents.

As the political parties jockeyed in 2000 and 2001 for political advantage in allocating the (now vanished) federal budget surplus, poll results again indicated that Americans' preferences looked different depending on how the alternatives were presented. For example, Stevenson (2000) asked citizens what they preferred "the leaders in Washington . . . do with the remainder of the surplus." Two versions of the alternatives were presented:

Mike Marland, *Concord Monitor*

Q: Should the money be used for a tax cut, or should it be used to fund new government programs?

Q: Should the money be used for a tax cut, or should it be spent on programs for education, the environment, health care, crime-fighting and military defense?

For the first alternative, 60 percent of Americans favored a tax cut and 25 percent preferred spending on new programs. But for the second alternative, only 22 percent favored a tax cut, and 69 percent supported spending for the listed programs. There is nothing necessarily inconsistent about these patterns of response because Americans may have felt that the "new programs" mentioned in the first alternative would be frivolous and not include the important, current programs mentioned in the second alternative. Whatever the case, the wording of the alternatives makes a major difference; support for tax cuts drops when the alternative is additional spending for specific programs and policies that Americans like. This pattern continued throughout 2002 and 2003, particularly when tax cuts were to be weighed against such programs as Social Security and Medicare or against such priorities as paying for the war in Iraq and the fight against terrorism.

Not only will the response alternatives explicitly offered to respondents affect the results of a poll, so too will the alternatives that are not offered. If respondents have to volunteer their preferred response because it was not explicitly included in the question, that will affect the pattern of responses, as shown earlier in our discussion of the presence or absence of a middle category or a "don't know" option. But it is also possible that the omitted alternative might be a much more substantive option. Solop and Hagen (2002) were critical of the polls conducted immediately after the September 11 terrorist attack on the United States, mainly because all of the options presented to Americans about how to respond were military in nature; they did not include diplomatic, economic, or other countermeasures. They argued that a more complete portrait of American public opinion would have included those other possibilities.

Sometimes the question format and response alternatives may be influenced by the way opinions are obtained—personal interviews, telephone interviews, or self-administered questionnaires, either mailed or over the Internet. Smyth et al. (2006) point out that the usual practice is to use a "check-all" question format in self-administered surveys but to rely on a forced-choice question format in telephone surveys. For example, suppose one wants to ascertain how citizens learn about politics and campaigns. One way to do this is to present citizens with a lengthy list of sources, such as friends, co-workers, family members, newspapers, newsmagazines, radio, television, Web sites, blogs, and so forth, and ask them to check off the sources that they use; this is a check-all question format. It works better when people can see the entire list, as happens with a self-administered questionnaire. Over the phone it is more burdensome to read a long list and expect respondents to remember all of the options as they answer. Thus it is more likely that in a telephone interview, people would be asked a series of discrete questions such as, "Did you rely on friends for information?" "Did you rely on co-workers for information?" "Did you rely on family members for information?" and so on. This is the forced-choice format. Smyth et al. (2006) found that even within the same mode of soliciting opinions, the question format made a difference in the responses. In an experimental study of Web and paper self-administered questionnaires, respondents selected more options under the forced-choice format and took more time to make their choices than under the check-all format. Thus we have an example of how alternative question formats, using the same interviewing procedure to measure the same phenomenon, yield somewhat different results. Smyth et al. (2008) extended their research to examine patterns of responses across different modes of data collection—Web self-administered versus telephone interview administered. They obtained similar results: Question format made a difference, this time across different data collection modes. The key substantive point here is that the results of a poll may look different depending on whether the investigator used a forced-choice versus a check-all format. Yet most often the consumer of the results of a poll will not be aware of the question format that was used.

Alternative Question Wording Does Make a Difference

As the Republican Congress and President Clinton waged their budget battles in 1995 and 1996, both sides tried to spin poll results to their advantage, and both complained about how the media were reporting the polls. For example, in late 1995 the *New York Times* published poll results showing that Americans, by 67 percent to 27 percent, preferred not to cut Medicare to balance the budget, a result described as a setback for the GOP budget plan (Budiansky 1995). The Republicans cried foul, claiming that the polling question was unfair and inaccurate and that their plan did not cut Medicare but simply slowed its growth. A subsequent *Newsweek* poll that talked about "limits" on Medicare rather than "cuts"—and incorporated the GOP tax cut plan—found less opposition to the Republican budget plan; respondents opposed it by only 51 percent to 41 percent. Americans were swayed, then, by whether the focus was on cuts to Medicare or limits to Medicare.

Two other surveys tapping opinions about Medicare found the same thing (Morin 1995c). One survey asked Americans, "Would you favor or oppose major reductions in the rate of increase in Medicare spending to balance the federal budget?" Forty-four percent of respondents supported such reductions in Medicare to achieve a balanced budget. But in another national survey conducted a week later, only 22 percent of respondents agreed with the notion of "cutting Medicare benefits to reduce the budget deficit." It is no wonder that throughout the budget debate the GOP spin doctors were encouraging Republican members of Congress to talk about reducing the rate of growth in Medicare, while their Democratic counterparts were telling Democrats to talk loudly and often about cuts in Medicare (Kolbert 1995).

Another example of the impact of question wording appeared in the furor over the impeachment of President Clinton, presumably a topic about which Americans were informed and felt strongly (whatever their preferences) and therefore one on which question wording was likely to have fewer effects. But even here the wording effects were dramatic, as summarized by Morin (1999a), who reviewed several polls. A *Washington Post*/ABC News poll asked half of a sample of Americans whether Clinton should resign if he was impeached or should "fight the charges in the Senate." The other half of the sample was asked whether Clinton should resign if impeached or whether he should "remain in office and face trial in the Senate." Fifty-nine percent said Clinton should resign rather than fight the charges, but only 43 percent said he should resign rather than face a Senate trial. Morin speculates that the key factor was the word "fight" in the first alternative; Americans do not like political combat. The second alternative—"face trial"—is less threatening. An even greater surprise resulted when Americans were asked the following two, very similar questions in a *New York Times*/CBS News poll:

Q: If the full House votes to send impeachment articles to the Senate for a trial, then do you think it would be better for the country if Bill Clinton resigned from office, or not?

Q: If the full House votes to impeach Bill Clinton, then do you think it would be better for the country if Bill Clinton resigned from office, or not?

In response to the first question, 43 percent of the sample favored a presidential resignation; in response to the second, more than 60 percent favored resignation. Morin speculates that because the second question did not mention a trial, respondents may have thought that impeachment was equivalent to being found guilty, and thus that the president should resign. But the first question explicitly mentions a trial, which suggested that the process was not yet complete.

An excellent example of how the inclusion of a key phrase can affect responses is provided by a 2006 CBS/*New York Times* poll on the use of government wiretaps in the battle against terrorism. Using a split-sample approach, CBS/*New York Times* asked the following two versions of the wiretap question:

Q: After 9/11, President Bush authorized government wiretaps on some phone calls in the U.S. without getting court warrants, saying this was necessary in order to reduce the threat of terrorism. Do you approve or disapprove of the president doing this?

Q: After 9/11, President Bush authorized government wiretaps on some phone calls in the U.S. without getting court warrants. Do you approve or disapprove of George W. Bush doing this?

In the first version, 53 percent approved and 46 percent disapproved; in the second version, 46 percent approved and 50 percent disapproved. While the results of the two versions are not all that different, it is likely that the phrase "saying this was necessary to reduce the threat of terrorism" stimulated more respondents to be supportive of wiretaps. In addition, the second question used "George W. Bush" rather than "the president" in asking about approval versus disapproval. Newport (2006) reviewed the many ways wiretap questions have been phrased by different polling organizations and concluded that questions that referred to the government or the National Security Agency rather than directly to George Bush tended to generate slightly more support for wiretapping.

Another example of question wording is public reaction to the news in May 2006 that the National Security Agency constructed a massive database of telephone calls made by U.S. customers. A one-day poll conducted on May 11, 2006, by *Washington Post*/ABC News showed Americans strongly supportive of the database by a margin of 63 to 35. Meanwhile, a *USA Today*/Gallup Poll conducted May 12 and 13 showed Americans disapproving this activity by a margin of 51 to 43. How can two polls done at approximately the same time yield such discrepant results? Let's first examine the actual wording of the questions:

Q: It's been reported that the National Security Agency has been collecting the phone call records of tens of millions of Americans. It then analyzes calling patterns in an effort to identify possible terrorist suspects, without listening to or recording the conversations. Would you consider this an acceptable or unacceptable way for the federal government to investigate terrorism?

Washington Post/ABC News

Q: Based on what you have heard or read about this program to collect phone records, would you say you approve or disapprove of this government program?

USA Today/Gallup

Clearly the wording of the two questions is different in some significant ways. The first question informs respondents that telephone conversations were not listened to or recorded. This information may address some potential concerns that citizens have and result in higher levels of support; certainly the second question does not provide these assurances. The first question also asks whether the program is acceptable rather than whether the respondent approves of the program, as in the second question. Perhaps it is easier for some respondents to say that the program is acceptable than to say that they explicitly approve of it. There are some other potential factors at work to explain the different results of the two questions. Even though the two surveys were done only a day apart, perhaps by the time of the second survey there had been substantial media coverage and criticism of the program, which generated more negative reactions. Respondents to the first survey were queried the day the news broke. Finally, there were differences in the questions that preceded these items in the two surveys. For example, in the *Washington Post*/ABC News survey, the immediately preceding question read:

Q: What do you think is more important right now—(for the federal government to investigate possible terrorist threats, even if that intrudes on personal privacy); or (for the federal government not to intrude on personal privacy, even if that limits its ability to investigate possible terrorist threats)?

Sixty-five percent of the sample said it was more important to investigate terrorist threats. It would be difficult for respondents who cited terrorism in this question to criticize the NSA program in the next question. Thus in this example we see that question wording, timing, and question context may all be part of the explanation for why the two survey questions yielded such different results. We'll say more about question order and context shortly.

Another example of how two different polls conducted at approximately the same time on the same topic can yield different results is provided by Fox News and Pew Research polls done in late July 2010 on the topic of tax cuts. The FOX News/Opinion Dynamics Poll asked:

Q. As you may know, a series of tax cuts passed at the beginning of former President George W. Bush's term are set to expire this year. If you were president, would you continue the tax cuts for everyone, continue the tax cuts for everyone except families earning more than $250,000 dollars a year, or allow the tax cuts to expire and let taxes go back up to their previous level?

Continue for everyone	44%
Continue for those under $250,000	36%
Allow to expire	14%
Unsure	6%

The Pew Research/*National Journal* question read:

Q. Which comes closer to your views about the tax cuts passed when George W. Bush was President? All of the tax cuts should remain in place. Tax cuts for the wealthy should be repealed, while others stay in place. All of the tax cuts should be repealed.

Keep all the tax cuts	30%
Repeal the tax cuts for the wealthy	27%
Repeal all the tax cuts	31%
Unsure	12%

These two questions were designed to measure the same phenomenon, and yet there are substantial differences in the patterns of response. Obviously, the questions are not worded identically so that may be a major reason for the differing results. For the sake of argument, let us assume that both questions are equally valid in their measurement of attitudes about tax cuts. Imagine a newspaper story based on each question. Based on the first question, the story might begin with the assertion that a sizable plurality (44%) of Americans favor continuing the tax cuts for everyone. In contrast, a story based on the second question might begin with the claim that a very narrow plurality (31%) of Americans favor repealing all the tax cuts. The choice of question clearly makes a difference.

Branching and Labeling Effects

Branching and labeling can have a big effect on the apparent stability of attitudes (Krosnick and Berent 1993). *Branching* refers to the follow-up questions asked after an initial query is presented to respondents. For example, political scientists typically measure political party identification by a series of questions. The first simply ascertains whether a person is a Democrat, a Republican, or an independent. If respondents say "Democrat" or "Republican," they are then asked whether they are strong or not-very-strong Democrats or Republicans. If respondents say they are independents, they are then asked whether they lean toward the Democrats or the Republicans. Note that at each stage of the questioning, the response alternatives are *labeled*—that is, each response option is specified in words. *Unlabeled* options are said to be used when, for example, respondents are asked to place themselves on a scale that ranges from one to seven, where only the endpoints are labeled with words; this type of scale is often used to measure citizens' policy attitudes and positions. Social scientists have shown that political party loyalties seem to be more stable than citizens' policy attitudes. But Krosnick and Berent (1993) argue that that finding may simply stem from polls measuring party identification by a labeled branching technique and assessing policy attitudes by an unlabeled procedure. Malhotra et al. (2009) argue that in branching from a question that has three options, the next question should provide three branching options for each of the end or extreme options, while no branching should be done for those respondents who initially chose the middle point. An example of this measurement strategy from the 2008 ANES would be the following set of questions:

Q. [initial question] Do you think the government should spend more on national defense, less on national defense, or about the same on national defense as it does now?

Q. [if more] Do you think the government should spend a lot more, somewhat more, or slightly more than it does now?

Q. [if less] Do you think the government should spend a lot less, somewhat less, or slightly less than it does now?

This question could also be asked in a different format similar to our discussion in chapter 2:

Q. Some people believe that we should spend much less money for defense. Suppose those people are at one end of a scale, at point 1. Others feel that defense spending should be greatly increased. Suppose these people are at the other end, at point 7. And, of course, some other people have opinions somewhere in between, at points 2, 3, 4, 5 or 6. Where would you place yourself on this scale, or haven't you thought much about this?

Both of these formats are legitimate, but they can yield different results. For the consumer of polls, it may be very difficult to understand the consequences and effects of alternative measurement strategies.

The Use of Multiple Items and Indexes

Often no single questionnaire item can adequately measure the complex construct that a public opinion analyst is studying. The researcher therefore may ask a series of questions and combine the results into an index, or the researcher may analyze the different items individually. For example, *political efficacy* is a concept that has long been of great interest to political scientists (Asher 1974a). It refers to a citizen's feelings of effectiveness in dealing with government. Early measures (since modified) of political efficacy generally relied on four statements:

1. I don't think public officials care much what people like me think.
2. Voting is the only way that people like me can have any say about how the government runs things.
3. Sometimes politics and government seem so complicated that a person like me can't really understand what's going on.
4. People like me don't have any say about what the government does.

These items usually appear in surveys in an agree/disagree format, with a "disagree" response representing the efficacious position on all four items. A researcher could construct an efficacy index by simply counting the number of items to which the respondent gave an efficacious answer. For the four statements listed, people giving three or four efficacious responses might be classified as high in efficacy, two efficacious answers as medium, and one or zero as low.

This kind of index is called a "simple additive index," in which the index score is a simple count of respondents' replies. For example, if we wanted an index of how informed citizens were about politics, we might simply present them a battery of, say, ten factual, knowledge questions and count how many they answered correctly. Scores on this index would range from zero (no correct answers) to ten (all correct answers).

Sometimes the terms "index" and "scale" are used interchangeably, but they should not be. An index focuses mainly on how many items a respondent agrees to or gets right; a scale would also be concerned with the pattern of the items that a respondent agrees to or gets right. For example, in our hypothetical knowledge index, a score of seven means that the respondent got seven questions correct. It does not matter which seven; any seven correct replies will result in a score of seven. In dealing with scales, one would also be concerned with the pattern of responses. For

Doonesbury

BY GARRY TRUDEAU

example, did people who got a score of seven tend to get the same seven knowledge questions correct? Was there a pattern to the responses such that certain items were easier and others more difficult?

The use of an index is justified on both substantive and methodological grounds (Asher 1974c). Substantively, the index does a better job of representing the complexity of the concept being studied than any single item could. Methodologically, the use of a multiple-item index can lessen the harmful effects of the random measurement error that is present in survey data: Whenever a researcher measures opinions, the very process of measurement may produce results that are not perfectly accurate. If the measurement error is random, the results obtained are just as likely to be above as below the true value. Thus, combining a number of items in an index will tend to cancel out some of the random measurement error, particularly if all of the items that make up the index are measuring the same underlying phenomenon. Unfortunately, consumers of public opinion polls are often not provided sufficient information about the components of an index, including the actual wording of the questions. Moreover, consumers are not informed about the ways in which separate items relate to each other and how they are combined into an index; they often must accept on faith that the index has been constructed properly, from individual items that themselves were appropriately worded.

There are cases in which one utilizes multiple items to measure some opinion but chooses to not combine the items into an index. There may be some concepts so inherently complex that no single item can do justice to them. Hence an investigator may construct multiple items each of which is trying to capture some aspect of the phenomenon under study. Indeed, one may want to compare the results of the separate items to get a sense of how effective the measurement strategy is. An example of this is the polling done on the issue of the public option as the country and the Congress were debating health care reform in 2009 and 2010. Different questions asked by different survey organizations generated very different levels of support for the public option. Small variations in wording resulted in different levels of support for the public option. For example, when the public option was described as similar to Medicare, support for it went up. Likewise, support for the public option differed according to how the role of government was described. When survey questions talked about a government-run public option, support was lower. But when questions made it clear that the public option was one more choice along with private options, support was higher. Blumenthal (2009a) argued that there was no perfect way to word a question about the public option, in part because many respondents had very little knowledge about it, and therefore their responses would be heavily influenced by slight changes in wording. He argued that it is helpful in understanding public opinion on the public option to have multiple questions on the topic; these multiple questions will enable one to see how sensitive responses are to question wording. Although Blumenthal makes an important point here, life is more complicated for the consumer of public opinion polls for a number of reasons. First, most Americans will not be aware of the different results of public option questions asked in different surveys; most often media reports will focus only on a particular poll and not multiple polls. Second, any single poll is unlikely to ask multiple questions on the same topic, in part because of time and cost constraints. Thus, the consumer of polls may learn about one finding on a topic when there are other, sometimes conflicting, results that are available.

Question Order and Context

Question order and context can dramatically affect responses to survey items by altering the framework and context within which a question is answered. An excellent example of the effect of question order occurred in 1980 when the Harris organization employed a "double vote" question to measure citizens' candidate preferences in the presidential primaries. Respondents were asked at the beginning of the interview whether they intended to vote for President Jimmy Carter or Senator Edward Kennedy in the hotly contested Democratic nomination battle. Next followed questions about domestic and foreign policy, including items about inflation and the economy, American hostages in Iran, and the Soviet invasion of Afghanistan. Toward the end of the interview, the respondents were again asked how they intended to vote. Surprisingly, over the course of the interview support for President Carter declined sharply. The only explanation for this drop was that as respondents thought about Carter's record and the problems that arose during his administration, their views of him became more negative.

A national poll conducted in 2002 further demonstrated the impact of question order (Morin 2002). Among the questions in the survey were two standard ones: whether Americans thought the country was headed in the right or wrong direction and whether they approved or disapproved of the job that George W. Bush was doing as president. For half the sample, the Bush performance question was asked first; for the other half the "direction of the country" item was asked prior to the Bush approval question. It turned out that asking the Bush approval question first (the president's poll ratings were very high at the time) increased the percentage of Americans who thought the country was headed in the right direction from 34 percent to 42 percent. But when citizens were first asked about the state of the country (respondents were not that positive) and then asked about Bush, his job approval rating fell by about 6 percentage points. Clearly, the response to the first question conditioned the response to the second.

The effects of question order and context were also evident in polling in the 2006 U.S. Senate race in New Jersey between Democratic incumbent Bob Menendez and his Republican opponent, Tom Kean (Woolley and Cassino 2006). In polling conducted by PublicMind, Fairleigh Dickinson University's independent survey research group, efforts were made to ascertain whether the unpopularity of George Bush would be a drag on the Kean candidacy. Thus, PublicMind asked about the choice between Kean and Menendez with different questions preceding and following the trial-heat query. One-third of the sample were asked about their support for Kean versus Menendez after being asked questions about their views about the direction of the nation, the performance of the president, and the war in Iraq. For these respondents who were cued to think about the unpopular president and the unpopular war, Democrat Menendez led Republican Kean by a margin of 44 percent to 36 percent. But for those who were asked about the president and Iraq after the trial-heat question was asked, the contest between Menendez and Kean was essentially even. A similar result occurred with respect to the generic ballot question for the House of Representatives that asked respondents which party's candidates they would vote for rather than which specifically named candidate they would support. Democrats had a seven-point lead in the generic ballot question among respondents who were not first reminded about Iraq and George Bush, but they had a 17 percentage point lead among the respondents who were first asked about Iraq and the president.

Many researchers have studied the effects of question order and context. Schuman and Presser (1981) demonstrated that the effects of question order are important—particularly when the questions are general, somewhat amorphous, and have little direct relevance to respondents—and they recommend that anyone examining the distribution of responses to identical questions asked at different times take into account whether the contexts in which the questions were asked also were identical. The significance of this point is supported by the work of Bishop, Oldendick, and Tuchfarber (1982). They argued that the decline in Americans' level of political interest that a 1978 survey uncovered was partly attributable to changes in the context and order in which questions were asked; the real decline in political interest was not nearly as worrisome as originally thought.

The ability of one question to affect responses to another has been demonstrated in some now-classic studies by Hyman and Sheatsley (1950), Schuman and Presser (1981), and Schuman, Kalton, and Ludwig (1983). Those studies examined responses to the following two items:

Q: Do you think the United States should let Communist newspaper reporters from other countries come in here and send back to their papers the news as they see it?

Q: Do you think a Communist country like Russia should let American newspaper reporters come in and send back to America the news as they see it?

When these two questions were asked in the order just given, support for letting communist reporters come to the United States was much lower than when the questions were asked in the reverse order. The explanation for this pattern seems clear: It was difficult for respondents to deny communist reporters the opportunity to come to the United States if they had already said that American reporters should be allowed to go to the Soviet Union. This effect of context is strong when the questions are contiguous in a survey, but it remains strong even when the items are separated by many other questions.

Another example of context effects is provided by Schuman, Presser, and Ludwig (1981), who studied the consequences of different orderings of a general and a specific question on abortion. Their items read:

Q: Do you think it should be possible for a pregnant woman to obtain a legal abortion if she is married and does not want any more children? [general]

Q: Do you think it should be possible for a pregnant woman to obtain a legal abortion if there is a strong chance of serious defect in the baby? [specific]

The authors found that responses to the general item were very much influenced by whether it came first or second—that is, support for abortion in general was much higher when the general item came first. Responses to the specific question were not affected by item order. Their explanation for this finding, although speculative, suggests the kinds of cognitive calcu-lations that may shape a response:

> One plausible explanation for the effect turns on the fact that there are a number of different reasons for supporting legalized abortion. A pos-sible defect in an unborn child is a specific reason that appeals to a large part of the population. When the more general item is asked first, some respondents may say yes but mainly with such a specific reason in mind. When the item on abortion because of a defective child is asked first, however, this indicates to respondents that the general item that follows does not refer to that specific case. Thus respondents who are reluctant to favor abortion except within narrow limits should find it easier to oppose the general rationale after having favored (and "subtracted") the more specific rationale about the defective child. (Schuman, Presser, and Ludwig 1981, 220)

In contrast to the example about communist reporters, in which a particular question order promoted consistency, here a particular ordering generated divergence because some respondents favored abortion in the specific case but opposed it more generally.

Sometimes poll respondents are asked comparative questions: Do you prefer X to Y? or Do you favor A over B? Research indicates that the order in which the alternatives are presented may affect the results—that is, ask-ing respondents whether they prefer X to Y versus asking them whether they prefer Y to X may generate different results (Wanke, Schwarz, and Noelle-Neumann 1995; Wanke 1996). For example, Wanke, Schwarz, and Noelle-Neumann asked samples the following questions:

Q: Would you say that traffic contributes more or less to air pollution than industry?

Q: Would you say that industry contributes more or less to air pollution than traffic?

When traffic was mentioned first, 45 percent of respondents said that "traffic contributes more" and 32 percent said "industry contributes more." But when industry was mentioned first, 57 percent stated that "industry contributes more," compared with 24 percent who cited traffic. Evidently, in these kinds of comparison questions people focus on the first item. In other words, asking people to compare X and Y essentially becomes a judgment on X, with many aspects of Y ignored. If so, the responses to the pollution questions are not that surprising. For the consumer of polls, the order of the items being compared becomes one more consideration in assessing the accuracy of poll results.

A final example of the effects of question order is taken from an analysis by Abramson, Silver, and Anderson (1987). They were puzzled to find that between 1980 and 1984 the percentage of citizens disagreeing with the statement "If a person doesn't care how an election comes out then that person shouldn't vote in it" dropped from 58.7 percent to 42.8 percent. This statement was one of four items that had traditionally been used to measure feelings of citizen duty. In surveys before 1984 the item had been preceded by two related statements with which Americans typically expressed high levels of disagreement. But in 1984 the item, although identical to earlier versions, was not preceded by the other two questions. Abramson and his colleagues provide convincing evidence that the apparent decline in citizens' feelings of duty between 1980 and 1984 was not real but was instead a consequence of the different questions that preceded this item in the survey. The lesson here is that before the users of polls conclude on the basis of survey data that an attitude change has occurred over time, they must be able to rule out other explanations for change, such as differences in question wording and question order.

One last point about the structure of the questionnaire is its length. Intuitively, one might expect that the longer the questionnaire and the more time and energy it requires from respondents, the more likely that the quality of the responses will lessen over the course of the survey administration. For example, one study (Galesic and Bosnjak 2009) found that the longer the questionnaire, the lower the completion rates and the shorter the responses to questions asked later in the survey. Certainly pollsters are very cognizant of the time demands they place on their respondents. Respondents themselves will often resist participation in lengthy surveys and will resent it if they have been misled to participate in a survey that took much longer than they were told at the outset.

Order, Context, and Visual Effects in Self-Administered Surveys

From our previous discussion it is clear that question order and context can affect responses in public opinion polls. In personal interviews and telephone surveys, the respondents typically hear the questions as they are read to them by the interviewer, but the respondents most often do not see the actual questionnaire. But in self-administered questionnaires (see chapter 5), whether sent through the mail or completed on the Internet, the respondents do see the actual questionnaire, which means that assessments of the effects of question order and context are more problematic. In telephone and personal surveys, the interviewer controls the order in which respondents are given the questions, and the order is consistent across respondents. But for self-administered mail questionnaires and many self-administered Internet surveys, respondents can answer the questions sequentially, they can read the entire questionnaire first, they can jump around and answer questions out of order, and they can go back and change answers after responding to other questions. It is possible to construct Internet surveys so that the questions are presented to respondents in a well-defined order, but many Internet surveys, especially the Internet pseudopolls, do not do this. There is evidence that in some instances question order is less consequential in self-administered mail surveys because respondents are likely to read all the questions before responding, or respondents can change answers after reading later questions (Schwarz and Hippler 1995). Thus perhaps in the earlier example about American and Russian reporters the order of the two questions would be less important in a mail or Internet survey because respondents may have read both questions, whatever their order, before answering them. Or respondents could have changed their responses when they realized they were being inconsistent by supporting freedom for American reporters in Russia but opposing freedom for Russian reporters in the United States.

There is also a growing body of literature suggesting that the visual design of self-administered questionnaires can affect responses. That is, the way in which the questions and response alternatives are laid out can affect responses, just as the actual question wording can. It could be things as simple as the spacing between response alternatives, whether alternatives are listed horizontally or vertically, whether the "don't know" or "no opinion" responses are in some way separated from the main body of alternatives, or many other features. This is an area of research that will continue to grow exponentially as Web-based, self-administered surveys become more commonplace. For examples of this type of research, see Tourangeau, Couper, and Conrad (2004); Christian and Dillman (2004); Couper, Conrad, and Tourangeau (2007); and Smyth et al. (2009).

Other Meanings of "Context"

Although the ordering of specific survey items among other questions is considered context, "context" also refers to the substantive framework within which questions appear. Pollsters can choose the framework within which they ask questions, and the choice can be very consequential. A survey about the U.S. military buildup posed in the context of the successful military campaign in Iraq would probably elicit more supportive attitudes toward defense spending than a similar survey framed in the context of the huge national debt. In their work on white Americans' attitudes toward affirmative action, Kinder and Sanders (1986) found clear differences in the factors that affect opinion depending on whether the questions were presented in the context of reverse discrimination (affirmative action discriminates against whites) or in the context of undeserved advantage (affirmative action gives blacks advantages they have not earned). For example, whites' opinions were more racially motivated when affirmative action was placed in the context of undeserved advantage.

"Context" can also refer to the broader environment in which an interview is occurring. Personal circumstances, recent societal events, and the content of media coverage can alter the meaning of a survey question for respondents. An identically worded question can mean dramatically different things to respondents depending on the frame of reference they bring to the interview situation, and that includes the broader social and political context at the time of the interview. For example, in their review of surveys on sexual behavior Michaels and Giami (1999) found major changes in how sexual activity and sexual relationships have been conceptualized and studied over time. Whereas surveys prior to the 1970s often linked heterosexual intercourse to marriage, more recently questions on sexual behavior accommodate other kinds of relationships and other sexual behaviors, as societal mores and practices have changed. In chapter 8, we discuss the analysis of trends in public opinion and note that even if the wording of questions has remained identical over time, the meaning of those questions differs because of changes in the broader societal context.

One dramatic example of the impact of societal context on poll responses occurred in mid-2003 after the U.S. Supreme Court decision striking down the Texas antisodomy law and affirming the privacy rights of gay adults. The decision was a victory for gay rights, but speculation about what it meant for a whole host of issues, such as gay marriage and gay adoption, went well beyond anything that could reasonably be construed from the case. There was widespread media coverage of gay marriage, for example. Although the Supreme Court decision was favorable to the gay community, public opinion polls conducted weeks and months after the ruling showed a decline in support for gay rights. For example, a Gallup Poll (Newport 2003a) conducted in May 2003, prior to the Court's ruling, asked Americans, "Do you think homosexual relations between consenting adults should or should not be legal?" A record high 60 percent thought that such relations should be legal. But when the same question was asked in two separate polls in July 2003 (after the Court decision and all its attendant controversy), the level of support for legal homosexual relations had dropped to 50 percent and 48 percent. Similar changes occurred on other survey items. Whereas 54 percent of the May sample thought that homosexuality should be considered an acceptable alternative lifestyle, only 46 percent of the July sample thought so. Support for a right of homosexual couples to legally form civil unions fell from 49 percent in May to 40 percent in July (Newport 2003b; 2003c).

What can explain these changes in opinion? One possibility is chance variations among samples, but the declines are statistically significant, exceeding sampling error. More likely the reason is that the July surveys were asked in a different political and social context than the May survey. In May, gay rights were not a prominent topic in the news, on talk shows, and in public discussion. But after the extensive coverage of the decision and its potential ramifications, gay issues were prominent on the agenda. Perhaps for some Americans it was easier to support gay rights as an abstraction in May than as a real possibility in July. Perhaps the scenarios that opponents of the Court decision presented convinced others to change their views. Whatever the case, surely the political and social context had changed. A parallel situation occurred with respect to attitudes about war with Iraq. It is one thing to query Americans prospectively, in the prewar era, about what the United States should do; at that stage, American opinions were more scattered, with support for a variety of diplomatic, economic, and military measures. But once war began, support for the military option soared. The prewar period was a very different environment in which to conduct polls than was wartime. Likewise, one would expect that poll results on the "Ground Zero" mosque or immigration reform or tax cut proposals would be very much influenced by whether the economic and/or political context had made these issues particularly salient.

Conclusion

For several reasons, citizens are in a better position to evaluate the effects of question wording than they are to assess the consequences of question order. Indeed, much of what is involved in question wording is common sense; people often recognize easily that a question is worded in a misleading and loaded fashion. News reports of survey results often provide the wording of the survey questions. Newspaper and television reports give consumers no information about the overall structure and content of the survey, however (although the major news organizations are very willing to mail the complete report of a poll to interested citizens who request it). Because information is limited, then, citizens normally do not have any basis to judge whether the responses to a particular item have been affected by its placement within the questionnaire. Moreover, the effects of question order and context are likely to be subtle.

The effects of question wording and question context are likely to be more pronounced for topics on which citizens have less information, lower levels of interest, and the like. Weissman and Hassan (2005) reviewed public opinion polls from 1972 to 2000 dealing with popular support for public financing of elections. They found that responses were very sensitive to how the questions were worded. When polls emphasized the cost of public financing, support for such proposals was very low. But when questions incorporated phrases about prohibiting large donations from wealthy individuals and special interest groups, support for public financing went up substantially. Weissman and Hassan recommend that efforts to measure popular views about public financing should be careful not to "prime" respondents in a positive or negative direction toward public financing. Their admonition is well taken, particularly so on a topic such as public financing, which is not at the forefront of citizens' concerns and is therefore more susceptible to question effects.

Fortunately, polling organizations are becoming more sensitive to the consequences of question order, and survey research textbooks are at last addressing the problem in more detail. Today reputable pollsters give more attention to effects of context and are more likely to inform the consumers of their polls about the potential consequences of question order. Nevertheless, it remains quite easy for the unscrupulous pollster, intent on generating a preferred response to a particular question, to manipulate the public by embedding that question in a survey in such a way as to yield the desired answer.

Exercises

1. Construct a ten-item poll designed to maximize the popularity of President Obama as measured by the question, "Do you approve or disapprove of the job that Barack Obama is doing as president?" Accomplish this by your selection and placement of items. Each question must be worded fairly and accurately; there must be no loaded words, inaccurate statements, and the like. You must manipulate the results by your careful choice of topics and how you order them.
2. Repeat exercise 1, but now maximize the unpopularity of the president.
3. Construct a ten-item poll designed to maximize the popularity of President Obama, using the same approval/disapproval question, but this time using loaded, misleading questions.
4. Repeat exercise 3, but now maximize the unpopularity of the president.

✔ 4 Sampling Techniques

Of the many aspects of public opinion polling, sampling arouses the greatest skepticism among Americans. One source of the skepticism is the actual composition of samples, as reflected in the plaintive question, "How come no one has asked me my opinion on that issue?"

An experience I had in October 1984 exemplifies Americans' suspicion of polls. I was to speak about the upcoming presidential election before a group of about seventy labor union leaders. As he introduced me, the president of the Ohio AFL-CIO, who was obviously disturbed by national polls showing Democratic nominee Walter Mondale badly trailing President Ronald Reagan, conducted his own two-part poll. He first asked the audience how many were for Mondale and how many supported Reagan. Everyone was for Mondale. He next asked how many people in the audience had been interviewed by national pollsters about their presidential preference. None had. He concluded by expressing disdain for the entire enterprise of polling. After that inauspicious introduction, he turned the platform over to me so that I might give my poll-based analysis of the 1984 campaign.

Sampling is the selection of a subset of respondents from a broader population. When the sampling process is conducted properly, the subset will be representative of that broader population. *Probability sampling* is typically cited as the number-one characteristic that makes a poll or survey scientific. Although all steps in the survey research process are critical, including measurement and question wording (chapter 3) and data collection procedures (chapter 5), it is probability sampling and statistical theory that enable one to determine sampling error, confidence levels, and the like, and to generalize from the results of the sample to the broader population from which it was selected. Other factors also come into play in making a survey scientific. One must also select a sample of sufficient size.

If the sampling error is too large or the level of confidence too low, it will be difficult to make reasonably precise statements about characteristics of the population of interest to the pollster. A scientific poll not only will have a sufficiently large sample; it will also be sensitive to response rates. Very low response rates will raise questions about how representative and accurate the results are. Are there systematic differences between those who participated in the survey and those who, for whatever reason, did not participate? Sampling methods, sample size, and response rates will all be discussed in this chapter.

Nonprobability Sampling

When we conduct scientific probability sampling, the results from the sample can be generalized to the broader population from which the sample was selected with the appropriate qualifications about sampling error and other sources of error. The aim of most public opinion polling is to be able to describe and analyze the opinions of some population of individuals based on a sample selected from that population. But *nonprobability sampling* is also done, some of it very legitimate and informative, and some potentially very misleading. We have already considered bad nonscientific sampling in our discussion of pseudopolls. In general, polls that allow respondents to select themselves into a sample should be viewed with great caution. For example, radio call-in shows, unscientific Internet polls, magazine postcard polls, and others may have huge numbers of respondents, but those respondents may not be representative of any well-defined larger populations. Any efforts to generalize beyond these self-selected samples may provide very misleading portraits of public opinion. Another form of nonprobability sampling is selecting respondents for reasons of convenience or happenstance. For example, one will often see on local television news reporters doing "man-in-the-street" interviews to ascertain public reaction to some event. Sometimes reporters are given informal quotas or targets—talk to men and women, young and old, black and white, and so on. These kinds of samples are in no way scientific, and while they may add some local color and provide some insights to a news report, they certainly are not a basis from which to generalize to a broader population.

Sometimes a nonprobability sample may be very informative in studying a particular topic. *Snowball sampling* is a procedure that often generates important information and insights. For example, suppose one wants to study interpersonal information transmission during a political campaign. One way to approach this topic is to select a respondent and ask him or her from whom they got information. Then one would go to the people named by the first respondent and ask them from whom they got information. This process would be repeated over and over, and the sample would soon snowball. Snowball sampling has been used to study the homeless because it would be very difficult, if not impossible, to select a probability sample of the homeless. Thus, one would contact a homeless person and ask him or her to identify other homeless people. Those homeless citizens would then be asked to name additional homeless people, and so on. The findings based on snowball samples may not be generalizable to broader populations, but they still may shed light on important political and social processes. There are other situations in which a nonprobability sample can be useful. For example, if one is conducting exploratory research where the major objective is testing survey items and examining relationships among responses, but not trying to generalize to a broader population, then a nonprobability sample may be satisfactory. Focus groups, an important election campaign tool discussed in chapter 7, utilize nonprobability sets of respondents, yet they still yield important insights about campaign messaging, the effectiveness of political ads, and many other topics. But our primary focus will be on probability sampling, which underlies the public opinion polls Americans hear about most frequently.

Sampling Designs

The aim of a good sampling design is to select a sample that is appropriate for the research topic and within the investigator's budget. Because it is impossible to interview an entire population—whether of the United States, of New York, of all doctors, or of all senior citizens—a researcher selects a sample. Typically the sample is of interest because of what it reveals about the overall population and not because of the actual sample characteristics themselves. Thus researchers try to select samples that accurately reflect the broader population from which they are drawn. The process can be carried out in a variety of ways, depending on the nature of the respondents, the objectives of the research, and the resources available to the investigator.

All the designs discussed here are examples of *probability sampling,* the dominant and preferred mode of sampling public opinion. Probability samples have several advantages. Foremost, they tend to be more representative than other kinds of samples because they generally avoid the selection biases inherent in nonprobability samples.

Another advantage of probability samples is that they allow researchers to use statistical theory to ascertain the properties of the survey sample. One such property is the *sampling error,* which enables the investigator to estimate, with a certain level of confidence, how discrepant the sample results are from the true population values. The defining characteristic of

a probability sample is that it permits the researcher to determine the probability of any single person's being selected for the sample. Nonprobability
sampling does not enable one to determine the sampling error, nor does it
enable generalizing to some broader population.

Simple Random and Systematic Sampling

In one method of probability sampling, simple random sampling, every
element in the population has an equal chance of being selected for the
sample. Moreover, every configuration of elements has the same chance
of composing the sample. The chief requirement for simple random
sampling is a list or an enumeration of the persons in the overall population.
For example, university settings are often very amenable to simple random
sampling, because of the availability of an up-to-date and comprehensive
list of faculty, staff, and students, as well as the fact that members of a
university community tend to be geographically concentrated. With such
a list, the actual process of sampling is straightforward. The researcher
assigns a unique number to each person and then selects a sample of
these numbers. A primitive way of selecting the sample would be to put
all the numbers in a hat, mix them up, and then draw the sample. A more
likely method today is to use a table of computer-generated random
numbers to select the sample. Simple random sampling is appropriate
when a reasonably complete and current listing of the population is
available.

Simple random sampling of individuals is not a feasible way to select
a national sample of Americans. For one thing, no complete and up-to-
date list of all Americans (not even the census list) exists. But even if there
were a good list, random sampling would not be useful, particularly if a
researcher planned to interview respondents personally rather than on the
telephone. Sending interviewers all over the country would make the cost
of the poll prohibitive (see the discussion later in this chapter of cluster
sampling techniques, which do allow the selection of samples from large
geographical areas when personal interviewing is to be used).

Systematic sampling is a variant of random sampling: the researcher
picks every nth name from the list, after picking the first name at random.
For example, to select a sample of 500 students from a student directory
of 25,000 names (a 2 percent or one-fiftieth sample), the researcher might
first pick at random a number between one and fifty. If that number was
twelve, the sample would consist of the twelfth name in the directory, the
sixty-second name, and every fiftieth name thereafter.

Systematic sampling is easy to conduct. The only caution is that the
list of names should have no cycle or periodicity to it, lest the skip interval

coincide with the periodicity. Normally, names listed in alphabetical order present no problems of periodicity, as opposed to, say, a list in which male and female names alternate. In the latter case, if the skip interval was an even number, the sample would be composed entirely of either males or females, thus introducing a bias into the study. A less-obvious example of a periodicity problem might be a list of homes in a major housing development. Anyone picking a sample of homes in order to interview the owners would want to ensure that there was no special pattern in the listing. For example, if every tenth house on the list is on a corner lot, the researcher might inadvertently select a sample that includes only corner homes. That could introduce a serious bias to the study because corner-lot houses tend to be larger and more expensive, and thus owned by wealthier people, than houses on the rest of the block. In systematic sampling, every element in the population has an equal chance of being in the sample, as is the case in random sampling. But unlike random sampling, every configuration of elements does *not* have the same chance of composing the sample.

Stratified Sampling

The key characteristic of stratified sampling is that the population is divided into subsets, or strata, according to characteristics of interest to the investigator. After stratifying the population, researchers may sample randomly or systematically within the strata. For example, to interview a sample of members of the U.S. House of Representatives, one might first stratify the members according to political party affiliation (Democratic versus Republican) and seniority (for simplicity, high versus low), two characteristics of relevance to the research, rather than pick a random sample. This stratification creates four categories: high-seniority Democrats, low-seniority Democrats, high-seniority Republicans, and low-seniority Republicans. One would then sample within each of the strata.

Stratification guarantees that a sample will include a sufficient number of cases with characteristics of interest to the researcher, because he or she can determine the size of the sample within each stratum. The major advantages of stratified sampling are a reduction in sampling error and a guarantee of representativeness with respect to the variables used in stratifying. The reduction in sampling error occurs when the strata differ from each other but internally are relatively homogeneous. For example, a researcher seeking to compare the attitudes of northern and southern Republicans in Congress would find it more efficient to set up these strata and sample within them than to pick a sample from among all Republicans.

Cluster and Multistage Sampling

Cluster sampling entails multiple interviews within the same geographical area, typically a neighborhood. The advantage of cluster sampling is economic. It is expensive to support an interviewer in the field and to send that interviewer to a particular site to conduct an interview. The overall cost of a field survey is lower if the interviewer conducts multiple interviews at one site.

Cluster sampling is often part of a multistage sampling scheme employed by organizations that wish to interview personally a national sample of Americans. The Survey Research Center (SRC) of the University of Michigan was one such organization; it used multistage sampling in which geographical areas, not individuals, are sampled at all stages except the last. (Today this is done under the rubric of the American National Election Studies [ANES] and under the leadership of the University of Michigan and Stanford University.) Typically, the SRC's sample design selected a sample of counties; then within the sample of counties a sample of cities, townships, and unincorporated areas; then from the sample of cities, townships, and unincorporated areas a sample of city blocks and land tracts; and then a sample of residential dwellings located on the sampled blocks and land tracts. For example, Cook County, Illinois, might be included in the sample of counties; the city of Chicago might be selected within Cook County; a number of blocks would be selected from within Chicago; and some dwelling units would be chosen from the selected blocks.

Note that up to this stage in the example geographical units and not individuals have been sampled. Sampling geographical units is relatively straightforward. It is easy to pick a sample of counties and a sample of localities within the counties because lists of counties and municipalities are readily available. Likewise, it is fairly easy to pick samples of blocks and dwelling units because local governments keep such information for the purpose of tax assessment. At each step in the typical multistage design, the probability of a geographical unit being included in the sample is proportional to its population. Thus Cook County and Los Angeles County are almost certain to be included in a sample of counties, whereas sparsely populated, rural counties will have very little chance of being included. A sample concentrated in the major metropolitan areas of the country helps to control the cost of supporting and transporting interview staff.

In cluster sampling, once interviewers arrive at the selected dwelling units they consult the instructions given them to determine whom to interview; it is not left to their discretion. The instructions are usually couched in terms of the age and gender composition of the households in the dwelling unit. For example, an interviewer might be instructed to survey the oldest male or the second-oldest female in a household. Note that this information about the characteristics of individuals within the household does not have to be known to researchers earlier in the sampling process; indeed, this kind of sampling scheme requires no prior knowledge about individuals—information that can be difficult to acquire—but only knowledge about geographical entities, which is easily obtained. There are multiple procedures available for determining which people will actually be interviewed; the common element in all of these is that respondent selection is done by an automatic procedure, not by the whim of the interviewer.

In its worldwide international sampling, the Gallup Organization uses a multistage area design when telephone interviewing cannot reach at least 80 percent of a nation's population over the age of fifteen. Thus, in much of Latin America, the former Soviet Union, and almost all of Africa, Asia, and the Middle East, Gallup uses an area frame design that first entails selecting a sample of primary sampling units, then selecting a sample of households, and then randomly selecting respondents using either the last birthday or the Kish grid method. While these multistage designs are very prominent in major social science research in the United States as exemplified by the ANES and in international research where the use of the telephone is not feasible, today telephone-based sampling and interviewing is the dominant approach in the United States, with Internet polling growing in importance. Thus we next turn to the telephone and its changing role in public opinion polling.

Sampling Techniques for Telephone Interviewing— Then and Now

The sampling designs just described are the classic ones covered in most textbooks on survey research. They do not, however, include the dominant technique used by major polling organizations: telephone interviews. Telephone surveys offer several advantages. The first is speed: Often pollsters want to assess as quickly as possible the public's reaction to a major event, such as the presidential debates in 2008 or some major presidential address to the nation. In such situations, personal interviews and mailed questionnaires take too much time. A second advantage is that telephone interviews are substantially cheaper to conduct than personal interviews, yet they still enable the interviewer to collect detailed and pertinent information from respondents. Although respondents tend to become fatigued more quickly in a telephone interview than in a personal interview, there usually is enough time to collect a reasonably extensive set of responses. Third, in many instances a telephone interview has the virtue of being less threatening and intrusive to private citizens; they do not have to let a stranger into their home to participate in the interview.

Over the past six decades, the challenges associated with telephone polling have changed dramatically. Decades ago telephone-based samples were considered suspect because of class bias: poor families were less likely to have phones. Today, almost all Americans have home phones, and that makes telephone samples more appropriate, even though some class bias still exists. According to the 2000 census, 97.6 percent of American households have telephone service, up from 94.8 percent in 1990. People without telephones are more likely to be uneducated, poor, in a minority group, of low occupational status, and living in a single-adult household.

In earlier years, telephone directories served as the basis for picking samples. Directories are still used today, particularly for local samples, but several problems are associated with their use. One is that telephone directories are always out of date because of the mobility of the U.S. population. Moreover, picking a national sample from telephone directories is a logistical nightmare—one would have to consult almost 5,000 directories. The most serious problem, however, is the popularity of unlisted telephone numbers. In 1996, an estimated 29.6 percent of American households had unlisted phone numbers, compared with only 21.8 percent in 1984 (Survey Sampling Inc. 1997). In some metropolitan areas, particularly in California, the percentage of households with unlisted phone numbers exceeded 60 percent.

Both Lavrakas (1987) and Piekarski (1989) refute the common assumption that upper-income white households are more likely to have unlisted telephone numbers. Instead, they find that unlisted households are more likely to be younger, unmarried, lower income, minority, less educated, and more mobile. National data confirm these patterns (*Genesys News* 1996). For example, *Genesys* found in 1996 that households headed by people eighteen to thirty-four years old had an unlisted rate of 51 percent, compared with 18.9 percent for those headed by persons over sixty-five. Black and Hispanic households had unlisted rates of 55.2 percent and 58 percent, respectively, compared with 31.2 percent for whites. Only 29.6 percent of homeowners had unlisted numbers, compared with 54.3 percent of renters. Lavrakas (1987, 33) cites a general rule: The farther from the central city a pollster samples, the more the proportion of households with unlisted phone numbers declines. He cites the Chicago area as an example, noting that within the city about 50 percent of households have unlisted numbers. Inner-ring suburbs have an unlisted number rate of about 20 percent to 30 percent, outer-ring suburbs a rate of 10 percent to 20 percent, and rural areas a rate of about 5 percent.

Households with unlisted numbers fall into two major categories: those that chose not to be listed and those that are unlisted because a change of residence resulted in a new telephone number unavailable to callers until publication of a new edition of the telephone book (telephone directories typically are published annually). There are differences between citizens who are unlisted through choice and those unlisted because of mobility. The "mobility unlisted" tend to be younger, more urban, lower income, and renters; the "choice unlisted" tend to be better off financially (Survey Sampling Inc. 1997). The third and smaller category of unlisted citizens is made up of subscribers who sporadically lose their telephone service because of financial problems and regain it later when their problems are resolved. In general, mobility increases the percentage of unlisted telephone numbers among all demographic groups (*Genesys News* 1996). For example, among households headed by persons eighteen to thirty-four years old the 51 percent unlisted rate increased to 69.9 percent among households that had moved in the past year. Likewise, the 18.9 percent unlisted rate for households headed by persons over age sixty-five soared to 54.2 percent for households that had moved in the past year.

Random-digit-dialing techniques were developed to address the shortcomings of telephone directories and unlisted numbers. With random-digit dialing (RDD), random numbers are generated to produce the telephone numbers to be called. In the simplest form of random-digit dialing, it is critical to know the area codes and the exchanges (the first three digits in the seven-digit telephone number) in an area. Once this information has been collected, a computer random-number generator or a table of random numbers can be used to provide the last four digits of telephone numbers to be dialed. This procedure does result in unlisted numbers being reached, as evidenced by the surprised reactions of respondents who ask, "How did you get my number? It's unlisted!" When a residential household is reached through random-digit dialing, the interviewer does not automatically interview whoever answered the phone. Instead, interviewers typically first collect information about the number of adults in the household and the number of males and females. Then the interviewers must follow a set of instructions that tell them, for example, to interview the oldest male in the first household, or the youngest female in the second household, or the second-oldest male in the third household. Sometimes interviewers ask to speak with the adult in the household who has had the most recent birthday. The combination of random-digit dialing and the instructions about respondent selection generates a sample highly representative of American households. (For more information about actual telephone sampling designs, *see* Tucker, Lepkowski, and Piekarski 2002.)

Even as RDD helped solve the problem of unlisted numbers, it encountered new challenges with the revolution in communications technology, particularly the tremendous growth in cell phone subscribers. Increasingly,

Americans are giving up their landlines and becoming only cell phone users. This is particularly pronounced among younger Americans. Estimates from Pew Research suggest that in 2010 approximately 20 percent of the American population are cell-only users, with the percentage still increasing. According to Pew Research (Christian et al. 2010), 41 percent of cell-only users are between the ages of 18 and 29; the comparable percentage for landline-only users is 7 percent. Pew Research estimates that among the overall population, about 18 percent are cell-only users, 16 percent use landlines only, and about two-thirds of the American population have access to both cell and landline telephones. This means that polling organizations now need to take into account the growing proportion of cell-only users, especially since this group is disproportionately young and the failure to include them in telephone surveys could introduce a bias in the responses. Thus, many polling organizations now explicitly incorporate cell phone numbers in their sample designs. For example, Pew Research routinely tries to have its samples consist of 75 percent landline and 25 percent cell phone numbers, a ratio that could change as the cell-only population continues to grow. The work of Fahimi, Kulp, and Brick (2009) reinforces the importance of incorporating cell phones in random-digit dialing. The failure to do so may result in the underrepresentation of households with distinct demographic characteristics.

Even with the inclusion of cell phone numbers in sampling design, cell phones still create some challenges. Landlines typically "belong" to a household, which allows the investigator to determine which resident of that household should be interviewed; that is, one can utilize any of a variety of methods (e.g., oldest female or most recent birthday in household) to determine who will be interviewed. But cell phones typically "belong" to individuals, which means that the interviewer may have to query the person who answers the phone. Even if the pollster is successful in getting through to a cellular subscriber, there may be greater problems with response rates, perhaps because cell phones are often shut off or because some cell phone users think of their cellular service as a private line that should not be available to telemarketers, pollsters, and the like. Also, the cellular respondent may be engaged in an activity, such as exercising, driving, working, or attending class, that makes it difficult to participate in and/or complete an interview.

As mentioned above, cell-only users are disproportionately young. To the extent that it is difficult to contact cell phone users, samples may thus underrepresent young adults. In a Pew study (Keeter 2006a), the percentage of young people (aged eighteen to thirty-four) interviewed in various Pew-sponsored studies declined from 31 percent in 2000 to 20 percent in March 2006, even though the proportion of young people in the overall population had hardly changed. In the Pew 2006 cell-only sample, nearly half of the respondents were under thirty, compared with only 14 percent in the landline-only sample and 21 percent in the population as a whole. If one examined college students, one would find even higher rates of cell phone use and landline nonuse. The key point here is that the rapid growth in cell phone use may result in younger citizens' being underrepresented in traditional telephone polling. The Pew study suggests that there are demographic differences even between young cell versus young landline users, although the two groups did not differ much in their political attitudes and partisan loyalties. Keeter (2006b) analyzed how the omission of voters who could be reached only through cell phones affected the accuracy of pre-election polls during the 2004 presidential campaign. Because cell phone–only voters are more likely to be young, and because young people are less likely to vote, omitting them from polls is likely to have little effect on the accuracy of the results, particularly when the polls are weighted for the underrepresentation of young voters. (Weighting is discussed later in this chapter.) Likewise, Christian et al. (2010) examined the differences in response patterns between landline-only versus landline plus cell–only results on a variety of survey measures and generally found only small differences. Ansolabehere and Schaffner (2010) demonstrate that cell-only users differ from landline users in ways other than age distribution—namely, differences in family structure and residential mobility. Those citizens with residential mobility and a spouse and children have greater need for cell phones for reasons of convenience and the need to contact family members. Their findings show that cell-only users were more likely to vote Democratic and less likely to turn out than were landline users, even when controlling for family structure and residential mobility. Thus they argue that surveys that do not include appropriate representation of cell phone users are likely to produce biased results. Hence, one consideration to keep in mind in evaluating polls—perhaps increasingly so—is whether the cellular population is adequately represented. For example, one might ask whether young citizens are properly represented, particularly if the poll deals with topics, such as gay rights, on which young Americans differ substantially from their older compatriots (in this case, younger people being more supportive of gay rights). The potential for cell phone bias will grow as more Americans drop their landlines in favor of cellular service. In a possible harbinger of future trends, about 23 percent of the landline respondents in the Pew study said that they were very likely or somewhat likely to give up their landlines and rely solely on cell phones (Keeter 2006a, 8).

There are other developments that are making traditional random-digit dialing more complicated. For example, more area codes are being added because of the proliferation of new telephone numbers. Typically telephone service providers divide an existing area code region into two new regions, each with its own area code. Thus people may find themselves with a new area code but with the same seven-digit telephone number. Pollsters and samplers then need to update their area codes.

Another challenge to telephone sampling is the increasing number of households in the United States having multiple phone numbers—and a greater chance of being selected for the sample. Today reputable pollsters correct their samples for this problem, lest they introduce an affluence bias. Piekarski, Kaplan, and Prestgaard (1999) argue that random-digit dialing has become a less-efficient way to sample residential households in recent years, since a smaller proportion of the phone numbers called will actually be attached to a residential household.

An additional development that lessens the advantages of random-digit dialing is number portability (*Genesys Q & A* 1997). The three-digit exchange in a telephone number had represented a well-defined geographical area within a community, a circumstance that could be useful to pollsters and other researchers. For example, the geographical information provided by the three-digit exchange may enable researchers to incorporate contextual data—information about the properties of the geographical region—into their analyses. With number portability, citizens are able to keep their telephone numbers when they move. At present, number portability is most common when individuals switch service providers but stay at the same address. But as number portability becomes commonplace, it will become difficult to use random-digit dialing to contact households in specific geographic areas.

Polling organizations have been creative in responding to the growing difficulty in contacting citizens by telephone brought on by the growth of cell phones, call-screening devices, and resistance to telephone interviews owing to intrusive telemarketing. One such response is address-based sampling, a methodology that includes most residential homes in a sampling frame based on the United States Postal Service Delivery Sequence File. This file contains all addresses the postal service delivers mail to, and because it is based on addresses, it includes all postal households, be they users of cell phone, landline, or cell and landline, or no phone users. When the Delivery Sequence File is combined with other lists, one comes up with a very comprehensive sampling frame amenable to Internet, mail, and telephone surveys. According to Survey Sampling International (SSI), its address-based sampling covers about 95 percent of postal households, matches about 85 percent of the addresses to a name, and can match 55 to 65 percent of the addresses to a telephone number. Address-based sampling illustrates one way the polling industry is responding to the changing telephone environment. For examples of how well address-based sampling works, see Link et al. (2008) and Messer and Dillman (2010).

Sample Size and Sampling Error

Many Americans wonder how a national sample of 1,500 respondents can accurately represent the views of 220 million adult Americans. Contributing to the confusion is that an equally accurate statewide survey requires a sample similar in size, even though any state's population is only a small proportion of the national total. In fact, few respondents are required for a good sample, and a very weak relationship exists between the size of the sample and the size of the population from which it is drawn. Many people who are aware of these apparent anomalies are skeptical of the validity of the entire polling enterprise.

Statistical theory and probability theory explain why such small sample sizes suffice to generate valid results, but those theories are not very enlightening to people who lack an extensive mathematical background. More helpful perhaps is an analogy. To perform a blood test, a medical technician only has to draw a drop or two of blood from the patient. This very small sample of the total amount of blood in the patient's body is sufficient to produce accurate results because any one drop has properties identical to those of the remaining blood. Another analogy is that of a chef trying to decide whether to add more spices to a large kettle of soup. The chef can sample the soup's flavor by tasting one spoonful, certainly a very small sample. Now, all spoonfuls of soup may not be comparable unless the chef first carefully stirs the mixture. But if the soup is stirred properly, a spoonful is sufficient to determine whether more spices should be added.

Because the biggest expense in public opinion polling is the cost of interviewing the selected sample, it is critical that the researcher select a sample that suits both the purposes and the budget of the project. There is no particular virtue in large samples. If poorly selected, they provide no guarantees of accurate results. The classic example is the infamous *Literary Digest* poll of 1936, which confidently predicted a sweeping victory for Republican presidential candidate Alf Landon based on a sample of more than two million people. In the election, however, incumbent Democratic president Franklin D. Roosevelt carried forty-six of the forty-eight states. The *Literary Digest* poll failed because of the unrepresentativeness of the respondents, who were selected from telephone directories and automobile registrations, a procedure that skewed the sample to the upper end of the socioeconomic scale. This method of sample selection had worked well for the *Literary Digest* in previous elections, but it failed in the Depression year of 1936. Moreover, additional problems with low response rates and a nonresponse bias were such that those who responded to the poll were more likely to be for Landon than for Roosevelt (Squire 1988).

One determinant of sample size is the amount of *sampling error* that can be tolerated in a poll. Sampling error is simply the difference between the estimates obtained from the sample and the true population value— for example, the percentage of people in the sample who approve of the president's performance versus the percentage in the overall population who do. Investigators often select national samples of sufficient size to generate a sampling error of about 4 percent. This means that if the sample indicates, for example, that 52 percent of respondents approve of the president's performance, the actual value is likely to be in the range of 48 percent to 56 percent (52 percent plus or minus four percentage points). How likely it is that the actual value will fall within that range is measured by the *confidence level.* In this example a 95 percent confidence level would mean that 95 out of 100 samples that might be selected would generate an estimate of approval within the range of 48 percent to 56 percent. One way to reduce the sampling error is to increase the sample size, but larger samples entail higher costs. Without going into the statistical explanation, in many sample designs, if one wanted to cut the sampling error in half, one would have to quadruple the size of the sample. In most instances, this is simply not feasible because of financial and time constraints. A 4 percent sampling error is normally considered acceptable.

Several caveats about sampling error should be kept in mind. First, in some instances a 4 percent error will be too large for the predictions that the investigator wants to make. For example, if the sample shows that in an upcoming election 51 percent of voters, with a 4 percent sampling error, are planning to vote Republican, the election outcome cannot be firmly predicted because the Republican vote could be as low as 47 percent or as high as 55 percent. But if the poll indicates that 70 percent plan to vote Republican, then a sampling error of 4 percent or even higher will scarcely affect the conclusions.

Second, although the sampling error of the overall sample may be only 4 percent, the sampling error associated with estimates based on subsets of the sample can be substantially higher, particularly for the smaller groups within the sample. In subgroup analysis the original sample is subdivided into a number of mutually exclusive subsets. For example, a researcher interested in comparing the political attitudes of Protestants, Catholics, and Jews based on a national sample of about 1,500 respondents would subdivide the sample into these three religious groups. The sampling error associated with estimates for the Jewish subgroup would be much greater than those associated with the other groups because Jewish respondents would number only 40–60, reflecting the percentage of Jews in the overall population (the sample would contain 350–400 Catholics and about 1,000 Protestants). To compare across religious and gender groups simultaneously, the researcher would divide the same sample into six categories: male Protestants, male Catholics, male Jews, female Protestants, female Catholics, and female Jews. The sampling error associated with these classifications would be even larger. In general, as the original sample is subdivided into smaller and smaller subsets, the sampling error becomes larger and larger.

Scores of polls were conducted throughout 2009 on Americans' views of the health care reform. In many of the releases that polling organizations provided and in many news media accounts of the polls, the typical lead focused on the overall levels of support for health care reform and for the president and how those numbers had changed since the last poll. Then some of the releases and news stories would examine the opinions of subsets of Americans, defined by political party affiliation, gender, age, and race. Many of these polls had a sample size of 1,000 or fewer respondents and a typical overall sampling error of about 4 percent. Thus, when the sample was subdivided by political party affiliation—defined as Democratic, Republican, and independent—or by gender—defined as male and female— there were still several hundred respondents in each of the subcategories, and the sampling error had not increased too much. Depending on how many age categories were used, the number of respondents in each subcategory became smaller and the sampling error grew. And if one examined subsets defined by two or more characteristics simultaneously (e.g., the youngest males vs. the oldest males), the number of respondents shrunk more and the sampling error grew larger. Yet in most cases the media reports failed to discuss the higher sampling error of the subgroups.

When investigators want to make comparisons across subsets of respondents but they recognize that the results for certain subgroups may be based on a small number of cases and therefore have high sampling error, they may decide to oversample certain categories of respondents. For example, if in a national sample of 1,000 Americans, one wanted to make race (e.g., black vs. white) and gender (e.g., male vs. female) comparisons simultaneously, one might choose to oversample black citizens. If 10 percent of the original sample is black and if there are equal numbers of men and women, then the results for black men and black women would each be based on about 50 cases, an N size that would generate less reliable estimates. But if one oversampled black citizens, one could generate more precise results. However, if one wanted to generalize back to the overall population, one would have to adjust the sample back to the proper proportion of black and white respondents.

Total versus Actual Sample Size

When a sample of citizens is interviewed, not every question is answered by every respondent. Some respondents may refuse to answer, other respondents may be screened out because of nonattitudes, and still others may have no opinion on the matter. In some instances there may be a substantial difference between the total sample size and the actual number of people responding to a particular question, whose responses thus are the basis of the reported results.

Consider the hypothetical situation in which 1,500 Americans are asked about their vote preferences one month before an election. Perhaps only 80 percent of the sample are registered to vote, and only 60 percent of those registered will actually vote on Election Day. If the investigator wants to report the vote preferences of likely voters only, and is able to identify that group (a difficult task), then the effective sample has shrunk from 1,500 to 720 (0.80 x 0.60 x 1,500), with an attendant increase in sampling error. Of those 720, 3 percent might refuse to reveal their preference, and another 22 percent might be unsure, thereby reducing the 720 to 540 likely voters with definite vote preferences, or just 36 percent of the original sample of 1,500. The 540 voters then are the actual sample out of the total sample. Of the 540 likely voters, 300 may intend to vote Democratic and 240 Republican, a 56 percent to 44 percent split. In reporting this split, the pollster also should describe the subset of the sample from which it is calculated.

A real-life example of the importance of reporting actual sample size is provided by a July 1985 ABC News/*Washington Post* poll on President Reagan's Strategic Defense Initiative, also known as "Star Wars." The three questions and responses were as follows:

Q. Have you read or heard about plans by the Reagan administration to develop weapons in outer space that could destroy nuclear missiles fired at the United States by the Soviet Union or other countries? Reagan calls the research on these weapons SDI, for Strategic Defense Initiative, and some people refer to it as "Star Wars."

Yes, have read or heard	84%
No, have not read or heard	16%
Don't know or no opinion	1%

Q. [For those who knew about Star Wars] Supporters say such weapons could guarantee protection of the United States from nuclear attack and are worth whatever they cost. Opponents say such weapons will not work, will increase the arms race, and the research will cost many billions of dollars. How about you: would you say you approve or disapprove of plans to develop such space-based weapons?

Approve	41%
Disapprove	53%
Don't know or no opinion	5%

Q. [For those who approved] Currently the United States and the Soviet Union have an anti-ballistic missile treaty that prohibits both nations from developing certain weapons. Suppose the U.S. had to violate or abandon that treaty in order to develop the space-based weapons. Would you still favor development of those space-based weapons or not?

Yes, would still favor	63%
No, would not still favor	32%
Don't know or no opinion	5%

Fortunately, *Washington Post* writer George Lardner Jr. (1985) was very careful in his reporting of the responses to the last question, for without the appropriate qualifications, citizens might interpret the result as showing strong support for development of the weapons even if the United States had to scrap the treaty. Note that the 63 percent favoring SDI represents only 26 percent (0.41 x 0.63) of those respondents who had read or heard about the plans initially and only 22 percent (0.41 x 0.63 x 0.84) of the original sample of 1,506. It would, then, be misleading and unscrupulous to release only the results of the last item, without the necessary qualifiers. Unfortunately, advocates of causes have at times been highly selective in their use of poll information, with the conscious aim of swaying the public to their position.

Response Rates

A growing concern among pollsters is the problem of nonresponse—meaning that some citizens selected for the sample either refuse to participate in the interview or cannot be contacted. Refusals are attributed to several reasons, including growing hostility to legitimate public opinion polling because of the excesses and intrusiveness of the telemarketing that bombards Americans. Moreover, reaching people is now more difficult because of the proliferation of technological barriers and cellular phones. According to Piekarski, Kaplan, and Prestgaard (1999), 50 percent of households have answering machines, 25 percent have "Caller ID," and 6 percent have voice mail. By 2003, Caller ID use had grown to close to 40 percent, although there was some indication that its popularity among subscribers was waning since many calls are never identified (Howe 2003).

Bierma (2002) mentions instances in which telephone poll response rates have fallen substantially—from 60 percent and higher down to 30 percent and 40 percent. Nagourney (2002) cites pollster Whit Ayres, who argued, "I can't fathom 20 years from now the telephone remaining the primary means of data collection. This industry is in a transition from telephone data collection to Internet data collection. In the meantime, we've got to get people to answer the phone." Evidence that lower response rates are due to both the greater difficulty in contacting respondents and the greater likelihood that contacted respondents will refuse to participate in the survey is provided in the Curtin, Presser, and Singer (2005) analysis of nonresponses in the University of Michigan's Survey of Consumer Attitudes from 1979 to 2003. They found that the decline in response rates was greater between 1996 and 2003 than it was between 1979 and 1996. They also found that the growth in nonresponses in the pre-1996 period was mainly due to the inability to contact respondents, whereas the increase since 1996 was primarily due to a greater rate of refusals.

Also contributing to the increased difficulty of contacting respondents is the growing tendency of pollsters to conduct overnight polls on salient political topics such as presidential candidates' debate performance or presidential addresses to the nation. In overnight polls there is insufficient time to do the multiple callbacks that may be needed to contact a member of the sample who was not at home or was otherwise unavailable when the first telephone call was made. As Kagay (1999) points out, most reputable pollsters make multiple calls to households over the multiple days that the poll is in the field to contact the designated respondent. These repeat calls are made at different times of the day to enhance the probability of a response. In many instances, interviewers leave phone messages explaining why they are calling and try to arrange a more convenient time to interview the respondent. Many polling organizations also field specially trained interviewers to re-contact respondents who had originally refused to participate to try to convert their refusals into completed interviews. But none of these special measures can be applied to an overnight poll, in which the actual interviewing period might be four hours or less. And all of these measures add to the cost of polling.

The American Association for Public Opinion Research (AAPOR) has called on polling organizations to provide more systematic and comparable information about response rates for random-digit-dialing telephone surveys, in-person household surveys, mail surveys of specifically named persons, and Internet surveys of specifically named persons. The AAPOR report "Standard Definitions" (revised 2009) wants people to be able to compare the response rates of different surveys, and it thus proposes standard definitions for response rates, cooperation rates, refusal rates, and contact rates. For example, for random-digit-dialing telephone surveys using landlines or cell phones or a combination of both, AAPOR advocates that the disposition or outcome of telephone calls be made available to the users of polls so that they can better evaluate the product. The outcomes would be (1) a successful interview with an eligible case (with a distinction made between a completed interview and a partial interview); (2) an eligible case that was not interviewed (for example, a refusal); (3) a case of unknown eligibility where no interview is obtained (for example, a constant busy signal or screening devices that prevent getting through to a number); and (4) a not-eligible case (for example, a telephone number at a household outside the sampling area's defined geopolitical boundary or a fax/data line or a nonworking number). With Internet surveys of specifically named persons, the possible outcomes are similar: (1) a completed or partially completed questionnaire; (2) an eligible case with no returned questionnaire (for example, a nonresponse); (3) a case of unknown eligibility with no questionnaire returned (for example, an undelivered e-mail); and (4) a not-eligible case (for example, a duplicate listing or a case that no longer fits the definition of eligibility, such as a student dropout in a study of enrolled students at a university). AAPOR recommends that survey organizations calculate and present response rates, cooperation rates, refusal rates, and contact rates. Traditionally, pollsters and media reports of polls have provided little information about response rates. One exception is the *Columbus Dispatch*'s reporting of its mailed election surveys, which have an outstanding record of accuracy in election predictions (see chapter 7) despite low response rates. In a September 2010 mail survey on the gubernatorial and U.S. Senate races in Ohio, the *Dispatch* listed as one of many sources of error "nonresponse bias": those who responded to the mail survey might not necessarily reflect the views of those who did not participate. The *Dispatch* then told its readers that the response rate was 14 percent. The scant attention given to response rates is often evidenced in major academic social science journals. Examining issues of some leading political science, sociology, and survey research journals published between 1998 and 2001, Smith (2002) found that in 73 percent of the cases, political science journals provided no information about response rates, compared with 59 percent for sociology journals and 53 percent for survey research publications.

There are two key aspects of response rates—the ability to contact a selected respondent and then the willingness of that respondent to cooperate and provide a reasonably complete interview (Langer 2003). Obviously a completed interview with a sampled respondent is the gold standard in evaluating the quality of a poll. But there are other measures of survey quality that could be analyzed, such as the fraction of missing information

(Wagner 2010), a relatively new approach that has not yet gained wide circulation and is almost never reported to the consumer of public opinion polls. Another measure is the rate of survey breakoffs—cases where selected respondents have started the interview (or started filling out the questionnaire) and then chose to end their participation in the survey process at an early stage. Peytchev (2009) found that Web surveys have higher rates of breakoff and examined properties of the questionnaire as well as characteristics of the respondents to help understand why breakoffs were occurring.

There is a substantial and growing body of research on techniques to increase response rates and cooperation rates in telephone, Internet, and mail surveys, focusing on steps that can be taken prior to the actual interview/data collection stage. Some of this research focuses on the format of the survey and how that affects response rates. Other research focuses on the use of incentives to increase response rates. Yet other research examines the impact of the interviewer on generating responses from contacted respondents, while other studies look at the instructions and deadlines that are provided to respondents. I will briefly mention only a few examples of these types of research to give the reader a flavor for them. Overall, the tremendous growth in this type of research demonstrates how seriously the public opinion research industry takes the problem of low response rates.

For example, with respect to the format of surveys and the instructions provided to the respondents, Fox, Crask, and Kim (1988) found that university sponsorship (as opposed to private business sponsorship) increased the response rate in mail surveys, as did notifying the respondents about the survey beforehand by letter, sending the survey by first-class mail, using a postcard follow-up, and providing return postage. Another significant factor was the color of the paper on which the questionnaire was printed. Rao, Kaminska, and McCutcheon (2010) found that advance letters and follow-up telephone calls had a positive impact on response rates. With respect to telephone surveys, Link and Mokdad (2005) found that sending respondents a prenotification letter informing them they would be asked to participate in a survey increased response rates by approximately six percentage points, but the increased response rate also made the sample obtained more white, older, and of higher socioeconomic status than it otherwise would have been. In a more elaborate study, Hembroft et al. (2005) found that sending advance letters was more effective in raising response rates than sending advance postcards but that postcards were better than doing nothing. With respect to Internet surveys, Heerwegh (2005) found that personalized invitations in a Web experiment among university students increased response rates, just as they did with mail questionnaires. And Martin (2009) showed that giving respondents clear deadlines and shorter time periods to complete the decennial census enhanced response rates.

The literature on incentives is very extensive and varied. According to James and Bolstein (1990), monetary incentives to complete the questionnaire increased response rates. Petrolia and Bhattacharjee (2009) examined the effect of prepaid and postpaid monetary incentives and found that these (especially prepaid) increased response rates to the overall survey but had little effect on item nonresponse. Brennan and Charbonneau (2009) showed that mail survey response rates could be improved by sending out chocolate with the first mailing or the first follow-up and by sending a replacement questionnaire with the first or second follow-up.

Although we discuss the importance of interviewer skills quite extensively in chapter 5, it is worth mentioning here that well-trained interviewers can have a major effect on the cooperation of respondents in an interview situation. One fascinating study (Durrant et al. 2010) was able to link the attributes of the interviewer to respondent cooperation on different kinds of surveys. Among the findings was that more experienced interviewers had higher cooperation rates with respondents. Interviewers with a positive attitude toward persuasion tended to have lower refusal rates. And interviewers who shared attributes (especially educational) with the households they contacted achieved greater cooperation from respondents.

What difference do lower response rates make to the accuracy of a public opinion poll? Here much more research needs to be done. Fortunately there is some work, albeit far from definitive, that suggests that lower response rates do not necessarily result in bias or inaccuracy in the results. For example, researchers have examined what happens to the properties of a sample when respondents who initially refused to be interviewed are converted to a successful interview through repeated callbacks and other methods. Wiese (1998) found that the inclusion of "converted refusals" does not make the sample more representative of the population from which it was drawn and that such respondents provide less-complete information than respondents who were successfully interviewed on the first try. In their study Curtin, Presser, and Singer (2000) found few differences on the Index of Consumer Sentiment among respondents who required varying numbers of telephone calls to complete a successful interview. Teitler, Reichman, and Sprachman (2003) found some differences between nonrespondent and respondent fathers in a national longitudinal survey of new parents, but they also argued that the efforts and resources required to convert nonrespondents into respondents reached a point of diminishing returns.

One of the most ambitious efforts to assess the effects of differential response rates was a study in which two national random-digit-dialing surveys were conducted using identical questionnaires (Keeter et al. 2000).

The first survey was conducted over a five-day period and used a sample of adults who were at home when the interviewer called. The second was conducted over an eight-week period that allowed for greater efforts to contact mobile and reluctant respondents. The first survey had an overall response rate of 36 percent; the second, a 60.6 percent response rate. Despite the large difference in the response rates, the two surveys produced very similar results across a wide variety of questions. What differences there were tended to occur on demographic items and not on attitudinal and opinion questions.

What conclusions can be drawn about the problem of response rates? Certainly it is important to monitor them. AAPOR's recommendations, if followed, will be very helpful here. Declining response rates are less a problem for those reputable survey organizations that work harder to secure completed interviews through multiple callbacks and other tactics. But for the overnight polls, low response rates can be a serious problem and need to be recognized as such. Much more research is needed on the fundamental question of whether survey respondents are indeed representative of nonrespondents. Even if numerous studies have shown that survey results have not been seriously biased by low response rates, there is no guarantee that the finding will hold in the future. And the situation gets more complicated if the survey items being studied are themselves thought to be correlated with the likelihood of responding in the first place. If so, there may be a greater problem of nonresponse bias due to lower response rates. (See Groves 2006 for an extensive discussion of nonresponse rates and nonresponse bias.) Obviously, high response rates are better than low rates, but lower rates do not automatically indicate that a poll is inaccurate. As America's telecommunications and Internet technology continues to advance and as individual concerns about the intrusiveness of telemarketing and protection of privacy continue to grow, the problem of response rates will become an even greater challenge for public opinion polling. The use of Internet surveys will become more prominent even as continuing modifications are made to telephone sampling.

Weighting the Sample

Although pollsters select their samples to be representative of the population from which they are drawn, sometimes they must adjust a sample before analyzing and reporting the results of a poll. The adjustments may be made for substantive reasons or because of biases in the characteristics of the selected sample. An example of an adjustment made for substantive reasons would be the pollster's attempt to determine who the likely voters will be and to base election predictions not on the entire sample but on that subset of likely voters. Another example of weighting would be adjusting for the underrepresentation of young people, who disproportionately rely on cell phones only and thus are less likely to be part of a representative sample.

Weights are used to correct for biases—that is, to make the sample's demographic characteristics more accurately reflect the population's overall characteristics. Because sampling and interviewing involve statistics and probability theory, as well as the logistical problems of contacting respondents, a sample may contain too few blacks, or too few men, or too few people in the youngest age category. Assuming that the true population proportions for sex, race, and age are known, the researcher, using weights, brings the sample numbers into line with the overall population values. For example, if females constitute 60 percent of the sample but 50 percent of the overall population, the researcher might weight each female respondent by five-sixths, thereby reducing the percentage of females in the sample to 50 percent (five-sixths times 60 percent). Although one typically weights demographic characteristics where there are known population distributions, in chapter 7 we will discuss weighting on the basis of the distribution of partisan loyalties and how that can affect the accuracy of poll results.

A 1986 *Columbus Dispatch* preelection poll on the gubernatorial preferences of Ohioans illustrates the consequences of weighting. In August 1986 the *Dispatch* mailed a questionnaire to a sample of Ohioans selected from the statewide list of registered voters. The poll showed that incumbent Democratic governor Richard Celeste was leading former GOP governor James Rhodes, 48 percent to 43 percent, with independent candidate and former Democratic mayor of Cleveland Dennis Kucinich receiving 9 percent. An "undecided" alternative was not provided (Curtin 1986a). Fortunately, the *Dispatch* report of its poll included the sample size for each category (unlike the practice of the national media). One table that the paper presented showed the following relationships between political party affiliation and gubernatorial vote preference (Curtin 1986b):

Gubernatorial preference	Democrat	Republican	Independent
Celeste	82%	14%	33%
Rhodes	9%	81%	50%
Kucinich	9%	5%	17%
Total %	100%	100%	100%
(N)	(253)	(245)	(138)

Given the thrust of the news story, that Celeste was ahead 48 percent to 43 percent, the numbers in the table were surprising. Rhodes was running almost as well among Republicans as Celeste was among Democrats, and Rhodes had a substantial lead among independents. Based on the numbers provided, one could calculate the actual number of Celeste, Rhodes, and Kucinich votes in the sample as follows:

Celeste votes   = $.82(253) + .14(245) + .33(138) = 287$
Rhodes votes   = $.09(253) + .81(245) + .50(138) = 291$
Kucinich votes   = $.09(253) + .05(245) + .17(138) = 58$

The percentages calculated from these totals show Rhodes slightly ahead, 46 to 45 percent, rather than trailing. At first I thought there was a mistake in the poll or in the party affiliations and gubernatorial vote preferences. In rereading the news story, however, I learned that the sample had been weighted. The reporter wrote, "Results were adjusted, or weighted, slightly to compensate for demographic differences between poll respondents and the Ohio electorate as a whole" (Curtin 1986b). Although the reporter informed readers that the data were weighted, nowhere did he say that the adjustment affected who was ahead in the poll. The adjustment was statistically valid because the poll respondents did not include sufficient numbers of women and blacks, two groups that were more supportive of the Democratic gubernatorial candidate. However, nowhere in the news story was any specific information provided on how the weighting was done. This example illustrates that weighting can be consequential, and it is typical in terms of the scant information that citizens receive about weighting procedures.

An ongoing problem in polling is the tendency of selected samples to overrepresent females and underrepresent males. This problem can be easily corrected by weighting the sample so that the proportion of male and female respondents reflects the overall population distribution. This solution, however, assumes that sampled males are representative of unsampled males. Males may be undersampled for several reasons. First, there are simply more female-only households than there are male-only households. Moreover, because fewer men live in male-only households, and a higher proportion of men live in mixed households, the probability of a male being selected in the sample is lower than for a female. The second factor relates to how the actual respondent to be interviewed is determined. Typically, interviewers (in telephone polling) ask the person who answers the phone if they can speak with the oldest female, or the second-oldest male, or some other designated person in the household. Sometimes the person who answers the phone is unwilling to transfer the interviewer to the household member requested. Because women are more likely to answer the phone in the first place and are less willing than men to bring their spouse to the phone, the number of male respondents is diminished. Finally, daytime calls are more likely to obtain female respondents because of the higher proportion of males who work outside the home.

In addition to the straightforward examples above of weighting to correct for the overrepresentation or underrepresentation of various demographic groups, weighting can also be much more complicated and statistically complex. Moreover, weighting can be applied to very different phases of the polling enterprise. For example, Merkle and Langer (2008) discuss phone line weighting to adjust for the fact that different households have different numbers and different kinds of phone lines. Blumberg and Luke (2007) discuss sample weighting procedures that help reduce coverage bias for multiple demographic characteristics (the failure to adequately represent certain population groups) in traditional telephone surveys, but they acknowledge that these adjustments may be insufficient for surveys of behavioral risk factors for low-income and young adults. Ehlen and Ehlen (2007) argue that weighting has not been particularly effective in adjusting for the undercoverage of cell phone users in surveys (although other techniques discussed earlier are being developed to address this problem). Probably the best advice about weighting for consumers of public opinion polls is to expect little detailed information about the use of weights from poll sponsors. But when such information is provided, try to be sensitive to the kinds of problems that are being addressed through weighting.

Conclusion

For many Americans, sampling is the most problematic feature of public opinion polling. Many citizens doubt whether the "small" samples reported in the media can adequately represent the population of whatever entity is being studied. And if the response rates noted are low, citizens are likely to be even more skeptical. They may question the wording of a poll, but it is difficult for individuals to offer informed criticism of sampling procedures unless the polling organization provides sufficient information about such matters as the size of the sample, sampling error and confidence levels, the dates of the interviews, response rates, and the method of interviewing. And even with that information, many people will still be unsure about the quality of the sampling procedures, which seem to be technical and statistical matters beyond the layperson. Even when the sampling is statistically and scientifically sound, sampling problems may undermine the substantive results and interpretations of public opinion polls. Normally, however, citizens must trust the polling organization to select a good sample.

Exercises

1. In exercises 1 and 2 in chapter 1, you kept a log of newspaper and newsmagazine public opinion polls. Now reexamine those same polls and look for information related to sampling. In particular, look for information about sample size, size of sample subset (where appropriate), sampling error, sampling error of sample subsets (where appropriate), response rates, and the use of weights. What type of information was provided most often? What type of information was provided least often?

2. Assume that you must select a sample of college students who live in officially sanctioned university housing, whether residence halls, fraternity and sorority houses, or university-run, off-campus housing. You are to design three different sampling schemes. The first one should be based on these housing units. The second one should be based on telephone numbers, but first you must determine what has happened to traditional landline telephone service in university housing. Does it still exist, or has it been partially or totally eliminated because most students have their own cell phones? If the latter, how would you sample students by phone? Finally, design a sampling scheme based on the printed student directory or its online equivalent. What kind of information is included in your student directory? Does it include residential addresses, e-mail addresses, telephone numbers, all of these, or what?

5 Interviewing and Data Collection Procedures

The interviewer's role in measuring public opinion is critical. Because polling organizations generally provide the public with little or no information about the interviewing process, the consumers of polls cannot make independent judgments and must assume that the interviews were conducted competently. That is a safe assumption with respect to the major polls. Nevertheless, when I have agreed to be a respondent in public opinion, market research, and academic research surveys, I have been surprised by the clear disparities in the training and competence of the interviewers I encountered.

Often, when I am a respondent, I ask the interviewer what a certain question means or complain about the range of alternatives available to me. Some interviewers are well trained to handle such reactions, but others are not. One interviewer agreed with my frustration about a particular item and informed me that there had been many complaints about the survey. Another interviewer—when I strenuously objected to the alternatives offered—pleaded with me to pick one of the choices given because he did not know how to handle volunteered responses. In yet another situation the interviewer told me that she would place my aberrant response in the category in which she thought it would best fit.

In some surveys there is no live interviewer. The most familiar example is the self-administered, mailed questionnaire, typically in paper-and-pencil format. Gaining popularity are the computerized self-administered questionnaire (CSAQ) and computer-assisted self-interviewing (CASI), which give pollsters greater flexibility. There are also automated telephone interviews with a recorded voice asking the questions. Finally, there is the growing phenomenon of Internet polls, which are typically self-administered and raise a variety of issues about sampling, representativeness, and the like.

The purpose of this chapter is to alert the consumers of polls about the potential effects of the interviewing process on poll results. The first section describes the methods used to collect data and the advantages and disadvantages of different approaches. That section is followed by a closer look at the interview situation and factors—such as the sex, socioeconomic status, race, and ethnicity of the interviewer—that can affect responses. The chapter ends with a discussion of the advantages and limitations of Internet surveys.

Methods of Collecting Polling Information

There are three basic ways to collect polling information: self-administered questionnaires, telephone interviews, and personal interviews.

Self-Administered Questionnaires

Organizations with access to good mailing lists are especially frequent users of mailed questionnaires, whose main advantage is their low cost. As discussed in chapter 1, interest groups often use mailed surveys in conjunction with their fund-raising efforts. Because mailed surveys are self-administered by the respondent, no interviewers must be trained and supported, dramatically reducing costs. Interviewer bias does not affect results. Moreover, the privacy in which they can complete a mailed survey may reassure respondents about the anonymity and confidentiality of their responses and encourage them to respond more frankly, particularly on sensitive topics. For example, a study by Aquilino (1994) showed that self-administered questionnaires used in the context of a personal interview generate a higher level of admitted illicit drug and alcohol use than does a telephone or personal interview without a self-administered questionnaire. Indeed, an extensive body of literature generally shows that self-administered questionnaires are more likely to produce higher estimates of illicit, illegal, or controversial behaviors than modes of data collection in which an interviewer directly interacts with respondents (Tourangeau and Smith 1996). Krysan et al. (1994) demonstrated that a mail questionnaire revealed more negative views among white respondents to questions about racial integration and affirmative action than did personal interviews. The explanation given for this finding was straightforward: white respondents were more open and honest about their views in the privacy of the self-administered mail questionnaire. In a personal interview the pressure to be socially and politically correct came into play, resulting in responses more supportive of civil rights.

These advantages of mailed questionnaires are typically outweighed by their limitations, foremost of which is that response rates tend to be lower for mailed surveys than for telephone and personal interviews. However, that disadvantage may be diminishing, in part because of growing refusal rates in personal and telephone interviews and improved techniques for generating satisfactory response rates to mailed questionnaires (Goyder 1985).

Ascertaining the extent to which respondents represent the actual population is a particularly acute problem when the response rate is low. A study by Bernick and Pratto (1994) concluded that it can be worthwhile to expend the extra resources required to enhance response rates; simply weighting or adjusting the responses obtained from smaller samples in their study would not have fully resolved the problem of response bias in a small sample. On the other hand, if the respondents are representative of the broader population even when the response rates are low, there is less need to incur the costs required to increase the response rate.

Another limitation of mailed surveys is that much information cannot be collected through self-administered surveys. For example, one cannot be sure who actually completes a mail questionnaire—a serious limitation when surveying elite populations, such as members of Congress or state legislators who, because they are bombarded with questionnaires, may have a staff person fill out the survey form. This is also a problem for mail surveys of the general citizenry: When a mailed survey is delivered to a household, who actually completes the questionnaire? As address-based sampling (see chapter 4) is becoming more prominent, there still is the issue of respondent selection within the household. One study (Battaglia et al. 2008) tested three respondent selection methods for mail surveys: have any adult in the household complete the survey, have the household adult with the next birthday do the survey, or have all household adults fill out the survey. While the results show strengths and weaknesses in all of these approaches, the key point is that address-based sampling along with related methodological advances may make mail questionnaires more useful to researchers in the future despite their obvious limitations. Certainly a shortcoming of mail surveys is that they provide no information about respondents' reactions to a survey or the environment in which it is completed. Because no interviewer is present to assist respondents who have difficulty with a questionnaire, instructions must be explicit and questions must be as unambiguous as possible. There is no opportunity for clarification.

Mailed questionnaires must not be too burdensome for respondents, or the response rate will plummet. Whenever I receive a questionnaire in the mail, I first check the number of open-ended questions that would require me to write mini-essays. If there are many, I'm likely to toss the questionnaire into the circular file, unless it addresses a topic of particular interest to me. Mailed questionnaires encourage response when they are largely limited to highly structured, fixed-alternative questions. However, even the structured items are often annoying to citizens, particularly to political elites, who complain that the political world is too complicated, and their own opinions are too complex, to be captured in a fixed-alternative item.

The burdens that a mailed questionnaire imposes are not uniform across the population. Poorly educated respondents will have more difficulty with a mailed survey, and illiterate persons may simply have to ignore it. In addition, there is no way of knowing the order in which any particular respondent answered the questions. The questionnaire may elicit different responses from individuals depending on the order in which they approach the questions. Finally, mailed questionnaires are inappropriate if an investigator needs a quick response on a topic such as a presidential debate or foreign policy crisis. Experienced researchers allow several weeks for questionnaires to be returned.

One response to some of the limitations of self-administered mailed questionnaires is computer-assisted self-interviewing (CASI), in which respondents answer survey questions on a computer. CASI permits more flexibility in questionnaire design. For example, it allows branching, in which respondents are presented with different survey questions depending on their responses to previous ones. CASI eliminates some of the errors that occur in the usual paper-and-pencil format and allows quick identification of any internal inconsistencies in item responses. Yet it maintains many of the privacy benefits of self-administered mailed questionnaires. Indeed, CASI appears to perform better than mailed questionnaires in generating accurate responses on sensitive topics. Studies of drug use (Wright, Aquilino, and Supple 1998) and sexual behavior (Harmon 1998) suggest that computerized administration of polls may make respondents feel more certain of privacy and therefore freer to offer honest responses about socially unacceptable and possibly illegal behavior.

A study by Epstein, Barker, and Kroutil (2001) found mode effects on another sensitive topic, respondents' reports of how often they experienced various mental health problems. Epstein and her colleagues compared two modes of data collection—audio computer-assisted self-interviewing (ACASI) and interviewer-administered, paper-and-pencil (I-PAPI) procedures. With I-PAPI, an interviewer asks respondents about mental health symptoms, the respondents answered, and the interviewer recorded their replies. With ACASI, respondents can listen to questions through a headset or read them on a computer screen and then enter their responses directly on the computer; they have greater privacy. It turned out that respondents cited more mental health problems with ACASI than with I-PAPI procedures, again suggesting that pollsters and investigators collecting sensitive information must be aware that the mode of data collection they employ can affect their results. Another study (Brener et al. 2006) examined whether the willingness of high school students to report health-risk behaviors was affected by where they were surveyed (home versus school) and how they were surveyed (CASI versus PAPI). The authors found strong setting (home versus school) effects, with mode effects (CASI versus PAPI) much weaker. Students who completed questionnaires at school were much more likely to report health-risk behaviors, particularly socially stigmatized behaviors such as drug use and sexual intercourse at a very young age. But mode effects and mode/setting interaction effects were much weaker and often different from the findings of previous research.

Telephone Interviews

Unlike mailed questionnaires, telephone surveys can be completed quickly (often in only two to four days and sometimes in a single evening), providing an almost instantaneous reaction to a political event. Another advantage, as detailed in chapter 4, is that by using random-digit-dialing techniques, researchers can pick a representative sample with a higher response rate than is possible with self-administered questionnaires, although lower than with personal interviews. Telephone interviews cost more than mailed questionnaires but less than personal interviews. In some situations telephone interviewing may succeed where other methods can fail, perhaps because of the sensitivity of a topic or because respondents will not allow a stranger in their home to conduct a personal interview.

Telephone interviews also have shortcomings beyond the dropping response rates discussed in the last chapter. Respondents become fatigued more quickly in a telephone interview than in a personal interview, and that limits the scope of a telephone survey (although recent experience indicates that telephone surveys can be lengthier than was originally thought). Training interviewers, to avoid unwanted effects from the interviewing process, adds to the cost of a project. Finally, use of the telephone eliminates the possibility of using visual aids during the interview unless materials are sent to respondents in a preliminary mailing.

Telephone interviews are now faster, more efficient, and more accurate thanks to recent advances, the foremost of which is computer-assisted telephone interviewing (CATI). With CATI, interviewers sit at video display terminals and feed responses directly into a computer, thereby eliminating a separate keypunching step. A computer program controls the overall flow and logic of the interview. Among other things, the program ensures that questions are asked in the correct sequence and that the responses are consistent with the questions being asked (Frey 1983, 144–145). Running totals are easily generated with CATI, so that survey results are available almost instantaneously. As CATI systems become more sophisticated, investigators who use them can save money, particularly as the sample size grows larger.

Moskowitz (2004) investigated how the use of CATI versus T-ACASI (telephone audio computer-assisted self-interviewing) affected teenagers self-report of smoking. With CATI, interviewers ask the questions and record the answers. With T-ACASI, respondents "listen to prerecorded, computer-controlled questions and respond by pressing the keypad on a touch-tone telephone" (Moskowitz 2004, 565). Moskowitz found, for example, higher reports of cigarette smoking among teenagers interviewed through T-ACASI techniques. The general point is that many surveys seek sensitive information that may make respondents wary. Surveys may deal with topics for which there may be social desirability pressures on respondents to give the right answer and therefore not appear to be ignorant or biased or any other negative characteristic. In such instances, survey methods and approaches must provide respondents greater confidentiality and privacy and general comfortableness in offering their true views. There is a huge body of research on mode effects that continues to expand rapidly. For a few recent examples, see Kreuter, Presser, and Tourangeau (2008), Chang and Krosnick (2010), and Holbrook and Krosnick (2010).

Personal Interviews

Personal interviews generally provide the richest and most complete information in public opinion polling and tend to have the highest response rates. Respondents are willing to participate in lengthy personal interviews, particularly if the interviewer is skillful in developing rapport with them. The presence of the interviewer is also helpful in other ways. He or she can assess respondents' problems with and reactions to the survey and can directly record not only the verbal responses of the interviewee but also nonverbal behavior such as fidgeting, nervousness, and other signs of unease or lack of interest in the interview situation. Moreover, the interviewer has more opportunities to ask follow-up questions and to probe in a personal interview than in a telephone survey. Holbrook, Green, and Krosnick (2003) compared the merits of telephone and personal interviewing and found that telephone respondents were not as forthcoming as face-to-face interviewees. Telephone respondents were less cooperative and less engaged in the interview, more suspicious about the interview itself, and more likely to offer socially desirable responses.

The obvious drawbacks of personal interviews are their high cost and the danger of introducing substantial interviewer effects and biases. The cost of training interviewers, supporting them in the field, often with housing, meals, and transportation allowances, and paying their salary is steep. Because the interview is a social situation, a poorly trained interviewer may alter its interpersonal dynamics and thereby influence the respondent's answers in undesirable and often unpredictable ways.

Interviewer Effects in Public Opinion Polling

Interviewer effects can emerge in both telephone and personal interviews, although they are likely to be more pronounced in personal interviews because of the face-to-face interaction between the interviewer and the respondent. For most respondents, the personal interview is a new experience, with all the attendant uncertainties and ambiguities of unfamiliar activity. Unsure of how to behave, respondents may look to the interview situation for cues. The two most important sources of cues are the survey instrument itself (the questionnaire) and the person who administers it, the interviewer. The cues that the survey instrument provides are direct (even if the questions are flawed); the cues that the interviewer provides may be far more subtle. If interviewers are inconsistent in the cues they give to different respondents, the reliability of the survey results may be undermined. At minimum, interviewers must not change the question wording, question order, or their voice intonation from respondent to respondent. And because most polls use more than one interviewer, the interviewing process must be standardized as much as possible, which requires careful training of interviewers.

This emphasis on consistency and uniformity in the interviewing process reflects a concern with the *reliability* of the measuring instrument. One type of reliability measure is based on *equivalence,* meaning the extent to which different investigators applying the same measuring instrument to the same individuals obtain consistent results. Ideally, the identity of the interviewer should not affect the responses that the questionnaire generates in the interview.

The reliability of an instrument can be distinguished from its *validity,* meaning the extent to which the instrument measures what it is supposed to measure. For example, consider one of the political efficacy items discussed in chapter 3: "Voting is the only way that people like me can have any say about how the government runs things." A "disagree" response to this item is considered an efficacious reply; it presumably means that the respondent believes that he or she can be influential in ways other than voting. But what if a respondent rejects this statement out of a belief that there is no way (not even by voting) that people can have influence? In this case, a "disagree" response signals a lack of efficacy, and the item itself is not a valid indicator of the underlying concept of political efficacy. Because of the problem with validity, this item has been eliminated from the American National Election Studies.

Reliability and validity are absolutely necessary attributes of survey instruments. After all, if a survey item is not measuring what the researcher intended, then the results may have little relevance to the topic of the research. For example, the question "Do you agree with President Bush that the United States should do more to fight AIDS in Africa?" is potentially flawed and invalid. What is it actually measuring? What might a "no" response actually mean? A "no" might more reflect one's opinion of the president than one's view about the problem of AIDS in Africa. Or a "no" response might indicate that one opposes doing more to fight AIDS, regardless of the president's stance. The reliability and validity of survey instruments are very rarely discussed in media reports of public opinion polls or even in the summary reports that polling organizations prepare. Most often it is left to poll consumers to form their own judgments about whether the survey questions are actually measuring what they are supposed to measure. Poll consumers may base their judgments on hunches, intuition, and common sense.

One way that pollsters can enhance the reliability and validity of their surveys is to pretest the poll before it is put into the field. Pretesting is basically a trial run, in which one tries to correct any flaws and shortcomings in the survey before it is administered to the population of interest. Very seldom are the consumers of a poll told anything about the pretesting stage, but it is very important. Pretesting can identify any problems that the interviewer or the respondent has with a question. One will certainly have greater confidence in the validity of survey items if respondents understand the concepts underlying the questions and if respondents' interpretation of the questions' meaning reflects what the researchers are trying to measure. Presser et al. (2004) discuss trends and strategies to enhance the effectiveness of pretesting.

Interviewer Skills and Demeanor

An interviewer's general demeanor, competence, and performance have much to do with the success of the interview. Interviewers must be able to make respondents feel at ease and receptive to the survey. If rapport is not established, respondents may refuse to cooperate or fail to provide complete and accurate information to interviewers. Ideally, interviewers are well informed about the purposes of the research and the intention of specific questions so that they know whether a respondent has answered a question fully and how to ask follow-up questions for clarification. They should not, however, inject themselves into the interviewing process by making editorial comments about respondents' replies.

Although they must follow instructions carefully and ask all appropriate questions, interviewers also should be able to handle the unexpected, such as a respondent who volunteers additional information. Equally important, interviewers must record and transcribe responses as accurately as possible, even when the answers do not fall neatly into one of the predetermined response categories.

How difficult an interviewer's job is depends on the nature of the questionnaire as well as the characteristics of the respondents. For example, highly structured survey items require less guidance and judgment from an interviewer; relatively unstructured instruments require more. For interviews of political elites that use open-ended questions, an interviewer not only must be a good listener and prober who takes few or no notes during an interview, but he or she must be able to write up the results after the question-and-answer session has ended. Sometimes such interviews are taped, which eliminates the need to take extensive notes, but taped interviews must be transcribed to be usable.

There is much research studying how interviewer characteristics affect respondents and the quality of the interview. For example, Olson and Peytchev (2007) examined the impact of interviewer experience and found that interviewer/respondent interaction changed as the interviewer gained more experience and conducted more interviews. But it was not clear how and why the interaction changed. As an illustration, with more experienced interviewers, interviews were completed more quickly. But was this due to interviewers asking the questions at a more rapid pace, or was it due to fewer deviations from the interview script? As interviewers gain more experience, are they less likely to engage in unnecessary conversation with respondents, or are they less inclined to probe and provide feedback to respondents? Does a faster interviewer pace lessen respondents' focus on the task at hand, thereby contributing to lower data quality? This study hints at the potential subtle effects interviewers can have on the information they collect.

Another study (Durrant et al. 2010) focused on characteristics of the interviewer that enhanced or lessened respondents' participation and cooperation in a survey. Among the many findings of this extensive study was that interviewer confidence affected cooperation rates, more so on more difficult, complex surveys. The authors found that interviewers with positive attitudes toward persuasion tended to have lower refusal rates and concluded that confident and engaged interviewers performed better. This may seem like common sense, but a confident and engaged interviewer will certainly make respondents more comfortable in the interview situation. Thus, survey organizations are becoming more sensitive to interviewer performance and how to measure it. One study (Durand 2008) examined alternative ways of evaluating interviewers and posited that the standard measure of performance—respondent cooperation rate at first contact—is not sufficient. Effective interviewers do so much more, including converting initial refusals into successful interviews, and this should certainly be recognized in any measure of performance.

Gender and Status

In addition to demeanor and skills, the personal characteristics of an interviewer can affect responses to a poll. For example, many interviewers are middle-aged women because this group is least threatening to both male and female respondents, particularly in a personal interview in a home. Also, female interviewers often are able to establish a rapport more successfully than men.

Morin (1990) cites research that shows that men and women answer poll questions differently depending on the gender of the interviewer. In a poll on abortion conducted by the Eagleton Institute, women were much more likely to give pro-choice responses to female interviewers than to males; the response pattern for men was weaker. For example, when given the statement "The decision to have an abortion is a private matter that should be left to the woman to decide without government intervention," 84 percent of the female respondents interviewed by women agreed, compared with only 64 percent of women interviewed by men. Seventy-seven percent of the male respondents interviewed by women agreed with the statement, compared with 70 percent of those interviewed by men.

A growing body of research indicates that women are more likely to give traditional, nonfeminist responses to male interviewers and more feminist responses to female interviewers. Likewise, men are somewhat more likely to give feminist responses to female interviewers than to males. Kane and Macaulay (1993) found that both men and women were likely to express more egalitarian gender-related attitudes and more criticism of gender-related inequalities to female interviewers than to male interviewers. Huddy and Bracciodieta (1992) obtained similar results in their research, except that they also found gender-of-interviewer effects on topics such as party identification and authoritarian attitudes, which are not directly related to gender. For example, both men and women gave more feminist, Democratic, and antiauthoritarian responses when interviewed by a female than when interviewed by a male. Therefore, on gender-related survey topics such as abortion, and perhaps even on gender-neutral topics, researchers must be sensitive to the potential for interviewer-gender effects.

Just as personal characteristics can, the social distance between interviewers and respondents can influence an interview. If an interviewer appears to be of higher social status than a respondent, the respondent may tend to defer or acquiesce to the interviewer by providing answers intended to win approval. Even an interviewer's manner of speech can affect a respondent's replies because a person's speech may reflect his or her geographical origin, social class, age group, or level of education.

Race and Ethnicity

An interviewer's race and ethnicity are additional factors that can affect responses to a poll (Schuman and Converse 1971; Hatchett and Schuman 1975–1976; Campbell 1981; Weeks and Moore 1981; Cotter, Cohen, and Coulter 1982; Meislin 1987). When black respondents are queried about the American political and judicial system, they are more likely to give supportive, positive answers to white interviewers than to black interviewers. Likewise, white respondents are less likely to reveal attitudes of racial hostility when interviewed by blacks than when interviewed by whites.

In late 1993 and early 1994 a major national telephone survey of African Americans was conducted using only black interviewers (Morin 1995b). A comparison of the answers of respondents who correctly believed they were being interviewed by blacks (76 percent) with those of respondents who incorrectly thought they were interviewed by whites (14 percent) revealed substantial differences. For example, only 17 percent of the respondents who thought they were queried by African Americans agreed with the statement, "American society is fair to everyone," compared with 31 percent agreement by those who believed their interviewer was white. Davis (1997) found that black respondents in a survey were likely to be more accommodating and deferential to white interviewers, even to the point of taking contradictory stances in evaluations of political figures and political parties.

Similar patterns of race-of-interviewer effects occurred in a 1989 ABC News/*Washington Post* poll (Morin 1989b). On a number of race-related questions, white responses shifted about five to ten percentage points depending on the race of the interviewer. For some questions the effect was greater. For example, 62 percent of whites interviewed by whites said that most of the problems now faced by blacks were "brought on by blacks themselves"; only 46 percent of white respondents interviewed by blacks gave that response. A study by Anderson, Silver, and Abramson (1988) found that "blacks interviewed by whites were much more likely to express warmth and closeness toward whites than were blacks interviewed by blacks" (289). Finally, in a study by Finkel, Guterbock, and Borg (1991) of race-of-interviewer effects in a poll prior to the 1989 Virginia gubernatorial contest between black Democrat Douglas Wilder and white Republican Marshall Coleman, white respondents interviewed by black interviewers were more likely to state a preference for Wilder (52.2 percent) than those queried by white interviewers (43.8 percent). This pattern was particularly pronounced among white Democrats and among whites who were less sure of their vote intention.

Davis and Silver (2003) identified a different kind of race-of-interviewer effect in a study in which they found that African American respondents answered fewer factual knowledge items correctly when queried by white interviewers than when queried by black interviewers. The researchers speculated that "respondents who belong to racial minorities may experience added anxiety when they risk being uninformed in the presence of the dominant racial group" (43), and that anxiety may lead to poorer performance in answering a battery of knowledge items.

A study by Reese and colleagues (1986) on the effects of interviewer ethnicity—white versus Hispanic—found that ethnicity also affected the responses to certain questions, especially items that related to the culture of the interviewer. When Anglos were asked questions by Hispanics about aspects of Mexican American life, they responded more sympathetically than when they were asked the same questions by fellow Anglos. Why? The general explanation is that respondents try not to give answers that might offend an interviewer, particularly on matters that relate to the interviewer's race and ethnicity.

Because of potential interviewer effects in personal and telephone interviews, some practitioners argue for the use of automated phone interviewing with prerecorded voices. That is, instead of a live voice on the phone asking questions, there is a prerecorded voice posing the questions. This procedure is controversial among pollsters, but it is becoming more commonplace. Its advocates, such as Rasmussen Reports and Survey USA, argue that the use of a single, digitally recorded voice ensures that every respondent hears exactly the same question; there will be no variations, as might occur with live interviewers who, even if well trained, may still have their own idiosyncrasies in asking questions, whether of tempo, accent, emphases, or whatever. Another argument made on behalf of using prerecorded voices rather than live interviewers is that it is cheaper; there is no need to spend time and money to train interviewers. Moreover, the turn-around time may be shorter. Prerecorded voices also cut down on fraudulent behavior and bogus responses; sometimes live interviewers engage in unethical behavior, completing questionnaires without ever having interviewed the respondents. Using our earlier terminology, proponents of prerecorded voices claim that their approach is more reliable than live interviewers, providing greater standardization and consistency.

Opponents of using prerecorded voices raise a number of criticisms, such as that prerecorded polling will have lower response rates, since respondents are more likely to talk to a live person than to a prerecorded voice. Another objection is that prerecorded interviewing eliminates (or at least makes very difficult) the opportunity for the interviewer to play an active role in the selection of the actual respondent to be interviewed. As we discussed in chapter 4, typically in telephone sampling, once a successful call has been achieved and an actual contact made, the interviewer then asks a number of questions to determine who within that household should actually be interviewed. That is almost impossible to do when the interviewer is a prerecorded voice. A related criticism is that with automated, prerecorded polling, it is difficult to know who answered the phone and

ᵗᵉᵈ ⁱⁿ ᵗʰe interview (although advocates say they do internal

suspicious interviews).

e is that prerecorded interviewing is here to stay and will

redibility, particularly in the area of election polling and

esults of prerecorded polls do as good a job in election

lls with live interviewers. Jacobson (2006) points out that

aces for governor, the U.S. Senate, and even the U.S.

entatives, at least one polling firm that uses prerecorded

llowing the campaign regularly. He notes that prerecorded

llarly prominent in smaller-population states and media

markets, where traditional polls are thought to be uneconomical and too expensive. In an era when many media outlets, especially newspapers, are cutting costs, the availability of free or low-cost polling results may be a genuine boon. The Internet is also a factor, since poll results can be posted and quickly disseminated throughout the Internet universe. Recounting an interview with Scott Rasmussen, the head of Rasmussen Reports, noted for its prerecorded interviewing techniques, Jacobson quotes Rasmussen: "The driving force behind all of this is the Internet, which makes more information of all kinds available, from polling data to amateur videos. The Internet and the online political community is reshaping politics. Our polling data is just a minor part of the change. Economically, our business model only works because of the Internet."

Internet Polling

Pollsters would benefit greatly from using the Internet to conduct public opinion polls of representative samples of citizens. First, they could interview large numbers of people quickly and economically. They also could provide respondents with audio and video materials as part of the interviewing process. Internet surveys could be self-administered, but an interviewer, either live or recorded, also could participate. Finally, Internet polling would permit researchers to tabulate and analyze data very rapidly.

With all these potential advantages, what is preventing the widespread use of Internet polling? The most obvious factor is access, although access to the Internet continues to expand. The most recent Pew Internet American Life poll (Rainie 2010) found that 74 percent of adult (18 and older) Americans use the Internet, almost double the rate from ten years earlier. According to the Pew poll, there were some predictable and sizable demographic differences in Internet usage with respect to age, education, and to a lesser extent income. For example, 93 percent of Americans aged 18 to 29 used the Internet, compared with 38 percent for those over 65. Likewise, 94 percent of respondents with a college education used the Internet, compared with only 39 percent for those citizens with less than a high school education. Ninety-four percent of respondents from households with income of more than $75,000 used the Internet, compared with 60 percent for households with income of less than $30,000. Differences based on race/ethnicity and place of residence were much smaller, yet clear. For example, 76 percent of non-Hispanic whites, 70 percent of blacks, and 61 percent of Hispanics used the Internet. Internet use was highest in suburban areas (77 percent), next highest in urban areas (74 percent), and lowest (but still very high) in rural areas (70 percent).

Accompanying the growth in the number of Internet users is the increase in home broadband connections; in 2009, 60 percent of Americans had a broadband connection at home, compared with 30 percent in 2005. Thus both the extent and quality of Internet connections continue to grow. Some observers compare the Internet today to the early days of the telephone and believe that just as telephone access became almost universal in American households, so too will Internet availability. Although there are marked demographic differences between citizens who go online and those who do not, these differences will lessen in the future. But for today, the issue of Internet access remains somewhat more complicated than simple use vs. nonuse of the Internet. Even as 74 percent of Americans have used the Internet, that does not mean that the Internet is readily available to them. In some cases, citizens must go to their local libraries or schools to access the Internet. It would certainly be more difficult for these citizens to participate in an Internet poll. For example, according to the U.S. Census Bureau, Current Population Survey of October 2009, 31.3 percent of American households had no Internet use at home.

For other Americans, Internet availability is much easier, either at home or elsewhere. For example, of the two-thirds of households with Internet access, almost 93 percent have broadband connectivity, while the rest rely mainly on dial-up connections. And, according to Pew, as of May

2010, 59 percent of all adult Americans go online wirelessly, either using a laptop or cell phone, or both. And, once again, there are demographic differences with respect to who has wireless access, with citizens of high socioeconomic status enjoying better access. Thus, Internet access in the United States is widespread though not universal. And given that citizens do have access to the Internet, there are still meaningful differences among Americans as to how that access is achieved.

Even if Internet access and use were universal, the most significant flaw in many Internet polls is that the respondents are not selected through a scientific sampling procedure. Instead respondents are self-selected—they choose to participate. Obviously such respondents may not be representative of the overall population, perhaps because they are more interested in the topic of that particular survey or because they have been stimulated by various groups to take part. Then there is the problem of respondents who participate in a survey more than once. Internet surveys with self-selected or voluntary samples are nonprobability samples, and that means that sampling error cannot be calculated. Nor can probability statements be made about the relationship between those sample results and the true population parameters. There is no sampling list from which a probability sample can be collected. This problem, however, is not inevitable. One can create Internet polls that are probability samples or that have elements of probability sampling. Couper has presented the following typology of Web surveys (2000, 477):

Types of Web Surveys

Nonprobability methods	Probability methods
1. Polls as entertainment	4. Intercept surveys
2. Unrestricted self-selected surveys	5. List-based surveys
3. Volunteer opt-in panels	6. Web option in mixed-mode surveys
	7. Prerecruited panels of Internet users
	8. Prerecruited panels of full population

On the nonprobability side, the first two methods are what we commonly think of when we talk about self-selected Internet polling, with large numbers of respondents, many of whom may participate multiple times. These are typically not particularly useful polls, even if it is fun to participate and read about the results. The third category of nonprobability Web polls is more interesting, and we will discuss one specific application shortly.

On the probability side, the intercept poll simply entails sampling people who visit a particular Web site, with features built in to account for multiple hits by the same people. Here the sample reflects the overall population that

visited that Web site, but results cannot be generalized to broader populations. The next category—list-based sample of high-coverage populations—
takes advantage of the fact that there are certain populations, such as those
on university campuses, in which access to computers, e-mail, and the Internet is universal, and comprehensive lists of the population exist. These circumstances make Internet polling of representative samples of university
populations very feasible and enable one to generalize from the sample to
the overall population from which it was drawn (assuming appropriate
response rates and the like). The mixed-mode design simply offers the
Internet as one way of participating in a poll; some respondents might use
the Web, while others might participate over the telephone or by filling out
a mail questionnaire.

Both of the final two categories involve using probability sampling
methods such as random-digit dialing to identify a representative sample,
then contacting them, identifying those with Internet access, obtaining
their e-mail address, and trying to recruit them to participate in a Web
survey. The major difference between the prerecruited panels of Internet
users and the prerecruited panels of the full population is that in the former
case, only those citizens who are already Internet users can be selected as
part of the sample. In the latter case, those who currently are not Internet
users are provided Internet access and training; thus one can conduct an
Internet survey of a sample from the entire population.

Two of the most creative and ambitious examples of Internet polling
have been conducted by Harris Interactive, using volunteer opt-in panels,
and Knowledge Networks, using prerecruited panels of the full population.
Harris Interactive puts together a large (more than 7 million in 2000)
national online panel of willing respondents. As described by Taylor et al.,
"the panel was recruited through multiple sources, including banner adver-
tisements and sweepstakes that have run across the Web, the Harris/Excite
daily poll, product registrations on Excite and Netscape, and telephone
surveys" (2001, 38). This results in a panel of Americans who already use
the Internet, but it is not representative of all Internet users or of the total
American population. Hence, statistical sampling and weighting procedures are used to adjust for the differential likelihood of different respondents' being included. On its Web site, Harris Interactive describes its
weighting process as follows:

> Completed interviews are weighted to figures obtained from the Current
> Population Survey (CPS) as well as key questions administered in Harris
> Poll monthly telephone surveys of national cross-sectional samples of
> 1,000 adults, aged 18 and older. We use several demographic variables
> (e.g., sex, age, education, race and ethnicity) as well as a variable represent-
> ing the propensity of an individual respondent to be online—a composite
> of several factors—to generalize survey results to the national population.

As early critics (e.g., Mitofsky 1999) of the Harris sampling procedures worried about representativeness and low response rates, a major
test of this type of online polling occurred in the 2000 presidential election.
The Harris Interactive online poll had Bush and Gore tied, a more accurate
prediction than the telephone polls sponsored by other organizations produced. Moreover, the individual-state-level predictions by Harris Interactive
were twice as accurate as all other telephone polls (Taylor et al. 2001, 38).
In the 2004 election campaign, the final Harris online poll showed Kerry
winning by three points (50–47), but that is not a major discrepancy in
predicting a very close election. Like most approaches to Internet polling,
the Harris methodology is continually being upgraded.

In contrast to Harris Interactive, Knowledge Networks tries to obtain
a representative sample of all Americans, whether or not they initially
have Internet access. This is accomplished by using random-digit-dialing
techniques to select a large panel (sample) from all households having a
phone. These households are then contacted to recruit them to participate in online surveys. Households that agree to participate are provided
Web access and Internet equipment. Citizens who previously did not use
the Internet thus are included in the sample. Various studies (Greenberg
and Rivers 2001; Smith 2003) comparing the Knowledge Networks
online polls with telephone and with face-to-face polls indicate that the
Knowledge Networks Internet surveys often yield reasonably similar
results, but some notable differences were observed. For example, there
tends to be a higher incidence of "don't know" responses in Knowledge
Networks polls, perhaps because they provided an explicit "don't know"
option and perhaps because it is easier to probe and elicit a response
from people in phone and personal interviews. Based on his own
research, Smith (2003) offered a cautionary note about the accuracy of
online polling:

> [I]t cannot automatically be expected that even Internet surveys based on
> probability samples and general populations will produce results equiva-
> lent to those from non-Internet surveys. Internet surveys intrinsically dif-
> fer from standard, non-Internet surveys in format and in what is required
> of respondents and will often differ on other characteristics such as pop-
> ulation coverage, response rate, and the use of panels. These factors will
> usually combine together to produce notable differences between Inter-
> net and non-Internet surveys. (175)

My own view is that whatever the current limitations of Internet polling, it will continue to grow, particularly as the challenges facing telephone
polling become more daunting. On grounds of cost, speed, the availability
of large samples, and the ability to incorporate audio and visual elements
in polls, Internet polling is increasingly attractive. Moreover, there may be

sensitive topics on which citizens are more likely to express their true views in a self-administered Internet poll than in a telephone interview.

Internet polling is the focus of much research and analysis. The research of Smyth et al. (2009) suggests conditions under which respondents could provide richer responses to open-ended questions on Web surveys. But Heerwegh and Loosveldt (2008) show in an experiment that data quality was lower in a Web survey than in a face-to-face poll as measured by the proportion of "don't know" responses, lesser differentiation on rating scales, and greater item nonresponse. On a more positive note, Couper and Miller (2008) point out that Web surveys offer new ways to pose survey questions by taking advantage of the graphical and interactive nature of the Internet. But Couper and Miller also point out that Web surveys may not provide the solution to the problem of declining response rates discussed in chapter 4. They note that there appear to be fewer Americans willing to participate in opt-in panels and that completion rates are low among those who do participate. Low cumulative response rates characterize probability-based Web panels. And indeed, the issue of response rates and nonresponse bias, long discussed in the context of telephone polling, is now a core topic of research for Internet polling. (See the 2008 special issue of *Public Opinion Quarterly* on "Web Survey Methods" for an interesting collection of articles on various aspects of Internet polling.)

For many practitioners the information collected in Internet polling is useful, even if it cannot be generalized to larger populations. And even though there are questions about the accuracy of specific, one-time estimates obtained in Internet polls, such surveys should do a good job of tracking trends over time. Nevertheless, one should be a bit cautious about directly comparing the results of polls on the same topic but carried out by different methods, such as Internet versus telephone (Fricker at al. 2005).

Technical and statistical developments and expanded access to the Internet will allow Internet surveys to become more scientific and more representative in the future. For example, one of the concerns about the use of Internet polls to make election predictions is that older people are less likely to have access to and use the Internet, yet older people are more likely to vote. Weighting techniques may address this problem, but so will time. As the reach of the Internet rapidly expands to a higher proportion of the citizenry, including older Americans, and as generational replacement occurs over a longer time frame, the concern about bias in Internet access and use will diminish dramatically.

As Internet polling of all kinds grows, the results of Internet surveys should be viewed with caution, particularly if they are conducted by entities with an agenda to promote. The National Council on Public Polls (NCPP), skeptical about the reliability of many Internet surveys, has provided journalists with ten questions that they should consider before reporting the results of Internet polls. According to the NCPP (2006), if an Internet survey is not designed to be representative, and if there is no evidence that it is representative, its results should not be reported. It also essentially dismisses self-selected call-in polls. Yet despite the NCPP's admonitions to journalists and the news media to be careful about publicizing and reporting Internet polls, Web-based surveys are becoming more prominent, and many are even sponsored by the news organizations themselves.

Conclusion

The method of data collection and the actual conduct of the interview measurably affect the responses to a public opinion poll. In most instances consumers of polls are in a weak position to evaluate those effects, mainly because pollsters provide little information about their interviewing procedures. Nevertheless, consumers might raise a number of questions about the interviewing process, particularly if they have been selected to be respondents in a poll. For example, consumers who refuse to complete a mailed questionnaire or an Internet survey might ask themselves why. Is it because the subject matter is of no interest, because the questions are too simplistic, or because the questionnaire is too time-consuming? Consumers who choose to participate in a survey might examine their reactions to question wording and question order, to the overall experience itself, or to other specific elements of the questionnaire.

One question that poll consumers will never be able to answer is whether the same results would have been obtained had a different data collection method been used. Some research suggests that the choice of interviewing method can affect the responses because of the different interpersonal dynamics that characterize different interviewing modes. For example, in two studies on substance use, personal interviews found higher levels of alcohol and drug use by respondents than did telephone interviews (Johnson 1989; Aquilino and Losciuto 1990).

Respondents to personal or telephone polls also should make some mental notes about the skill of the interviewers. How effective was the interviewer in establishing a good climate for the interview? How well did the interviewer handle the respondent's questions and problems? Did the interviewer do or say anything that seemed to lead the person to respond in certain ways? Did the interviewer have any characteristics or traits that either facilitated or hindered the interview? The answers to these and other questions should alert poll respondents to biases that can influence the interviewing process and the answers it generates.

Exercises

1. Go to the Web site of the American National Election Studies, Gallup, or the Program on International Policy Attitudes and download an actual questionnaire. Then assume that you are an interviewer who will administer that questionnaire (or a subset of it) in a face-to-face setting. Find five friends who are willing to serve as respondents and administer the survey to each of them separately. What problems did you encounter in conducting the interviews? How did the fact that you were interviewing friends affect the interpersonal dynamics of the interview situation? How do you think the experience would have differed if you were interviewing strangers?

2. Design a ten-item Internet survey to be self-administered on your college campus. How might your survey differ if you were to interview the respondents directly (in person or on the phone) rather than use the Internet?

6 The Media and the Polls

Newspapers and television are still the major sources of what Americans learn about polls, although the Internet and specific Web sites such as pollingreport.com and pollster.com (today huffingtonpost.com/news/pollster) are increasingly important sources of polling information. That is, most of what citizens learn about the polls does not come directly from the reports prepared by the organizations sponsoring the polls. Instead, citizens' awareness of poll results is largely channeled through the media. And because newspapers and TV are the major sources for information on polls, citizens need to recognize that many of the organizations that sponsor surveys try to manipulate those media to cover poll results in ways that promote the organizations' objectives. Candidates for office also often try to obtain advantageous media coverage of private campaign polls by selectively leaking the results. And the media themselves play a critical role in terms of which polls they cover and the content of that coverage.

Moreover, the national television networks and their local affiliates, the major newsmagazines, and newspapers throughout the country themselves sponsor some of the most publicized and widely disseminated public opinion polls. Thus the media generate much of the public opinion data that in turn become the subject matter for the news stories that they present. For some observers, this situation raises questions about a conflict of interest—meaning that the definition of what is newsworthy may be unduly influenced by media-sponsored polls on particular topics. One critic (Schier 2006) goes further, arguing that the media may choose to cover a particular story, subsequently conduct a poll on that topic, and then use the poll results as confirmation of the significance of the story itself. In addition, the fact that news organizations make substantial investments in developing their capability for public opinion polling may result in a tendency to use that capability even when it is not necessary or appropriate to the topic at hand.

Because of the media's pivotal role in developing citizens' awareness of polling, this chapter evaluates the media's reporting of public opinion polls, both the ones they sponsor and those sponsored by other organizations. The discussion focuses on two distinct aspects of poll coverage—the treatment of the polls' technical features (for example, sampling error and question wording) and the presentation of substantive results and interpretations based on the polling data. It concludes with some caveats about the reporting of polls.

Standards for Reporting Results

Because media reporting of polls may not always be reliable, various organizations have adopted standards to govern the disclosure of poll results to citizens. For example, the National Council on Public Polls (NCPP), a group of polling organizations, has adopted the following Principles of Disclosure (Level 1 Disclosure):

> All reports of survey findings issued for public release by a member organization will include the following information:
>
> —Sponsorship of the survey
> —Fieldwork provider (if applicable)
> —Dates of interviewing
> —Sampling method employed
> —Population that was sampled
> —Size of the sample that serves as the primary basis of the survey report
> —Size and description of the subsample, if the survey report relies primarily on less than the total sample
> —Margin of sampling error (if a probability sample)
> —Survey mode (for example, telephone/interviewer, telephone/automated, mail, internet, fax, e-mail)
> —Complete wording and ordering of questions mentioned in or upon which the release is based
> —Percentage results of all questions reported

The recommendations go on to state:

> Member organizations reporting results will endeavor to have print and broadcast media include the above items in their news stories.

Like the NCPP, both the American Association for Public Opinion Research (AAPOR) and the Council of American Survey Research Organizations (CASRO) have codes of conduct that specify standards for disclosure of how a poll was conducted. Both organizations specify two sets of standards for disclosure, one a minimum and the other more encompassing. Both organizations recognize that it is difficult to expect the media, polling organizations, and the like to devote substantial time and attention to the methodological aspects of a poll, but they both agree that there is at least a minimum body of information that must be disclosed. For example, AAPOR advocates that at minimum the following items be disclosed:

1. Who sponsored the survey, and who conducted it.
2. The exact wording of questions asked, including the text of any preceding instruction or explanation to the interviewer or respondents that might reasonably be expected to affect the response.
3. A definition of the population under study, and a description of the sampling frame used to identify that population.
4. A description of the sample design, giving a clear indication of the method by which the respondents were selected by the researcher, or whether the respondents were entirely self-selected.
5. Sample sizes and, where appropriate, eligibility criteria, screening procedures, and response rates computed according to AAPOR Standard Definitions. At a minimum, a summary of disposition of sample cases should be provided so that response rates could be computed.
6. A discussion of the precision of the findings, including estimates of sampling error, and a description of any weighting or estimating procedures used.
7. Which results are based on parts of the sample, rather than on the total sample, and the size of such parts.
8. Method, location, and dates of data collection.

Effectiveness of the Standards

But how much protection do these standards provide for consumers of public opinion research, assuming that polling organizations adhere to them? The answer is that they provide less protection than is apparent at first glance, although the standards have contributed to improved media coverage of the polls. One reason why the standards are not as effective as they appear is that they apply primarily to the survey organizations and pollsters who release results, rather than to the news organizations that are covering the results. In cases when the survey organization and the disseminator of the results are part of the same news organization, the coverage is usually more in line with the NCPP and AAPOR standards.

Here is an example of how the standards may be applied when the survey organization and the disseminator of the results are the same. Reports of the results of a CBS News/*New York Times* poll may emanate from four distinct sources:

1. A story that appears in the *New York Times.*
2. A story presented on the *CBS Evening News.*
3. A news release issued by the *New York Times.*
4. A news release prepared by CBS News.

The first two sources are readily available to citizens; the latter two are not. Normally, the news releases prepared by CBS News and by the *New York Times* and the news story in the *Times* comply closely with the NCPP and AAPOR standards; the story presented on the *CBS Evening News* is less complete because airtime is limited. Fortunately, television networks and major newspapers often provide complete poll releases on their Web sites, although citizens may not be aware of this.

If the organization reporting the poll is different from the group that sponsored it, the poll release and the actual news story may show major discrepancies in meeting the NCPP, CASRO, and AAPOR recommendations. For example, most newspapers do not conduct their own polls. Instead, they rely on syndicated polls from organizations such as Gallup or on news releases in the public domain that are issued by polling organizations. In these situations the NCPP recommends that the sponsoring organization attempt to ensure that the medium that reports its results conforms to the NCPP standards. But there really is no way to enforce this recommendation with news organizations once the poll release has become public. Moreover, the interests of the sponsoring organization may not be well served by full disclosure of the technical features of the poll, particularly if the sponsoring organization has manipulated the poll to generate a desired set of results. Overall, then, compliance with the standards is voluntary, and that diminishes their effectiveness.

A more serious problem arises, however, when a news organization prepares a news analysis based on a subset of items from a questionnaire and does not inform readers or viewers about item selection, question wording, and question order. Then the news analysis may or may not accurately represent the content of the entire survey. Obviously, the items chosen for analysis and the perspective taken on them can dramatically affect the resulting coverage. (For potential examples of this problem, see the discussion on substantive interpretation of polls later in this chapter.)

The NCPP and AAPOR minimum standards ignore some of the technical characteristics of polls. For example, NCPP standards do not require reporting of the actual adjustments made to a sample, such as weighting (used to achieve demographic representativeness—see chapter 4) or filtering (for example, to identify likely voters within a sample). A poll release will often state that weighting and filtering have been done, but in most cases it will not tell how. As a result, the poll consumer, ill equipped to

cathy®

assess the soundness of the poll, is at the mercy of the decisions made by the news organizations. For example, pollsters identify likely voters using different methods that can generate divergent predictions of election outcomes (see chapter 7).

Finally, the NCPP minimum standards do not address response rates or the procedures, such as callbacks, that were used to increase them. Poor response rates may make it necessary to adjust the interviewed sample to make it representative of the broader population. If respondents who are called back multiple times in order to complete an interview differ in systematic ways from those who are interviewed on the first attempt, then the decision whether to use multiple callbacks can affect the substantive findings of the poll. Unfortunately, in most situations poll consumers receive little, if any, information about response rates and related matters.

Observing the Standards

How closely do the media actually conform to these professional standards in their reporting of polls? An early study by Miller and Hurd (1982) examined how well three newspapers—the *Chicago Tribune,* the *Los Angeles Times,* and the *Atlanta Constitution*—followed the AAPOR guidelines. In a sample of 116 polls reported between 1972 and 1979, compliance was highest for sample size (reported 85 percent of the time) and sponsorship (reported 82 percent of the time) and lowest for sampling error (reported only 16 percent of the time). Miller and Hurd found that compliance with the AAPOR standards on sampling error was better for election polls than for nonelection surveys. In general, compliance on sampling error was better when newspapers reported on their own polls than when they reported on polls provided by external sources, a finding that was repeated in a study of major newspaper performance in the 2000 general election (Welch 2002).

Overall, Miller and Hurd did see signs that newspaper reporting of polls had improved over the years. The improvement can be attributed to increased collaboration between journalists and social scientists, the availability of readable books on polling, and the increased frequency of in-house polls (newspapers do a better job of reporting their own polls because of local interest in them and because reporters have greater access to information about the polls' technical aspects).

The positive findings of that study must be tempered by the fact that it dealt with major daily newspapers of reasonably high quality. One expects such papers to be competent in reporting polls. Moreover, many of the polls the researchers analyzed were election surveys, which are more likely to report information such as sample size and sampling error than are nonelection surveys. A different study found that reports of nonelection polls were more descriptive of question wording and method of interviewing than were election polls (Salwen 1985). That finding was speculatively attributed to the fact that question wording and interviewing method are more self-evident in election polls and therefore need not be reported. In smaller daily and weekly newspapers, without the resources to conduct their own polls or employ their own survey research experts, poll coverage is probably much poorer.

If newspaper reporting falls short of the NCPP and AAPOR standards, what must television coverage be like? Newspapers have obvious advantages in reporting polls, one of which is that they provide the reader with hard copy that can be reread and referred to. In contrast, the television message (unless taped) "disappears" as soon as it is presented. It is also easier for newspapers to present a lot of information, such as full question wording.

Paletz and colleagues (1980) conducted one of the few empirical studies of the treatment of polls by network television. They examined every poll reported on the CBS and NBC evening news shows and in the *New York Times* in 1973, 1975, and 1977, years deliberately chosen to avoid presidential elections. Their conclusion was that the television networks generally did a poorer job of reporting details about polls than did the *Times,* although the latter's performance was not stellar. Among the findings was that the sponsor of a poll was almost never mentioned on the networks and mentioned only about 25 percent of the time in the *Times.* Sample size was presented in two-thirds of the *Times* stories but in only 26 percent of the television reports. The time of interviewing was given in 43 percent of the *Times* accounts and in 30 percent of the television reports. And in only 30 percent of the *Times* stories and 5 percent of the television reports was the complete wording of particular questions provided. Beyond these details, the reports provided virtually no other technical information about the polls (Paletz et al. 1980, 504–505).

One study focused on how well the television networks treated sampling error in their coverage of polls in the 2000 general election campaign. Larson (2003) found that although more than half the television stories included mention of sampling error, a major improvement over what used to be the case, the coverage often demonstrated a lack of understanding of how the sampling error was to be applied to the reported percentages. Too often, the news report compared the sampling error directly with the percentage gap between contenders Gore and Bush, rather than applying the sampling error (plus and minus) to the Gore and Bush percentages, concluding incorrectly that the margin separating the candidates was statistically significant. Larson also found that when the news reports talked about subsets of poll respondents, the stories generally failed to acknowledge that the margin of error for the subgroup was higher than for the overall sample. This finding was echoed by Langer (2000), who found that media coverage of the presidential preferences of subgroups (such as Hispanics) often ignored the fact that the sampling error was so great that no definitive statements about the patterns of voter movements could really be made.

Another study (Welch 2002) analyzed how well newspapers covered presidential election polls from September 1, 2000, through Election Day. The study examined eight newspapers, including four national papers (*New York Times, Wall Street Journal, USA Today,* and *Washington Post*) and four small local papers. Overall, the study concluded that the papers did not do a good job of meeting the AAPOR and NCPP standards in their coverage of election polls and that this was true for both the national and the local newspapers. Newspapers did do a much better job when they were reporting the results of one of their own in-house polls, a finding repeated in a separate study (Marton and Stephens 2001) that found that the *New York Times* did a much better job meeting AAPOR standards in stories using *New York Times*–sponsored polls. Welch noted that the worst offenders were newspaper stories that used a poll result to illustrate a point; these newspaper articles tended to ignore nearly all the AAPOR and NCPP standards.

In summary, the available evidence suggests that the media could do a much better job of adhering to the NCPP and AAPOR standards in reporting poll results, especially for surveys not conducted in-house. If they did, citizens could become more proficient in evaluating poll results. Methodological sophistication in poll reporting is increasing as journalists, political practitioners, and even media audiences acquire survey research skills.

Moreover, as more news organizations conduct their own polls and ignore those from other sources, the overall quality of poll reporting will probably improve. An appropriate way to end this section is to provide two excellent examples of newspaper reporting of the mechanics of polls. The first is from the *Columbus Dispatch* and the second from the *New York Times;* both of these were in-house polls.

About its own poll the *Dispatch* said:

> The *Dispatch* poll was based on returns from 1,445 registered Ohio voters who said they intend to vote in the 2010 general election. *The Dispatch* obtained a computerized list of all registered voters in Ohio from the secretary of state. Those who had not voted since 2005 were eliminated. A *Dispatch* computer then randomly chose who would receive ballots. Ballot recipients were asked to describe themselves by party affiliation, age, sex, race, education, income, religion, union membership and the candidates they voted for in the 2008 presidential race and 2006 gubernatorial election. Ballots of different colors were mailed to various regions of the state so *The Dispatch* could ensure that each area was represented in proportion to its actual voting strength. The results were weighted slightly so these proportions were reflected accurately. The standard margin of sampling error in a poll of the size conducted by *The Dispatch* is plus or minus 2.3 percentage points in 95 out of 100 cases. This means that if a poll is conducted 100 times, the result in 95 cases will not vary by more than 2.3 percentage points from the result that would be obtained if all registered Ohio voters were polled and responded. Like all polls, the *Dispatch* Poll is subject to possible error other than sampling error. Other sources of error include unintentional bias in the wording of questions, data-entry error and nonresponse bias. Nonresponse bias means that those who responded might not necessarily reflect the views of those who did not participate. The response rate for this poll was 12 percent. The poll was designed, conducted and financed solely by *The Dispatch*. *The Dispatch* is a supporter of the American Association for Public Opinion Research's transparency initiative. (*Columbus Dispatch,* October 31, 2010, p. A8)

The *New York Times* provided the following information about its poll:

> The latest *New York Times*/CBS News Poll is based on telephone interviews conducted Oct. 21 through 26 [2010] with 1,173 adults throughout the United States, including 1,073 who said they were registered to vote. The sample of landline telephone exchanges called was randomly selected by a computer from a complete list of more than 69,000 active residential exchanges across the country. The exchanges were chosen so as to ensure that each region of the country was represented in proportion to its share of all telephone numbers. Within each exchange, random

digits were added to form a complete telephone number, thus permitting access to listed and unlisted numbers alike. Within each household, one adult was designated by a random procedure to be the respondent for the survey. To increase coverage, this landline sample was supplemented by respondents reached through random dialing of cell phone numbers. The two samples were then combined and adjusted to assure the proper ratio of landline only, cell phone only, and dual phone users. Interviewers made multiple attempts to reach every phone number in the survey, calling back unanswered numbers on different days at different times of day and evening. For purposes of analysis, black respondents were over-sampled in this poll. Phone numbers at which a self-identified black respondent had been interviewed in polls over the last 14 months were recalled and a random member of the household was interviewed. If that person was black, he or she was included in the oversample. All blacks were then weighted back to their proper proportion of the population. The combined results have been weighted to adjust for variation in the sample relating to geographic area, sex, Hispanic origin, age, education, marital status and number of adults in the household. Respondents in the landline sample were also weighted to take account of the number of telephone lines into their residence. Some findings regarding voting were also weighted in terms of an overall "probable electorate," which uses responses to questions dealing with voting history, attention to the campaign, intention to vote in 2010, and other indicators of engagement as a measure of the likelihood of respondents' turning out in November. In theory, in 19 cases out of 20, results based on such samples of all adults will differ by no more than three percentage points in either direction from what would have been obtained by seeking to interview all American adults. Results based on smaller subgroups have a larger sampling error. For example, for the 273 black respondents it is plus or minus six points. Shifts in results between polls over time also have a larger sampling error. In addition to sampling error, the practical difficulties of conducting any survey of public opinion may introduce other sources of error into the poll. Variations in the wording and order of questions, for example, may lead to somewhat different results. Michael R. Kagay of Princeton, N.J., assisted *The Times* in its polling analysis. Complete questions and results are available at nytimes.com/polls.

Note that in addition to the standard information about sampling error and confidence levels, both of these descriptions discussed weighting or adjusting the data, with the *Times* talking about three aspects of weighting. Both newspapers mentioned response rates and nonresponse bias and also referred to other sources of error, although they did not develop this point. It is clear the *Times* and the *Dispatch* both provided their readers with a lot of information about their polls. What is not clear is whether readers are willing and able to make use of this information.

ABC News, among others, does a superb job of presenting its polling methodology and discussing the role of polls on its Web site (Langer and Merkle 2006; Langer 2006). Langer and Merkle summarize the sampling, interviewing, and weighting procedures that ABC uses in general and provide a very informative discussion of sampling error, standards, and response rates. In addition, they provide a very insightful discussion of the challenges of preelection polling, including an analysis of alternative likely voter models. Although the complete information is not included in every specific poll report ABC issues, it is available to citizens on the ABC Web site.

Substantive Interpretation of Polls

Without access to the complete results of polls, citizens cannot easily evaluate how well the news media report the technical aspects of polling. It is even more problematic for them to evaluate how well news organizations describe and interpret the substance of public opinion polls. Because interpretation of polling data can be highly judgmental and value laden, it may be difficult to demonstrate that one particular interpretation is superior to another except in cases where obvious misreading of the data has occurred or blatant biases have been built into the analysis. Even a simple description can pose a problem if a news story covers only a subset of the items on a topic because there is insufficient time or space.

In this section I will present several examples illustrating how the news media use and interpret polls and how much leeway they have in deciding which parts of a poll to emphasize. A good example of the choices that face the analyst is Adam Clymer's *New York Times* story on attitudes toward abortion, based on a survey of Americans conducted in late 1985. Though there have been countless surveys on abortion attitudes since the one that Clymer discussed in his article, it remains rare to see a reporter explicitly point to the deep complexity of public opinion on a topic. In Clymer's view, the wording of questions about abortion has a tremendous impact on the responses, and that is a "clear indication of uncertainty and conflict" in the public's attitudes on the topic (Clymer 1986b). Three items in the survey illustrate the complexity of popular attitudes:

Q. What do you think about abortion? Should it be legal as it is now, legal only in such cases as saving the life of the mother, rape or incest, or should it not be permitted at all?

Legal as is now	40%
Legal only to save mother, rape or incest	40%
Not permitted	16%
Don't know, not ascertained	4%

Q. Which of these statements comes closest to your opinion? Abortion is the same thing as murdering a child, or abortion is not murder because a fetus isn't really a person.

Murder	55%
Not murder	35%
Don't know, not ascertained	10%

Q. Do you agree or disagree with the following statement? Abortion sometimes is the best course in a bad situation.

Agree	66%
Disagree	26%
Don't know, not ascertained	8%

A journalist could write markedly different stories based on this survey, depending on which items are emphasized and how particular items are interpreted. By focusing only on the first item, a reporter could write a pro-choice story that points out that 40 percent of Americans favor the current abortion law, another 40 percent favor legalized abortion in limited circumstances, and only 16 percent oppose abortion outright. Another reporter could write an antiabortion story based on the first item, by stressing that 56 percent of the sample (40 percent plus 16 percent) favor limiting somewhat the current availability of abortion. Likewise, the second item could be used to document an antiabortion story that emphasizes that a majority of Americans think abortion is murder. But a story based only on the third item would suggest that a strong majority of Americans think abortion is sometimes the best course of action. The article that Clymer wrote reflects the complex and even contradictory nature of popular attitudes on abortion (1986b). Imagine the advocacy piece he could have written if he had adopted a blatantly pro-choice or antiabortion perspective.

Now consider the very divergent news stories that could be written based on the following questions asked of a national sample of adult Americans in a *Newsweek* poll conducted February 17–18, 2010, by Princeton Survey Research Associates International. The first two questions address health care reform overall and focus on the major political actors dealing with the issue. The next eight items focus on specific proposals that fall under the general rubric of health care reform. And the last item ascertains Americans' opinion of health care reform after being told that all of the specific proposals were included in the Obama plan.

Q. "Now thinking about the issue of health care reform, please tell me if you approve or disapprove of the way each of the following is handling this issue."

	Approve	Disapprove	Unsure
Barack Obama	39%	52%	9%
Democrats in Congress	27%	61%	12%
Republicans in Congress	21%	63%	16%

Q. "As you may know, Barack Obama has proposed a plan to change this country's health care system. From what you have seen or heard about what he has proposed, what is your overall opinion of Obama's health care reform plan—do you favor or oppose it?"

	Favor	Oppose	Unsure
All	40%	49%	11%
Republicans	15%	78%	7%
Democrats	72%	17%	11%
Independents	26%	62%	12%

Q. "Now I'm going to read you some specific proposals people have made to change the health care system. As I read each one, please tell me if you personally favor or oppose this change."

Q. "Creating a new insurance marketplace—the Exchange—that allows people without health care insurance to compare plans and buy insurance at competitive rates."

Favor	Oppose	Unsure
81%	13%	6%

Q. "Requiring health insurance companies to cover anyone who applies, even if they have a pre-existing medical condition."

Favor	Oppose	Unsure
76%	19%	5%

Q. "Requiring most businesses to offer health insurance to their employees, with tax incentives for small business owners to do so."

Favor	Oppose	Unsure
75%	20%	5%

Q. "Requiring that all Americans have health insurance, with the government providing financial help to those who can't afford it."

Favor	Oppose	Unsure
59%	36%	5%

Q. "Preventing insurance companies from dropping coverage when people are sick."

Favor	Oppose	Unsure
59%	38%	3%

Q. "Creating a government-administered public health insurance option to compete with private plans."

Favor	Oppose	Unsure
50%	42%	8%

Q. "Imposing a tax on insurers who offer the most expensive health plans, the so-called Cadillac plans, to help pay for health care reform."

Favor	Oppose	Unsure
34%	55%	11%

Q. "If health coverage is required for everyone, imposing fines on individuals who don't obtain coverage and on larger businesses that don't offer it."

Favor	Oppose	Unsure
28%	62%	10%

Q. "Now please think about the proposals I just described to you. All of these proposals are included in Barack Obama's health care reform plan. Having heard these details, what is your overall opinion of Obama's plan—do you favor it or oppose it?"

	Favor	Oppose	Unsure
All	48%	43%	9%
Republicans	18%	74%	8%
Democrats	83%	10%	7%
Independents	34%	57%	9%

Imagine the incredibly different stories that could be written about health care reform if reporters decided to cover only a subset of the items. There are questions that demonstrate support for health care reform and others that demonstrate opposition. Often because of space constraints or other reasons, journalists cannot (or will not) report on all the relevant items in a poll and focus only on a subset of the items. But if the reader is not aware of the full set of questions, then he or she will not know whether the journalistic account accurately reflects the results of the survey. The last exercise at the end of this chapter will ask the reader to write very divergent stories about support for health care based on different subsets of the above items.

The following examples suggest that media reports of polls conducted by other organizations are particularly susceptible to misinterpretation and faulty reporting. Krosnick (1989) investigated the *New York Times* coverage of a poll commissioned by Aetna Life and Casualty on the public's attitudes toward the civil justice system and tort reform; the poll was conducted by Louis Harris and Associates. Aetna had a vested interest in tort reform. When the poll was completed, Aetna issued a press release that began, "An overwhelming majority of Americans support a number of specific reforms to improve the nation's civil justice system." Throughout the press release and the Harris report of the survey results were assertions that Americans supported and favored many changes. The survey questions themselves, however, did not ask respondents whether they supported or favored those changes; instead, the questions asked whether respondents found the changes acceptable. Clearly, finding something acceptable is not the same thing as supporting or favoring it. Nevertheless, the news story on the poll that appeared in the *New York Times* failed to recognize this distinction and made strong claims that the poll results demonstrated "broad public support for *changes* in the civil justice system" and "reflected the public's *demand* for reform" (Krosnick 1989, 108). As Krosnick concluded, the *Times* coverage of the poll results most likely overstated public support for the changes that Aetna desired.

Another example, one with serious international ramifications, of news media misreporting and misinterpreting polls occurred in the late 1970s, as the U.S. Senate considered ratification of the treaties that would lead to Panamanian control of the Panama Canal. Smith and Hogan (1987) found that as the debate progressed in the Senate, many media organizations were reporting that public opinion was shifting toward support of the treaties—a finding that, if true, would obviously make it easier for senators sympathetic to the treaties to vote for ratification. But when Smith and Hogan examined the myriad poll results from the period, they found a pattern of stable opinion (which was hostile to the treaties), not one of change. They attributed the misleading interpretations to the variety of questions asked by different polling outfits, flaws in those questions, misinterpretation of key findings, and other factors. Here, though, the key point is the researchers' evaluation of how different news organizations actually reported the polls. They wrote:

> In general, CBS and the *New York Times* provided accurate and perceptive accounts of public opinion on the treaties. But the *Time, Newsweek,* and NBC stories . . . display serious flaws. During the crucial period of

Senate deliberation (January through April 1978) all claimed a massive shift in approval based on comparison of responses to different questions asked, in most cases, by different pollsters. Furthermore, the coverage is littered by errors of fact and inference and shows little understanding of the complex issues involved. . . .

Equally disturbing are certain common omissions. After January 1978, most findings of continued public opposition were simply ignored. . . . Also omitted were the methodological details that would have allowed an educated reader or viewer to discover the misinterpretations embedded in the media coverage. Only two articles, both in the *New York Times,* provided the complete text of a question; only one, also in the *Times,* included all of the information required by the American Association for Public Opinion Research (AAPOR) Standards of Disclosure for poll reports. In *Time* and *Newsweek* almost no information was given. (Smith and Hogan 1987, 27)

Morin (1998b) has pointed out that much of the media coverage (including some of his own) of the U.S. role in Bosnia in the late 1990s ignored poll results indicating strong support for some form of multilateral involvement and instead emphasized public opposition to U.S. involvement.

The coverage of domestic policy issues also is often flawed. Morin (1997c) cites the work of Jacobs and Shapiro (1995; 1995–1996), who investigated how the media use polls to report on entitlement programs. Their conclusions are very critical, claiming that news stories often fail to provide context and background from which to interpret survey data. They also point out that polling on topics such as entitlements is focusing increasingly on the politics (for example, the performance of various political actors) of the issue rather than the substance. Certainly it is possible that the way the news media portray public opinion on controversial issues, such as the canal treaties or Bosnia or entitlements, may affect the public policy decisions that are ultimately made.

Jack Rosenthal (2006) of the *New York Times* points out two polls that received more media coverage than they deserved. The first was an American Medical Association report on binge drinking and unprotected sex among college women on spring break. The report was allegedly based on a random sample of women and received extensive media coverage, including some mention of the data in the *New York Times.* It turned out that the sample was not random but was self-selected, and only a quarter of the sample had ever gone on a spring break trip. Many media outlets that reported the story had to issue corrections. The second poll story was in the *Wall Street Journal* and reported on a major survey conducted for liquor retailers, which purported to show that millions of kids buy alcohol online. It turns out that this also was not a scientific poll. Both of these examples demonstrate that the news media have an obligation to report legitimate polls accurately and to prevent illegitimate polls from being reported as valid research. Thus the *New York Times* issued a document on polling standards for editors and reporters that included the following statement: "Keeping poorly done survey search out of the paper is just as important as getting good survey research into the paper" (Rosenthal 2006, 10). Clearly, as the number of unscientific polls continues to grow, the media will have a greater responsibility to evaluate which polls merit coverage and which do not.

The above examples focus on news media coverage of polls conducted by other organizations. But the media can also stumble in reporting their own commissioned polls. In 2002 the state of Ohio was addressing the issue of science education in public schools. A controversy arose about the teaching of evolution versus other explanations of life, including "intelligent design," a perspective supported by creationism advocates. The *Cleveland Plain Dealer* sponsored a poll to ascertain Ohioans' attitudes about what should be taught in science education and ran a major, page one story on the results titled "Poll: Teach More Than Evolution," with the subtitle, "A majority of those surveyed want evolution, intelligent design to get equal time in school" (Stephens and Mangels 2002). And in the second paragraph of the story (on the first page of the paper), the reporters wrote, "A clear majority of the state's residents—59 percent—favor teaching evolution in tandem with intelligent design in public school science classes." Their evidence for that conclusion was the following poll question and responses:

Q. Currently, the Ohio Board of Education is debating new academic standards for public school science classes, including what to teach students about the development of life on Earth. Which position do you support?

Teach only evolution	8%
Teach only intelligent design	8%
Teach both	59%
Teach the evidence both for and against evolution, but not necessarily intelligent design	15%
Teach nothing about human development	9%
Not sure	1%

The thrust of the story was that Ohioans were very supportive of teaching intelligent design, and its proponents cited the *Plain Dealer* as evidence for their position. But a very different story could have been written had the reporters chosen to focus on other questions in the survey and had they adopted a different analysis strategy. For example, one item asked respondents,

Q. Which of the following is the best place to teach about beliefs regarding the development of life that differ from evolution?

In a science class	23%
In a class other than science	17%
At home or in a religious setting	51%
Not sure	9%

Based on these responses, a different story lead might have been that Ohioans overwhelmingly preferred that intelligent design be taught somewhere other than in a science class and that a majority of them preferred that intelligent design be taught outside the school altogether.

One might also question whether Ohioans responding to the poll even knew what evolution and, especially, intelligent design were. Respondents were asked about their familiarity with intelligent design and evolution. Eighteen percent said they were very familiar with intelligent design, 37 percent said "somewhat familiar," and 45 percent said "not that familiar." The comparable percentages for evolution were 42, 43, and 15. Perhaps the reporters should have replicated their analysis for those respondents who were at least somewhat familiar with intelligent design and evolution. Doing so would undoubtedly have eliminated some nonattitudes and might provide a more accurate portrait of Ohio public opinion.

One challenge the media may face occurs when there are multiple polls conducted on a topic that yield discrepant results. Which polls should be covered? Will all the divergent results be presented? Too often the media report certain polls and largely ignore others. An example of this phenomenon occurred in the 2010 election for governor in Ohio, where, at different stages of the campaign, there were multiple polls conducted in close temporal proximity that yielded highly divergent results. What should the media do in this case? One answer, of course, is to report all the polls and let the viewer/reader decide what these polls mean. Or the media could suggest a strategy by which to evaluate the multiple polls, perhaps calculating an average of all the results.

Unfortunately, this was not the practice when it came to the reporting of the Quinnipiac polls, especially in the *Columbus Dispatch.* At multiple points in the gubernatorial campaign, the Quinnipiac results generally showed the largest lead for the GOP candidate for governor, reaching a high of 17 percent when other polls were showing a narrower margin. Contributing to the excessive coverage of the Quinnipiac polls was the fact that Peter Brown, assistant director of the Quinnipiac Polling Institute, repeatedly made himself available to Ohio media, especially to the *Dispatch,* to discuss the Quinnipiac results and opine about the likely election outcome (when Quinnipiac showed a 17 percent GOP lead) with comments such as "Whatever the governor is doing is not working. . . . At this point, things obviously look very good for Mr. Kasich. . . . If those poll numbers are born out on Election Day, it won't be close" (Rowland, 2010a). And when a subsequent Quinnipiac poll showed the Republican lead down to 9 percent, Brown opined, "If the governor can continue to increase his numbers . . . anything's possible. But I'd sure like to be in John Kasich's shoes" (Rowland, 2010b). Perhaps nonpartisan pollsters should be more restrained and cautious in their comments to the media.

Did the Quinnipiac result get so much coverage because its results were so definitive? Or was it because a Peter Brown of Quinnipiac was so available to the media and offering pithy quotes? When a later Quinnipiac poll showed the Republican margin at ten points (still larger than what most other polls were showing), the Democratic campaign for governor, angry at the extensive coverage the Quinnipiac results were receiving, released some of its own internal polling showing a much closer race. And despite Quinnipiac showing a substantial GOP lead, the state Republican Party chairman dismissed the Quinnipiac results, stating that the contest was a dead heat. The last Quinnipiac poll done right before the election was in harmony with most other polls, showing a Republican lead of only 1 percent. And Peter Brown commented, "The governor's race is a statistical tie. It could go either way" (Rowland, 2010c). The actual election result was a Republican victory of slightly more than 2 percent.

Sometimes the news media use pseudopolls of self-selected respondents to embellish a news story in a misleading way. In one example, ABC used a pseudopoll in its coverage even though genuine polling data were available (Morin 1996a). ABC's newsmagazine show *20/20* devoted a segment to "physical attraction"—that is, whether women were satisfied with their physical appearance and what aspects of the physical appearance of women were most important to men. ABC's own scientific survey on these topics had found that the vast majority of women were satisfied with their physical attributes. The show decided, however, to build its story about physical attractiveness around a pseudopoll conducted by *Self* magazine, and it went on to report that 50 percent of the women who completed the magazine survey and mailed it in said that "they were inadequate because of their breast size." But the genuine poll that ABC itself conducted found quite different results: only 23 percent of the respondents had ever wished their breasts were a different size, and contrary to the thrust of the *20/20* segment, with its emphasis on breast enlargement, more than half of the dissatisfied women in the genuine poll had wished that their breasts were smaller, not larger. In this case, entertainment value overrode any responsibility to use appropriate polling data.

The statistical analysis that poll stories most commonly present is simple percentage distributions for individual questions in the survey—something that most adults understand. Sometimes reports include a breakdown by demographic subgroups, such as men and women or blacks and whites, but they seldom offer a cross-tabulation that shows the relationship between two survey items. Measures of association, correlation analysis, and multivariate statistical analyses almost never appear in news stories, probably because of the media's fear of intimidating and alienating the audience. It is fair to say, however, that news organizations' use of statistics is reasonably accurate, as far as it goes, in part because the data analysis is not very ambitious given media executives' perceptions of what audiences want and are able to comprehend.

Media, Polls, and the News Reporting Emphasis

The news media are frequently criticized for elevating polls to such a position of prominence that the polls themselves become regular topics for news stories. Indeed, some observers complain that the media, in their role as sponsors of polls, have gone into the business of creating the news rather than simply reporting it. More and more news organizations have developed their own polling capabilities, and to justify this sizable expenditure they may increasingly report poll-based stories that are not newsworthy in the traditional sense. Fitzgerald, Rule, and Bryant (1998) documented the rise of poll-based reporting on television news and the growing tendency of the networks to use their own polls. Consider this hypothetical example: A news organization conducts a poll on American attitudes toward mass transportation. Even though this topic is not on the national agenda and not a focus of public debate, the news organization publishes a story reporting the results of the survey. Such a story comes very close to being news that is created by the media rather than news that is coverage of real events. The media also come close to generating news in their constant reporting of presidential popularity polls, in that the latest blip in the trend line of presidential popularity becomes a news story. This certainly occurred in the lead-up to the 2006 midterm elections. Because the 2006 elections were seen by some as a referendum on President Bush and the war in Iraq, great attention was given to the various polls that measured presidential approval and popularity. Too often, a small shift upward or downward—for example, two percentage points—received media coverage that was excessive given that such a change was well within sampling error.

Another concern is that as more news organizations develop their own polling capabilities, they will less and less cover polls conducted by their rivals. Many polls by news media query citizens on matters such as presidential election trial heats, but usually their news reports do not mention the results that their competition's polls obtained, particularly when those results disagree with their own.

The media's treatment of election polls has received especially harsh criticism. The most common complaint is that the news organizations treat elections as sporting events—the comparison is usually to horse races (see chapter 7)—and use the polls to handicap the outcome. Indeed, Fitzgerald, Rule, and Bryant (1998) found that between 1969 and 1996 only four topics accounted for 90 percent of the poll-based stories on TV news, and number one on the list was candidates and elections. These stories frequently emphasize candidates' relative standing as measured by the polls (Broh 1980; Asher 1992), rather than their stances on the issues. As Robinson and Sheehan (1983) argue,

> The main problem with polling . . . is that it is objective and so "newsworthy" (at least for the moment) that it drives out all other forms of news. Polls have a higher priority in the newscast than most other forms of campaign reporting. And, of course, polls tend to be among the least substantive kinds of political journalism. (252)

In the 1988, 1992, 1996, 2000, 2004, and 2008 presidential campaigns, much of the criticism of presidential election polls focused on their frequency, their intrusiveness, their inconsistency, and the quality of media coverage of them. For example, Elving (1989) notes that in August 1988 fourteen major polls on the Dukakis-Bush presidential contest had results that varied by nineteen percentage points, a situation that generated confusion and annoyance with the polls. In defending their enterprise, many pollsters shifted blame to the media:

> "Did I see [1988] polls that annoyed me? No, but I did see reporting on them that did," says Linda DiVall of American Viewpoint Inc. "I wish the press had less desire to be conclusive and say the race is over when it's 10 points and it's May."
>
> Ed Goeas, president of Tarrance & Associates, says newspaper polls can be manipulated by the campaigns. "When newspaper polls are in the field the campaign can learn of it and do things to pump their guy up."
>
> But, Goeas contends, the real problems come when the data are in hand: "Newspapers are hurting the credibility of the industry because they are not prepared to analyze the data correctly.". . .
>
> "They're getting better, but I am always amazed at how many reporters are covering polls . . . without training or background," says Bud Lewis, the veteran pollster for the *Los Angeles Times*. "It's like sex—everybody thinks they're good at it automatically." (Elving 1989, 2187)

The 1992 elections offer another example. In the preconvention period, different polls had either George Bush or Ross Perot ahead (though not by large margins). The media coverage of these polls was often very dramatic and definitive, giving little recognition to how unstable early presidential preferences can be (Morin 1992d). Harwood (1992) argues that the media then did a poor job of accounting for dramatic postconvention swings in polled support for Bill Clinton and Bush, often simply attributing them to convention "bumps," when in fact much of the fluctuation might have stemmed from the limitations inherent in the polls themselves.

A similar situation occurred in the preconvention period in the 1996 presidential campaign. Most polls in May 1996 showed Clinton with a sizable double-digit lead over Bob Dole. Most of the next round of poll results, in mid-June, showed Clinton still ahead by a double-digit margin but a smaller one than in May. Of the June polls, the one that received the greatest media attention was the survey that showed the smallest gap between Clinton and Dole; the *Time*/CNN survey revealed that Clinton's lead had dropped from 56 percent to 34 percent, to 49 percent, to 43 percent. Why did the news media focus on the *Time*/CNN poll when other polls showed Clinton with a larger lead? The probable answer is twofold: First, the media love a close horse race that generates excitement, and that is what the *Time*/CNN poll showed. Second, the *Time*/CNN poll showed the greatest fluctuation over time, which intrinsically made it more interesting to those who report the news.

In the 2000 election, Bush-versus-Gore poll results bounced around substantially through the Republican and Democratic conventions, past Labor Day, and into the presidential debates in October. The volatility perplexed some observers and led others to be critical of the media for their breathless reporting of slight changes in poll standing.

In the 2004 election there were similar criticisms of the tendency of the media to overreport small differences and small changes in poll results, criticisms also made about the 2008 presidential election polls. Some media outlets in 2004 were criticized for premature release and dissemination of exit poll results and for the subsequent confusion in explaining what had happened. And, as has been the case for decades, the media were criticized for allowing polls to shape their campaign coverage, thereby contributing to the horse race approach to elections (discussed in chapter 7).

Other problems inherent in public opinion polling by news organizations reflect the structural characteristics of the polling and news-reporting enterprises. Ladd (1980, 576) questions whether polling and journalism can ever fit together well, given that *newsworthiness* for the media entails speed and timeliness, whereas good polling, despite the current technology for quick assessments of public attitudes, requires "extensive, time-consuming explanation and exposition." This conflict is exacerbated by the space and time constraints that news organizations face, which often do not allow them to present a poll-based story that includes complete details about the poll itself plus substantive background and context. Ladd also argues that good reporting is generally sharply focused, with relatively unambiguous conclusions; good survey research, however, usually reveals uncertainty, ambiguity, and low levels of public information and interest on matters of public policy. Often the portrait of public attitudes that polls reveal is a complex, contradictory one that may not make a "good" news story.

News treatment of polls also is shaped by journalists' ability to analyze and report on them. Because of changes in the curricula of university journalism programs and the availability of specialized training programs, reporters are becoming increasingly skillful in reporting on polls. Even so, Crespi (1980, 473) argues that journalistic requirements affect polling in both positive and negative ways:

Positive	Negative
Journalistic requirements place a high value on factual documentation of poll results, in the form of actual percentages rather than fuzzy generalizations.	There is a preoccupation with reporting numbers, the "objective" poll results, with a corresponding lack of interest in their underlying meaning or patterning.
Subjective editorializing is devalued insofar as poll reports are concerned, reducing the likelihood that the personal views of pollsters will introduce bias.	Superficiality and lack of analysis too often characterize coverage of even the most complicated issues.
Attention is focused on opinion regarding specific events and issues, thereby making poll results relevant to the real-life experiences and problems of the public, and to the political process.	Topics that can be expected to create front-page headlines dominate, leading to a spasmodic coverage of the agenda of public concerns.
Sensitivity to changes in public opinion, resulting from the effects of events, is enhanced.	There is limited continuing coverage of long-term trends, and background news is often neglected.

Rosenstiel (2005) has described six trends that affect how the press uses polls in contemporary election coverage. He argues that these trends result in citizens' learning more about the horse race aspects of campaigns and about the tactics employed by practitioners. But the upshot is that citizens learn less about what elections actually mean and less about what citizens are actually saying through their vote choices. Rosenstiel claims:

Changes in journalism—including newsroom cutbacks, an emphasis on repackaging, secondhand material, and the demands of 24-hour news—have expanded the reliance on polls as news, including polls of a sort once considered not reliable for publication, reduced the vetting that these polls are getting, and led to a more superficial understanding of the political race.

The proliferation of outfits offering news, which has resulted in greater competition for audience, has intensified the motivation of using polls in part for their marketing value rather than purely their probative journalistic value.

The more "synthetic" style of contemporary journalism has increased the tendency to allow polls to create the dominant context by which journalists explain and organize other news. . . .

These trends are reinforced by a growing reliance in the press on reporting daily horse race tracking polls as news, which due to their superficial nature, is further thinning the press's and the public's understanding of campaigns.

Growing audience skepticism and political polarization have created an environment of distrust about the methodology and integrity of polling.

And all of these factors, in turn, are frustrating the efforts of academic and commercial pollsters to maintain standards and deepen understanding among journalists about public opinion research and how to use it as journalism. (700)

Conclusion

The relationship between polling and the media can be difficult and complex. But if poll sponsors recognize both the uses and the limitations of polls, the relationship also can be beneficial and informative for citizens. News organizations need to take whatever steps are necessary to ensure that they provide their audiences with sufficient information to make informed judgments. Reporting sample size and sampling error is the beginning of good poll coverage, not the end. Standard practice should include presenting question wording and question order, factors that can have a much greater effect on the responses than can sampling error.

Beyond this, the journalism profession must be more sensitive to and reflective about the possible links between polls and news coverage. The media can easily play an agenda-setting role by bringing certain issues to the public's attention through news reporting, sponsoring and conducting polls on those issues, and reporting the results, activities that will reinforce the visibility of an issue to the electorate. Indeed, citizens can become highly concerned about an issue even though its prominence is largely due to media coverage and media-sponsored polls. For example, Morin (1994a) says that public concern about drugs in the late 1980s and fears about crime may have been largely driven by media coverage of those issues and of polls about them. He points out that in January 1989, only 19 percent of poll respondents cited drugs as the most important problem facing the nation. By October of the same year, the percentage had increased to 53 percent. But less than a year later, only 16 percent of Americans named drugs as the country's major problem. Morin attributes much of the rise and fall in the public's concern about drugs to the news media's heavy attention to the problem, which subsided when news organizations turned their attention elsewhere.

Journalists also need to be more perceptive about the frailties and limitations of polls and about how the reporting of polls can influence people in unintended ways. Gawiser and Witt (2006), in a pamphlet sponsored by the National Council on Public Polls, compiled a list of twenty questions that journalists should ask about poll results. Their elaborations of and answers to the following questions should be required reading for journalists:

1. Who did the poll?
2. Who paid for the poll and why was it done?
3. How many people were interviewed for the survey?
4. How were those people chosen?
5. What area—nation, state, or region—or what group—teachers, lawyers, Democratic voters, etc.—were these people chosen from?
6. Are the results based on the answers of all the people interviewed?
7. Who should have been interviewed and was not? Or do response rates matter?
8. When was the poll done?
9. How were the interviews conducted?
10. What about polls on the Internet or World Wide Web?
11. What is the sampling error for the poll results?
12. Who's on first?
13. What other kinds of mistakes can skew poll results?
14. What questions were asked?
15. In what order were the questions asked?
16. What about "push polls"?
17. What other polls have been done on this topic? Do they say the same thing? If they are different, why are they different?
18. What about exit polls?
19. What else needs to be included in the report of the poll?
20. So I've asked all the questions. The answers sound good. Should we report the results?

Even if news organizations are becoming more responsible and thorough in reporting some of the technical details of polls, one must wonder whether readers actually read and can understand the information. The person who wishes to be a discerning consumer of polls must take some responsibility for using the technical polling information that the paper provides. And when the news media (or other polling outfits) do not provide basic information about their polls, the consumer should be wary. Finally, even when a news organization provides technical information about its polls, it still must ensure that the substance of the story accurately reflects the polling data. Only conscientious, well-trained reporters and editors can guarantee that.

Exercises

1. Take the *New York Times'* description of the technical details of its polls on pages 144-145 and try to determine whether five friends of yours can actually understand what the *Times* is saying. Do this by constructing a brief questionnaire that attempts to determine whether people know what sampling error, random-digit dialing, weights, question order, and other technical aspects of polls actually are. Then administer your questionnaire to the five friends and draw some conclusions as to how helpful the *Times* discussion is.
2. Try to find one news story about a poll whose tone, thrust, or emphasis you disagree with. That is, try to find one example where you would have written a different story than the reporter did, even though both of you were looking at the same data. To do this you will likely need to track down the actual question wording used in the poll.
3. Find five reports of public opinion polls, either news articles or releases from polling organizations, that adhere to the AAPOR minimum standards for disclosure. Now find five additional reports in which the guidelines are not followed. Can you make any generalizations from these ten reports about which outlets are most likely to adhere to the AAPOR standards? Feel free to use the Web sites listed on pages 253-255 to find the reports.
4. Using the health care reform questions on pages 147-149, write two very different reports about Americans' opinions about health care reform. One report will "demonstrate" support for reform; the other report will "demonstrate" opposition. You will accomplish this by selecting different subsets of items to prove your point in each case.

☑ 7　Polls and Elections

Election surveys are probably the polls that are most familiar to Americans. As do surveys on presidential performance, election surveys receive substantial and continuing news coverage. They also generate the most controversy, particularly when preelection polls incorrectly predict the Election Day outcome, or when exit polls appear to contradict the actual election returns. Although the most prominent election polls focus on the presidential contest, polling has expanded to congressional contests as well as to many state and local races, on both candidates and issues. Indeed, election polling has become an international phenomenon, even in countries where the history of free and open elections is relatively short.

Sponsors of Election Polls

A variety of individuals and organizations such as candidates for office, political parties, the news media, and polling organizations themselves all conduct election polls. The candidates and parties use polls as research tools, collecting information to devise winning campaign strategies. Typically, candidate-sponsored polls survey citizens on their sociodemographic characteristics, their perceptions of the candidates, and their views on issues. The candidates can then determine how well they are running overall, how their campaigns are going within important subgroups, and how campaign events and advertising affect their standing among the voters. For polling organizations, election polls can be a revenue source as well as an opportunity to get free publicity when the media cover the organizations' surveys.

As for the mass media, election polls are a central focus of their election coverage, and they have been criticized for treating elections as if they were horse races, emphasizing not what the candidates say on the issues but their relative standing in the polls (Asher 1992, 273–278): Who's ahead? Who's behind? Who's gaining? Who's falling back? Yet polls also often go beyond recording levels of support for the candidates and address topics such as patterns of support for the candidates among groups of voters defined by their demographic characteristics and issue stances.

This chapter describes the types and uses of polls that are common in election campaigns. It examines candidates' and parties' attempts to use polls for purposes other than research and to manipulate media coverage of polls. It addresses the role of polling during the presidential primary season, as well as the general election campaign, and how and why polls can go wrong in making election predictions. The chapter concludes with some thoughts on how polls can affect the way citizens vote.

Types of Election Polls

The many kinds of election polls differ less in their methods than in the purposes they serve. For example, some of the candidate- and party-sponsored polls, such as tracking surveys, serve as the private tools of a campaign; media-generated surveys, such as exit polls, often become topics of public controversy as well as a tool for media reporting of election results. It is important for consumers of public opinion polls to be aware of the different kinds of surveys and what they can say about elections.

Benchmark Surveys

A candidate usually commissions a benchmark survey at the time he or she decides to seek office. It collects standard information about the candidate's public image and positions on issues and about the demographics of the electorate to provide a baseline for evaluating the progress of a campaign. Three important pieces of information often gathered in a benchmark survey are the candidate's name recognition level, the candidate's electoral strength vis-à-vis that of opponents, and citizens' assessments of an incumbent officeholder's performance.

One problem with a benchmark survey is its timing. The earlier it is done, the less likely it is that the respondents will know anything about the challenger and the more likely it is that the political and economic situation will change dramatically as the election nears. Nevertheless, useful information can be collected about voters' perceptions of the strengths and weaknesses of the incumbent, their perceptions of the ideal candidate, and their views on major policy issues. The results of a benchmark survey normally are not publicized or leaked unless they show the candidate doing surprisingly well.

Candorville

Trial Heat Surveys

Technically, a trial heat survey is not a survey but a question or series of questions within a survey. Trial heat questions pair competing candidates and ask citizens who they would vote for in such a contest.

Typically, a trial heat question reads, "If the election were held today, would you vote for X or Y?" Sometimes questions are asked about hypothetical matchups, particularly in the earlier stages of the presidential selection process. Even before the 2010 midterm elections were over, pollsters were already asking the American electorate about hypothetical matchups in the 2012 presidential contest, such as Barack Obama versus Mitt Romney or Barack Obama versus Sarah Palin. The results of these trial heat questions facilitate the "horse race" emphasis in media coverage of election campaigns; they are fun and often become the grist for interesting political speculation and gossip.

Several caveats apply, however, to the results of trial heat questions, the most important of which is that much can change between the time a question is asked and the actual voting on Election Day. This observation is best illustrated by the dramatic fluctuations in support for the presidential candidates in 2000. For example, a Reuters/MSNBC/Zogby poll in early August of that year gave Bush a seventeen-point lead over Gore; by early October the poll was indicating that Gore had a four-point lead. Equally dramatic changes can occur in a much shorter time. For example, a *New York Times*/WCBS-TV poll less than two weeks before the 1993 New Jersey gubernatorial contest showed incumbent Democratic governor Jim

Florio with a 49 percent to 34 percent lead among registered voters, and an even larger lead among likely voters, over his Republican opponent, Christine Todd Whitman. But on Election Day, Whitman was the victor. In California's 1994 gubernatorial race Democratic challenger Kathleen Brown was more than twenty points ahead of the Republican incumbent, Pete Wilson, in trial heat polls conducted months before the election. But Wilson defeated Brown by a fifteen-percentage-point margin. In the 2010 special election to fill the seat of the late U.S. senator Ted Kennedy, a poll done two weeks before the election showed Democrat Martha Coakley ahead by 15 percentage points, a lead that grew to 17 points when undecided leaners were allocated (Viser and Phillips 2010). Yet on Election Day, the Republican Scott Brown won by five points. In this contest, which had great national significance, there were signs that Coakley's lead was not as insurmountable as it seemed. Indeed, in the *Boston Globe* poll that had her ahead by 15 points, the two candidates were tied among the 25 percent of the respondents who said they were extremely interested in the race and Scott Brown had a good favorable-to-unfavorable rating given that he was a relatively unknown candidate at the outset. The lesson of all these examples is that it is not over until it is over.

Trial heat questions asked far in advance of an election measure name recognition more than anything else, particularly in less-prominent election contests. The consumers of such surveys must be careful not to view trial heat placements as immutable, nor should they be surprised when the standings of the candidates change dramatically over the course of the campaign. Moreover, consumers must also be careful in assessing the results of a trial heat question because those results depend on how the question is constructed. For example, when the political party affiliation of the candidate is given, the outcome is bound to be affected. With well-known candidates it makes little difference whether party affiliation is mentioned, but in races between less well-known candidates, it can make a substantial difference if the question is phrased, "Mary Doe versus Joe Blitz" or "Mary Doe, the Democrat, versus Joe Blitz, the Republican."

Tracking Polls

Tracking polls provide the most up-to-date information on which to base changes in campaign strategy and media advertising. A tremendous resource for candidates, these polls are often conducted on a daily basis near Election Day to monitor closely any late shifts in support. Because tracking polls are expensive, they rely on rolling samples. For example, samples of 200 different people may be collected on four consecutive days. Although an N of 200 is small and has a large sampling error, an N of 800

Steve Kelley Editorial Cartoon ©Steve Kelley. Used with the permission
of Steve Kelley and Creators Syndicate. All rights reserved.

is much more reliable. But much can happen between the first and fourth
day of interviewing, perhaps making the oldest interviews less interesting
to the campaign. Thus on the fifth day another 200 people are interviewed
and added to the sample, and the first 200 responses are discarded. And
on the sixth day another 200 people are interviewed, and the 200 interviews
done on the second day are eliminated. This procedure guarantees an
overall sample of 800 that includes 200 new interviews each day, thereby
allowing a close and timely monitoring of voters' reactions to the campaign.
One danger of tracking polls is that any single day's interviews could be
highly aberrant; the candidate and campaign must be careful not to
overreact to what might be only a statistical blip.

Tracking polls were prominent in the 2000 presidential campaign but
less so in 2004 (Traugott 2005) and 2008, when more resources were
devoted to polling in key battleground states and more media attention
was given to those battleground state results. Undoubtedly, the key role
played by Florida in 2000 and Ohio in 2004 sensitized the media that a
presidential contest is not simply a national popular vote contest to be
measured by national tracking polls but is also an Electoral College competition where the key battleground states will determine the outcome in

a close contest. In 2000, as Election Day approached, the results of various media-sponsored tracking polls converged to yield predictions very close to the actual election outcome. But throughout the campaign one particular tracking poll—that conducted by the Gallup Organization for CNN and *USA Today*—showed dramatic fluctuations over very short time periods. For example, one set of results showed Gore ahead by eleven points, yet two days later Bush was up by seven. Such substantial volatility surprised observers, who questioned the accuracy of the Gallup results. It turned out that one reason for the results was dramatic variation in the proportions of Democrats and Republicans in their samples over short periods of time (Morin and Deane 2000). When the sample had relatively more Democrats, Gore did better, and vice versa. Gallup argued that the short-term fluctuations in the distribution of partisanship were genuine. Other polling organizations made different decisions and weighted their results so that the proportion of Democrats and Republicans did not vary as much with each night's sampling, and their results did not show as much volatility. Abramowitz (2006) argues in general for weighting the number of Democrats and Republicans in any particular sample, based on a moving average of the proportion of Democrats and Republicans taken from surveys conducted over several weeks. This procedure will lessen the dramatic changes observed from sample to sample in such measures as vote intention and presidential approval when the changes are largely an artifact of the different proportion of Democrats and Republican from one sample to another. Whether or not to weight on party identification remains a topic of controversy.

While tracking polls are typically conducted either by campaigns or by news organizations, the 2000, 2004, and 2008 presidential elections saw the most ambitious and extensive use of rolling samples to measure the dynamics of the presidential campaign. The National Annenberg Election Survey conducted in each of those election cycles entailed a complex research design with rolling samples, panel surveys, and other impressive design features. This elaborate design enabled researchers to study campaign dynamics over a lengthy period to ascertain what voters learned about the candidates and how their views changed over time in response to particular campaign events and media coverage.

Cross-Sectional versus Panel Surveys

When the major polling organizations conduct multiple polls over time on an election contest, they generally use a *cross-sectional design* in which different samples of citizens are selected for each round of interviewing. For example, in the 2004 presidential contest, CNN/*USA Today*/Gallup polls conducted before and after the Republican convention tried to assess the postconvention bounce in the polls that Bush gained. The preconvention poll showed Bush ahead of Kerry 50 percent to 47 percent among likely voters, whereas the postconvention poll showed Bush ahead 52 percent to 47 percent. Each of these surveys provides a picture of where the electorate stood at a single point in time, and each is based on a different sample.

A comparison of the two surveys reveals that the Bush lead went from 3 percent to 5 percent (subject to sampling error) and that the net gain for Bush was 2 percent. But what pattern of movement produced this net gain? Perhaps 2 percent of the undecided moved to Bush. But perhaps 10 percent of Kerry supporters moved to Bush, while 10 percent of Bush supporters moved to Kerry and 2 percent of the undecided moved to Bush. Either hypothetical scenario yields a net gain of 2 percent, but the total percentage of citizens changing their preferences varies dramatically—2 percent in the first instance and 22 percent in the latter.

Unfortunately, cross-sectional surveys reveal only the net change; they cannot tell poll consumers about the gross change or about the pattern of individual changes that produced the net result. Thus cross-sectional surveys are fine for revealing net changes in the relative standing of the candidates, but a *panel design* is needed if the total volatility of voters' attitudes and preferences is the chief concern.

In a panel survey, the same individuals are interviewed two or more times—a more costly and difficult process because the same respondents must be located repeatedly, no easy task in view of the mobility and mortality of respondents. For example, conducting panel surveys of college students over a period of months or years can be burdensome because of the high mobility of that group. Another problem is that respondents may not be willing to participate in multiple interviews, and respondents who do agree to be reinterviewed may differ in distinct ways from those who do not. A final problem with panel surveys is that the experience of being interviewed the first time may affect the respondent's answers at the next interview. Despite these difficulties, panel surveys provide better information about the dynamics of the campaign and voter decision making than do cross-sectional surveys. Panel surveys reveal more volatility in voters' preferences than do cross-sectional surveys.

Focus Groups

Focus groups can be an important campaign tool, even though voters may never hear of them. Technically, focus groups are not polls but in-depth interviews with a small number of people (usually ten to twenty), who often are selected to represent broad demographic groups. A focus group might watch a candidate debate and offer reactions, thereby helping the candidate to prepare better for the next debate. Or a group might be asked to react to a political commercial, so that campaign managers can gain some insight into its effectiveness before spending money to air it. Focus group discussions also are useful in raising and developing questions that later may be incorporated into a public opinion poll.

The effectiveness of focus groups was illustrated most famously in the 1988 election, when the Bush campaign team called on a group to identify the "hot-button" issues that it later used with devastating effect against Bush's Democratic opponent, Massachusetts governor Michael Dukakis, in the general election. The campaign team invited two dozen New Jersey residents to a local hotel to talk about the candidates. Many of the participants were blue-collar and Catholic Democrats who had supported Reagan but intended to vote for Dukakis even though they knew little about him. Because these Reagan Democrats were seen as critical to a Bush victory, the focus group leader pushed until issues emerged that moved the participants away from support for Dukakis. The issues turned out to be Dukakis's opposition to the death penalty, his opposition to a bill requiring Massachusetts schoolchildren to recite the Pledge of Allegiance, and his support of a weekend furlough program for prisoners (among them the infamous Willie Horton). The reactions of the focus group participants told the Bush team that it had found the issues it needed to undermine the Dukakis campaign. It would have been much more difficult to generate this information through a public opinion survey. As Bush campaign manager Lee Atwater commented, "Focus groups give you a sense of what makes people tick and a sense of what's going on with people's minds and lives that you simply don't get from reading survey data" (Grove 1988b).

Many years ago Morin (1992e) pointed out that focus groups have become very popular with newspapers and television networks, which frequently commission them. Although Morin applauds focus groups as another tool for journalists, he warned that the media often fail to recognize the limitations of this method. Certainly one caveat is that focus groups are not mini public opinion surveys. Focus groups may suffer from problems of external validity—that is, the results of the focus group may not be generalizable to any broader population because the participants may not be representative. Nevertheless, the process of intensive discussion within a focus group may provide insights into what factors are motivating citizens, insights that a standard public opinion survey does not readily reveal. In the early 1990s a report prepared for the Kettering Foundation relied heavily on focus group methodology (Harwood Group 1993). Titled "Meaningful Chaos: How People Form Relationships with Public Concerns," the report argued that if political leaders really want to engage citizens in key public policy concerns, they and the media may need to devise new ways to reach that goal. Among the report's recommendations was a call for more "mediating institutions" where citizens can interact directly and discuss the issues of the day. Sensitive to the limitations of the focus group method, the Kettering report stated in its appendix on methodology:

> There are, of course, limitations to group discussions. The research is qualitative. Thus, the observations detailed in this report should not be mistaken for findings from a random sample survey. They are, technically speaking, hypotheses, or insights, that would need to be validated by reliable quantitative methods before being considered definitive. Still, the insights are suggestive of how citizens view public concerns and their relationships to them.

In observing focus group sessions dealing primarily with local government topics, such as the quality of city services or the performance of the local school system, I have been struck by how often the sessions take a critical and negative turn. One focus group participant relates a horror story, leading others to join in with their own awful anecdotes. Soon the focus group becomes a gripe session. Would public opinion polls on the same topics elicit as much intensely negative content? I doubt it. A 1996 book on gender relations by Roberta Sigel, who employed both focus groups and surveys in her work, supports my speculation. In general, Sigel's focus group data—more than her survey information—showed women to be angry about gender discrimination and mistreatment they had endured as women. Sigel attributed the differences in the focus group responses and the survey responses in part to the different modes of data collection. In other words, focus groups do not yield the same kinds of information as surveys and polls. Focus groups are fine research tools for certain purposes, but citizens should be wary of accepting general descriptions and explanations of people's attitudes and behavior based solely on a focus group. But for candidates and their campaigns, a focus group can be an effective tool for testing campaign themes, messages, and commercials.

Deliberative Opinion Polls

A deliberative opinion poll combines elements of both the focus group and the standard public opinion poll—that is, it brings together a representative group of citizens, provides them with information and the opportunity for discussion on issues, and then polls them on those issues. Fishkin sets out the rationale and need for deliberative polls (1992, 1996), arguing that public opinion surveys measure what the public thinks, but not what people would think if they had the opportunity to meet and become immersed in the issues through discussion and study. A deliberative poll is an expensive and challenging undertaking because it requires bringing together a representative sample and providing fair and balanced materials about the issues at hand.

The first major deliberative poll in the United States took place in Austin, Texas, in January 1996 in the context of the presidential election (Merkle 1996; Winkler 1996). A representative sample of Americans was surveyed about their opinions in three main issue areas: foreign policy, the economy, and family concerns. Then a subset of the sample attended the National Issues Convention in Austin where, after extensive presentations and discussions on the same issue domains, members of the subset were polled again to determine whether and how their views had changed. Attitude changes did occur. For example, support for U.S. military engagement abroad rose, and support for a flat income tax declined. The respondents' views about the biggest problems facing American families moved toward economic concerns and somewhat away from the breakdown of traditional family values.

The key question arising from this deliberative poll is to what extent its users can generalize its conclusions to the broader population. Fishkin (1996) would argue that because the sample was representative, similar attitude changes might be expected in the population at large. But one of the major criticisms of Fishkin's claim is that citizens in the real world, and the election campaign itself, do not operate in the same way as the National Issues Convention (Mitofsky 1996). Most people do not take the time to learn, nor are they exposed to information about the issues or candidates in such a concentrated and thorough way. Even though small group discussions may occur in the real world, much of what citizens experience and learn comes directly from campaign ads, news coverage, and the like. Moreover, critics faulted the representativeness of the 1996 sample and also cited the intrusive effects of television, which heightened the respondents' awareness that they were participating in a very special event. That awareness might have unduly influenced participants' reactions to the deliberative polling experience.

Even if the real-world prospects for deliberative polling are less than its adherents believe, the rationale for the enterprise is clear. Traditional public opinion polls capture what is immediately on the voters' minds, and as noted in chapter 2, they often are plagued by nonattitudes. Moreover, candidates tend to treat citizens' opinions as something to manipulate through political advertising and campaign rhetoric. A deliberative poll, by contrast, can reveal what citizens think once they are informed about an issue. Whether such results would ever constrain candidates or influence politics and elections remains doubtful. Sturgis, Roberts, and Allum (2005) argued that even if participation in a deliberative poll influenced attitude distributions and information levels, there was little evidence of any increase in the internal consistency of the attitudes participants held.

Interest in deliberative polls waned in the 2000 election, but a fascinating example of a deliberative poll occurred in January 2003 (Fishkin, Luskin, and Brady 2003). A scientifically selected sample of 343 Americans was polled by phone on topics such as Iraq, international security issues, and foreign aid. The respondents were then brought together to experience the deliberative process and subsequently reinterviewed on the same topics. Participants in the deliberative process became more likely to see Iraq as a threat, but they also grew more skeptical about the United States going it alone on Iraq and other matters. They became more supportive of U.S. rebuilding of Iraq once the prospective war was over. And they became generally more positive about the United States exercising leadership in world affairs and being more generous in providing foreign aid to other nations. That the results of this deliberative process received little media attention was frustrating to the sponsors of the deliberative poll. They argued that their results were important and worthy of news coverage because they showed what citizens' preferred policies were once they had become informed on the issues.

Fishkin (2009) has argued that a deliberative polling approach to the traditional town hall meeting may be more beneficial to both citizens and elected officials. He noted that in 2009 many of the town hall meetings conducted by members of Congress back in their districts turned into ugly shouting matches dominated by the most extreme voices. A deliberative polling approach would enable a more civilized, informed discussion where reasoned opinions would not be drowned out by theatrics. But would citizens want to participate in such an enterprise? Neblo et al. (2010) argue that this is the case in their research where they found that Americans were more willing than expected to participate in a deliberative process. Moreover, those citizens who were less likely to engage in traditional partisan politics were more receptive to trying the deliberative approach.

Exit Polls

Exit polls, as noted in chapter 1, are interviews with voters as they leave polling places. These very visible and controversial polls typically ask voters whom they voted for. They also collect some information on the issue positions and demographic characteristics of the respondents. The most prominent exit polls are conducted by the major news organizations to predict and explain presidential election outcomes, as well as the results of congressional and major state-level races.

Exit polls have several advantages and uses. First, they are polls of actual voters, and so they avoid the enduring problem that preelection surveys face of determining who will actually vote. Second, exit poll samples are collected in many states, allowing state-by-state analysis of the presidential election—an endeavor not feasible with national surveys of 1,500 respondents, which are not amenable to breakdowns by state. Third, exit polls can be tabulated quickly, allowing almost instantaneous predictions and descriptions of election outcomes. Indeed, this advantage became a central selling point for exit polls, as the television networks competed with one another to be the first to call an election. Finally, exit polls generate rich information that enables both journalists and social scientists to understand better the factors that help to shape the voters' choices.

Exit polls are generally accurate, although recent developments in the mechanics of how Americans vote might affect their predictive ability. Numerous states are making it easy to vote by absentee ballot. Oregon votes entirely by mail, and more states are permitting voting prior to Election Day. For example, the key battleground state of Ohio moved to no-fault absentee voting in 2006, as well as early, in-person absentee voting. Early voting is on the increase, with estimates suggesting that 14 to 15 percent of the 2000 election vote was cast early, about 20 percent in 2004, and approximately 29 to 30 percent in 2008. Election Day exit polling will not capture those votes. Pollsters therefore must conduct preelection polls in states with a substantial amount of early voting to estimate how the early voters behaved and then combine those estimates with the exit polls that are done on Election Day to generate accurate predictions. This makes exit polling a more challenging task and raises the possibility of errors as the preelection and the Election Day votes are combined.

Occasionally exit poll results are inaccurate. For example, an exit poll in the 1989 Virginia gubernatorial race showed the black Democratic candidate, Douglas Wilder, winning by 10 percent of the vote, when he actually won by less than 1 percent. The explanation for this inaccuracy is that some white respondents in the exit poll indicated that they had voted for Wilder when they had not (Traugott and Price 1992). As another example, the exit poll in the 1992 GOP presidential primary in New Hampshire showed George Bush with only a six-point margin over Republican challenger Pat Buchanan, when his lead in the actual vote count was sixteen points. The discrepancy was attributed in part to the greater intensity of Buchanan supporters and their greater willingness to participate in the exit polling (Mitofsky 1992; Morin 1992b).

Exit polls helped create storms of controversy on election night in 1980 and again in 2000 and 2004 (but not in the 2006, 2008, and 2010 elections). In 1980, the national preelection polls had indicated a close race between Jimmy Carter and Ronald Reagan, but the results from the eastern time zone revealed that a Reagan landslide (especially in the Electoral College) was developing. What troubled many observers was that within minutes after the polls closed in a state, the television networks would declare—on the basis of exit polls and not official election returns—that Reagan had carried that state. By 8:30 p.m. eastern standard time (EST), it was clear from exit poll results that Reagan had won enough states to ensure his election, no matter what happened in the states west of the Mississippi, where the polls were still open (strong Reagan states in any event). Thus the networks declared Reagan the victor while parts of the country were still voting. Moreover, Carter conceded the election before all of the polls had closed. Understandably, many concerns were raised about the effects of news media declarations of victory when some voters had not yet cast their ballots. There were reports that voters in line at polling places left when they heard that the presidential race was already decided and that other citizens decided not to go to the polls at all. In 1984 Democrat Walter Mondale wisely waited until the polls were closed on the West Coast before conceding, as did Michael Dukakis in 1988.

Did the early call of the 1980 presidential election actually deter citizens from voting? The empirical evidence is mixed (Jackson and McGee 1981; Jackson 1983; Epstein and Strom 1984; Delli Carpini 1984; Sudman 1986). It is clear that the early projections had no significant impact on the outcome of the presidential race in 1980, but in state and local contests turnout effects, no matter how small, could have been much more consequential. In those elections fewer votes are cast, and the margin between victory and defeat is sometimes very small.

In the 2000 election, the major television networks twice made predictions about the outcome of the presidential contest in the key state of Florida that never should have been made. Early on election night, the networks projected Vice President Gore as the winner. Much later in the evening, they projected that Governor Bush had won Florida—another forecast that had to be withdrawn but one that nonetheless gave Bush a major strategic advantage in the postelection Florida recount battle. Mitofsky (2001) explained that the incorrect Gore prediction may simply have been a case of the sampled precincts yielding a bad estimate, whereas the later Bush prediction was less a problem with exit polling than a case of flawed communications among entities tabulating the vote.

Election night in 2002 witnessed a computer programming problem with respect to the exit polls. It led the networks to ignore exit polls in their election night coverage and rely instead on the actual vote tabulations (Torry 2002; Kurtz 2002; Plissner 2003). The problems in 2000 and 2002 led six news organizations—ABC, CBS, CNN, Fox, NBC, and the Associated

Press—to disband the Voter News Service, which had been the umbrella organization responsible for collecting exit polling data, and create a new consortium called the National Election Pool, which had the responsibility for constructing exit polling capacity for the 2004 and 2008 elections. (For a comprehensive discussion of the exit polling fiasco in 2000 and how the Voter News Service performed, see the "Review Symposium: Election Night 2000 in Perspective," a collection of articles in the spring 2003 issue of *Public Opinion Quarterly.*)

In 2004 a major exit poll controversy erupted as exit polls were leaked throughout Election Day by various media sources. Most of the leaks suggested that John Kerry would carry such key states as Ohio and Florida and, if that were true, would oust George Bush and be the next president of the United States. When the votes were actually counted, Bush had carried Florida by a sizable margin and Ohio by a much smaller margin. Some citizens believed the exit polls, and not the actual vote counts, and therefore concluded that the election system had been compromised, or even that the election had been stolen. Postelection analyses were conducted to try to account for the discrepancies between the exit polls and the actual vote and to determine whether anything sinister had occurred. One study was conducted by the National Election Pool and its sponsors, the same group responsible for the exit polls in the first place. They (Edison Media Research and Mitofsky International) criticized the media leaks, arguing that any partial, early results could be inherently misleading, particularly since the final adjustments to the data had not yet been made. They also acknowledged that the precincts they sampled in the exit polls were a bit too pro-Kerry. They suggested that Republicans were less likely to participate in the exit polls, thereby creating a misleading pro-Kerry bias, and they also cited some problems with the exit interviewers. Some critics did not accept these explanations and still wondered whether more systemic problems occurred in the conduct of the 2004 election. Traugott, Highton, and Brady (2005) present a concise summary of the controversy and a very helpful bibliography of key sources.

Projecting election results for a state before that state's polls are closed raises concerns about the behavior of broadcast news organizations. Although there is some dispute about how late in the day exit polls must be taken to obtain a representative sample and make accurate projections (Busch and Lieske 1985), it is clear that if the polls close in a state at 7:30 p.m., exit polls could in most cases accurately predict the winner by late afternoon. But widespread reporting of such projections by the broadcast media could measurably depress turnout within a state. The television networks claim they are very careful not to make projections about a state until after its polls have closed, but a 1983 study by the League of Women

Voters and the Committee for the Study of the American Electorate pointed to numerous instances in the 1982 elections when projections were broadcast while the polls were still open. In 2000 there were deliberate leaks of exit poll results while the polls were still open in some of the key, early-primary states. During the general election only the threat of lawsuits prevented certain media outlets from prematurely leaking exit poll results. Even some of the major television news anchors have become careless about revealing exit poll results for a state before that state has completed voting and all too often are heard speculating on election night that the early exit poll results suggest that it will be a good evening for a particular candidate. In 2006 the major television news anchors said that the exit polls showed that the concerns and motivations pushing voters on Election Day suggested a good Democratic evening once the votes were tallied. The anchors emphasized that they were not revealing anything about any specific contest until the polls were closed, but they certainly sent out strong signals while the polls were still open in many states that election night would be a good one for Democrats.

The opposition to exit polls has been fierce in many circles. Congress and state governments have sharply criticized exit polls, but legislative efforts to ban or restrict exit polling have largely come to naught. Newspaper columnist Mike Royko once urged readers to lie to exit poll interviewers, thereby undermining the usefulness of the entire enterprise. Some pollsters have themselves been critical of exit polls and early projections. Although Roper (1985) and others believe that exit polls have few if any effects on elections, they argue that their use should still be curtailed because most citizens believe that exit polls can influence election outcomes. Exit polls, they claim, cause citizens to lose confidence in the electoral process and become increasingly suspicious of the mass media. Morin (2004) welcomed the 2004 controversy, hoping that the experience of 2004 would make citizens more skeptical about early exit poll results and more aware that exit polls, like any other poll, have inherent problems and imperfections.

The controversy surrounding exit polls will likely continue to ebb and flow depending on their performance and their use and misuse. When controversy is high, there will be calls to regulate and restrict exit polls. The television networks argue strenuously that government-imposed limitations on the reporting of exit polls would be a form of censorship and a violation of their First Amendment rights. The news organizations also note that if the polls were open simultaneously for twenty-four hours in all fifty states, the problem of early projections would be resolved. State officials reject that option as too expensive and point out that the networks could still make premature projections for those states for which they had sufficient information. Many years ago, Broder (1984) proposed the Canadian solution:

the networks could begin their election coverage by time zone from east to west, beginning each regional broadcast just as polls in that region are closing. Thus the networks might begin election coverage in the East at 8:00 p.m. EST, in the Midwest at 9:00 p.m. EST, in the Mountain States at 10:00 p.m. EST, and on the Pacific Coast at 11:00 p.m. EST. But today, with so many media outlets and so many Internet-based ways to access election returns, such a proposal would provide little relief.

Consumers of exit polls should carefully evaluate the news reports throughout Election Day. Any news about patterns of voting among various groups is most likely based on the exit polls completed to that point. Consumers should ask themselves whether such reports might affect their likelihood of voting or their chosen candidate. They also should note the time of the announcement of any election projections. If the projection is made before the polls have closed, then it is based on exit polls and not on official election returns, which are not available until after the polls close. The next question is whether the projection is for a state contest or a national race. If the latter, consumers should note whether the polls are still open in some states. Finally, consumers should try to keep a mental list of the number of early projections that subsequently are contradicted by the actual vote totals.

It is unlikely that exit polls will ever be regulated except by the self-policing of the networks themselves. In the early days of exit polling, the television networks, aiming to beat the competition and to improve ratings, invested heavily in the technology of polling and election coverage. (The polls play a somewhat different role for newspapers, which are not in a competition to predict election outcomes on election night. Instead, newspapers use exit polls primarily to describe voting patterns and to explain why the election turned out as it did.) Beginning with the 1990 midterm elections, however, the competition was somewhat mitigated when ABC, NBC, CBS, and CNN decided to conduct one joint exit poll under the auspices of the Voter News Service (and, later, the National Election Pool). The major reason for the change was financial; exit polling is very expensive. But as Schneider (1989) has pointed out, when different exit polls have been conducted for the same election, the results have differed; multiple polls enabled investigators to compare the results and decide which were more likely on target. This cannot happen when there is only one exit poll consortium.

Push Polls

Push polling gained notoriety in the 1996 elections, even though the practice had been around for years, particularly in U.S. House races and in some state and local contests. As push polling has become more common, the American Association for Public Opinion Research and the National Council on Public Polls have condemned the practice. AAPOR describes push polling as:

> . . . an insidious form of negative campaigning, disguised as a political poll. "Push polls" are not surveys at all, but rather unethical political telemarketing—telephone calls disguised as research that aim to persuade large numbers of voters and affect election outcomes, rather than measure opinions. (2007)

The National Council on Public Polls further explains the difference between legitimate political polls and push polls:

> [Legitimate political polls] use samples representative of all voters. "Push Polls" use telephone banks to canvass large numbers of voters. Legitimate polls may seek out weaknesses of candidates and attempt to ascertain the impact on voters of knowledge of these weaknesses, as well as issues and other facets of a political campaign. "Push Polls" attack selected candidates. The intent of legitimate polls in each case is research; a sample is interviewed, not a canvass, and the survey is not designed to deceive. . . . The results of "Push Polls" should never be reported by the media, but the use of such polls by a candidate may, of course, be a legitimate news story. (1995)

In 1996 a push poll was used in a Republican congressional primary in Texas (Clymer 1996). Representative Greg Laughlin was the preferred choice of the Republican Congressional Committee, which financed a push poll designed to hurt the other two contenders, Ron Paul and Jim Deats. About 30,000 calls were made. If respondents said they preferred Ron Paul, they were asked if they would still support him if they knew that Paul supported legalization of drugs, pornography, and prostitution. Likewise, if respondents said they favored Deats, they were asked how strong their support was given his campaign debt of $200,000 and four previous unsuccessful runs for office. The information provided to respondents was misleading and designed to push them away from Paul and Deats and toward Laughlin. During the 2000 presidential primaries, a major controversy emerged in the South Carolina Republican primary when the McCain campaign accused the Bush team of engaging in massive push polling that included the following question: "Would you be more or less likely to vote for John McCain for president if you knew he had fathered an illegitimate black child?" The Bush campaign denied the charge, pointing out that the thousands of phone calls being made were simply advocacy calling, not done under the guise of a poll. The intent, the Bush camp said, was to disseminate negative information about Sen. John McCain to South Carolina voters.

Push polling was common in the 2006, 2008, and 2009 elections, often relying on automated calling rather than live callers. For example, in Maryland voters received automated calls sponsored by a conservative group, asking whom they supported in the race for U.S. Senate: Republican Michael Steele or Democrat Benjamin Cardin (Marimow 2006). Respondents were then asked whether medical research should be done on unborn babies. If they said no, they next heard on the phone: "Fact: Ben Cardin voted to allow stem cell research to be done on unborn babies. Fact: Michael Steele opposes any research that destroys human life." The same conservative group (Common Sense Ohio) was active in push polling in other key U.S. Senate contests in Ohio, Tennessee, Montana, and Missouri and in an anti-abortion referendum in South Dakota (Drew 2006). Hundreds of thousands of these calls were made. And in the Ohio gubernatorial contest in 2006, the campaign of Republican candidate Ken Blackwell used push polling to suggest that his opponent was soft on sexual abuse of children (Hallett 2006).

In 2007, in the lead-up to the Iowa Republican precinct caucuses, a group supporting Mike Huckabee for the Republican presidential nomination organized telephone calls against three Huckabee opponents—Fred Thompson, John McCain, and Rudy Giuliani (Martin 2007). After beginning with some relatively innocuous questions, the poll then presented negative information about Thompson, McCain, and Giuliani. For example, for Giuliani, respondents were told that he was pro-abortion, supported civil unions, and his police chief and business partner had been indicted on various charges. Mitt Romney was also the target of push polls in the months prior to the Iowa caucuses and the New Hampshire primary (Elliott 2007; Lightman 2007). The calls would ask whether the fact that Romney was a Mormon, that Mormons consider the Book of Mormon to be superior to the Bible, that Romney received military deferments when he served as a Mormon missionary, and that none of his five sons served in the military made respondents more or less favorable to Mitt Romney.

During the general election in 2008, Jewish voters in Florida and elsewhere were asked whether they would be more or less likely to vote for Barack Obama if they knew he had donated money to the Palestine Liberation Organization, had met with Hamas leaders, and belonged to a church that had made anti-Semitic statements (Kennedy 2008). As a final example, the 2009 campaign to reelect Michael Bloomberg as mayor of New York City was accused of conducting push polling against a potential Bloomberg opponent, U.S. representative Anthony Weiner

(Hernandez 2009). The interview began with appropriate questions, but then respondents were asked whether their views of Mr. Weiner would be changed if they knew that he had missed votes in Congress, had difficulty keeping staff, and had accepted campaign contributions from foreign fashion models.

How can citizens protect themselves from push polls? The American Association of Political Consultants, another organization that has denounced push polling, has provided some advice for spotting such polls. First, reputable polling begins by providing the name of the sponsor of the research or the organization conducting the research; push polls typically do not provide that information. Second, legitimate telephone surveys usually last at least five minutes and often much longer; the typical push poll is less than a minute in duration. A third sign of a push poll, more apparent to news reporters than the average citizen, is the number of calls made in a particular election contest. The fact that thousands and thousands of calls have been made to citizens about a particular race is a clear sign that push polling is under way because most genuine polls require fewer than a thousand respondents. Indeed, when the news media hear of such an activity they should publicize and condemn it. And citizens who believe they have been called as part of a push poll might tip off their local media in the hope that a news organization would investigate and expose the situation. Because push polling is more likely to be used in less-visible, lower-level elections, where media scrutiny is often less extensive, it is important that citizens be particularly vigilant in those circumstances. But as the previous examples show, push polling occurs even in the more visible presidential selection process.

Uses of Polls by Candidates

Candidates use polls to test the political waters in a variety of ways. Prospective candidates might commission a private poll and also examine public polls to assess their chances. How they assess the results can steer their expectations and actions. For example, bad poll news might lead to a decision not to seek office. In 1986 New Yorker Geraldine Ferraro decided not to run for the U.S. Senate against incumbent Republican senator Alphonse D'Amato in part because poll results showed her trailing substantially. A party organization with the financial resources to conduct polls and to provide other election services may use that capability to provide services to recruit candidates. At the national level the Republican Party has been much better able than the Democrats to offer such assistance to its candidates and would-be candidates because of its more successful fund-raising operations based on computerized direct mail. In 2006 late polls sponsored by the

Democratic Congressional Campaign Committee (DCCC) identified some U.S. House contests in which the Democratic challenger was running surprisingly well against the heavily favored Republican incumbent. The DCCC then channeled funds to those contests and wound up gaining some unexpected victories. In 2010 the DCCC cut off funding to some Democratic incumbents when polls showed them losing and transferred the money to other contests where Democratic prospects were more promising.

Sometimes candidates use positive poll results to generate campaign contributions or to deter contributions to their opponents. In 1985 Idaho's Democratic governor, John Evans, sent the results of a poll he had conducted to many political action committees (PACs) and potential contributors. The poll showed Evans in a virtual tie with the state's Republican U.S. senator, Steve Symms, in a trial heat for Symms's Senate seat. Evans's action was clearly a signal to contributors that he had a good chance of unseating Symms in the 1986 election and therefore was worthy of their donations (Rothenberg 1985, 11). Evans ultimately lost by a narrow margin.

Often when published polls show a candidate running poorly, the candidate may try to minimize the potential damage to fund raising and volunteers' morale by attacking the credibility and relevance of the poll. "The only poll that counts is the poll taken on Election Day," the candidate might argue, citing examples of the polls having been wrong in the past. In a systematic analysis of the reactions of the 1992 Bush campaign to negative poll results, Bauman and Herbst (1994) found three dominant responses. First was the (often valid) assertion that it was too early to give much credence to poll results. Second was an attack on the pollsters themselves and the journalists who reported the polls. Finally, the campaign tried to counter the results of published polls with the results of its own private polls. In other instances, the attack on a poll may be more method related, challenging the sample, question wording, or question context.

Whatever the merits of these criticisms, it is clear that a candidate "harmed" by polls has a strong incentive to cast doubt on their credibility, so that a campaign is taken seriously. If a campaign is not taken seriously, it will have difficulty raising money and attracting other resources, such as free media coverage. As mentioned in the previous chapter, in the Strickland/Kasich campaign for governor of Ohio in 2010, the Strickland campaign released its own internal polling data in a very forthcoming fashion in order to counter the potential effects of some public polls showing a much larger deficit than was the case.

There are times when candidates allow their campaigns to be too poll driven. When asked why a campaign did not utilize a particular messaging strategy, the campaign sometimes replies that it tested that message or theme and found it did not move the poll numbers. This is certainly a correct response in some cases. But in other situations it will not be. Testing a message or theme in a poll is not the same thing as having a major media buy or an ambitious earned media strategy and then assessing whether the poll numbers moved. Items in a public opinion survey cannot fully capture the actual political and media context and impact of a real-world campaign.

Sometimes candidates deliberately manipulate aspects of their campaign or the polling process to generate poll results that will advance their candidacies. For example, in the four-way contest for the Republican nomination for governor of Ohio in 1982, one of the candidates, Seth Taft, scheduled his early television advertising to go on the air before the Ohio Republican Party conducted a statewide poll assessing the standing of the candidates. The poll showed Taft running first, thereby enhancing his credibility. Undoubtedly his famous last name and the skillful timing of his commercials gave Taft an early advantage in the polls, but he eventually lost the primary. To demonstrate greater electoral strength than they actually have, candidates often schedule television commercials and mailings in conjunction with party- and media-sponsored polls.

Candidates and campaign managers are also very skillful in selectively leaking information from in-house, private polls. Sometimes in-house polls are deliberately designed to generate the desired results. For example, before asking a trial heat question about the contenders, pollsters might ask a series of issue questions or candidate qualification items that will predispose the respondent to support one candidate over another. But in leaking the results of the trial heat item to the media, the campaign will not include information about the questions that preceded it. A candidate can also try to control poll results through sample selection. For example, if a candidate is thought to be more popular among women than men, interviewing might be conducted mainly during the day to obtain a predominantly female sample. When the results of the poll are leaked, however, the pollsters will not mention the gender composition of the sample, thereby inflating the standing of the candidate.

Voters and reporters should be wary of such selective leaking. One tip-off is refusal by a campaign to reveal additional information about a poll, such as question wording and question order. Although this kind of manipulation is not widespread, many campaigns use whatever tactics they believe will work because the objective of most campaigns is to win the election. "Good" poll results—whether valid or not—can make fund raising easier, generate more serious media coverage, and invigorate the campaign team and volunteers. Consumers can only endeavor to exercise good judgment in evaluating election poll results and hope that reporters and other journalists will not be easily victimized by manipulative campaigns.

Polls in the Presidential Selection Process

Polls pervade all stages of the presidential selection process. During the primary season, media polls in key states are common, as are national polls measuring the presidential preferences of Democrats and Republicans throughout the nation. During the general election campaign, the major news organizations and the campaigns themselves regularly conduct polls. When a major campaign event occurs, such as a televised debate among presidential contenders, a slew of polls follow immediately assessing the effect of the event.

One result of the ubiquity of polls in presidential campaigns is the increasing prominence of pollsters. Over the past two decades, individual pollsters such as Pat Caddell, Richard Wirthlin, and Stanley Greenberg achieved celebrity status during the Carter, Reagan, and Clinton campaigns. Today pollsters are part of individual candidates' core strategy groups that decide on themes and tactics, media advertising, public speaking schedules, and other key aspects of the campaign.

Polls do much more than simply reflect the current standings of the candidates in the presidential contest. The polls and the reporting of them shape the very course of the campaign. They also have been instrumental in campaign fund raising, although their impact has lessened in that area. Since 1976, presidential campaigns in the general election have been publicly funded, leaving major party nominees free from worry that poor poll performance will cut off the flow of money to their campaigns. In 2008, some candidates declined public financing because they believed they could raise much more money privately; for these candidates, their standing in the polls would have more consequences for their fundraising. In 1968, many Democrats complained that early polls showing Hubert Humphrey losing the election badly hindered fund raising, so that when it became clear near the end of the campaign that Humphrey had a chance to win, the money available for the final push was inadequate. In contrast to the general election, during the primary season eligible candidates receive only partial public funding, and the amount of public matching money they receive depends on their ability to attract private financial support. Bad poll results, as well as poor primary and caucus showings, may deter potential donors from supporting a campaign that appears to be failing.

The Caucus and Primary Season

The combined effect of polls and media coverage of polls is particularly critical during the caucus and primary season for at least two reasons. First, many candidates may seek a party's presidential nomination. In 1988, for example, six Republicans and seven Democrats sought party nominations.

Because there was no incumbent president seeking reelection in 2008, there was a large field of candidates for both the Democratic and Republican nominations that exceeded the 1988 numbers. Unable to cover all candidates equally, the news media give more attention to the most serious and viable candidates, with viability defined foremost by candidates' standings in the polls and how much money they have raised.

Second, the caucuses and primaries are a sequence of elections in which news media coverage of the outcome in just one state can dramatically affect later polls and primaries. For example, in 1984 John Glenn's campaign conducted a poll in New Hampshire about one week before that state's primary. The actual interviewing was conducted around the time of the Iowa precinct caucuses, in which Glenn did much worse than expected. The media coverage of the Iowa results stressed how badly the Glenn campaign was hurt there. Glenn's New Hampshire survey then showed that interviews completed before the reports of his poor finish in Iowa had him running much more strongly in New Hampshire than did interviews completed after the reports of the Iowa results. The combined effect of media coverage and the polls is particularly significant in Iowa and New Hampshire, the states in which the formal process of selecting delegates to the parties' national nominating conventions begins. The "winners" in Iowa and New Hampshire almost invariably enjoy a sizable gain in support in the national polls because of the positive and extensive media coverage they receive.

The presidential primary season is something of a sequential, psychological game. In it, the perception that a candidate is running strongly, as indicated by good poll results, makes it easier for the campaign to attract money, volunteers, and media coverage; bad poll results have the opposite effect. But strong performance in the polls is itself a function of the amount and content of media coverage that a candidate receives. That is why Iowa and New Hampshire are so critical. Because they are small states, in which both a personal and a media campaign can be conducted, they enable a relatively unknown or underdog candidate—such as Jimmy Carter in 1976, Gary Hart in 1984, Bill Clinton in 1992, John McCain in 2000, John Edwards in 2004, or Barack Obama in 2008—to do better than expected and thus receive substantial media coverage. The coverage can move a candidate higher in the public opinion polls, which in turn enhances the candidate's media coverage and credibility.

During the primary season candidates appeal for support on the grounds that they are more electable than their opponents, as demonstrated by the polls. Probably the best examples of this phenomenon occurred in 1976 and earlier in 1968. In 1976 Gerald Ford and Ronald Reagan were locked in a tight battle for the Republican presidential nomination; the winner would most likely face former Georgia governor Jimmy

Carter in the general election. The Ford campaign conceded the South to Carter no matter who won the GOP nomination but argued, citing public opinion polls, that Ford was much the stronger candidate to run against Carter nationwide (Phillips 1976). In 1968 Nelson Rockefeller's campaign to win the GOP nomination also depended heavily on the public opinion polls because Rockefeller knew he would have great difficulty winning presidential primaries and caucuses. Rockefeller challenged Richard Nixon, the front-runner, to cosponsor fifty state polls to see which candidate was the strongest. He also commissioned and released polls of states whose electoral votes were key that showed him running better than Nixon against Democratic candidate Hubert Humphrey (Crossley and Crossley 1969, 7). Rockefeller hoped to sway Republican delegates to his cause by the argument that he was the strongest candidate the party could offer. More recently, John Kerry's strong first place finish in the Iowa precinct caucuses in 2004, in conjunction with the attendant media coverage and national polls, earned him the title of most electable Democrat. That perception of electability, fueled in part by the polls, facilitated Kerry's path to the Democratic nomination.

Presidential Debates and the General Election

The interaction between poll results and media coverage is well illustrated by the treatment of the presidential and vice-presidential debates before the general election. Often polls taken immediately after a debate produce very different results than ones taken a few days later. The difference is attributable to the dominant media message in the interim. For example, in the Ford-Carter debate in 1976, President Ford mistakenly asserted that Eastern Europe was not under the domination of the Soviet Union, when in fact, at the time, Soviet troops were stationed in Poland and the Polish government, among others in the region, was following the dictates of Moscow. Telephone polls immediately after the debate showed Carter winning, but only by a narrow margin. When Ford received negative media coverage after the debate for his mistake, his campaign officials did not display much skill at putting the matter to rest. As a result, Carter's narrow margin burgeoned in the follow-up polls, which showed that Americans overwhelmingly viewed him as the winner of the debate.

"Winning" a debate may be a function less of a candidate's actual performance than of the media's coverage and interpretation of that performance. That is why the call-in poll that the ABC News organization sponsored after the Carter-Reagan debate in 1980 was particularly offensive. ABC News invited its viewers to call one of two numbers to indicate whether they thought Reagan or Carter had won; the call cost fifty cents.

Despite the self-selection and economic biases inherent in this procedure and the technical difficulty many citizens experienced in trying to complete their calls, ABC News announced that Reagan had won the debate by a two-to-one margin over Carter. Ideally, Americans should have dismissed this instant poll as foolish and unsound. Unfortunately, because it was the first large-scale reaction to the debate to be publicized, the poll and ABC's reporting of it shaped subsequent perceptions of who won the debate. After the first Bush-Gore presidential debate in 2000, scientific polls generally showed Gore to be the victor, albeit by a small margin. Many Internet and radio call-in polls, however, characterized by self-selected and unrepresentative samples, showed Bush the big winner. Fortunately, when the news media discussed the debate polls, they focused on the scientific ones. Broadcasters were criticized, however, for their reliance on instant and overnight polls.

As polling has become an integral part of media coverage of major campaign events, such as convention speeches and presidential debates, news organizations have increasingly incorporated overnight and instant polls into their coverage. The National Council on Public Polls (NCPP) (2000), however, has urged caution:

> One issue where news values and good polling methods clash is the media's appetite for "instant" polls which provide an immediate reaction to dramatic events. . . .
>
> A key question for poll watchers, and the media who report polls, should always be *"How many days was the survey in the field?"* In general, the quality of the sample improves the longer the survey is in the field. . . .
>
> All surveys fail to interview many people . . . because they are on vacation, on a business trip, visiting, shopping, eating out or just too busy to take the call. That is why the most reliable telephone surveys make three, four or more calls, on different days, to try to complete an interview. Obviously, this is not possible for polls that are conducted overnight or over a few hours, and their response rates are much lower.
>
> Given the very real possibility that those who are not interviewed, because they are not available, have even slightly different opinions than those who are interviewed, overnight polls, with their very low response rates, are much more likely to have substantial biases than polls with multiple call-backs over several days.

Polls also play a big role in determining which candidates are allowed to participate in presidential candidates' debates. In 1980 the League of Women Voters, the sponsor of the debate, decided to invite candidates whose support in public opinion surveys was more than 15 percent. The real issue at the time was whether independent candidate John Anderson would meet the 15 percent test. In 1996, unlike 1980, all independent and minor-party candidates were excluded from the debates. Ross Perot and other candidates asked the courts to overturn the decision, but to no avail. The decision had been made by the Commission on Presidential Debates, a ten-person body of five Republicans and five Democrats, which determined the debates' format and who would participate. The Democratic and Republican nominees (Clinton and Dole) were automatically included, but the candidates of other parties had to demonstrate that they had a realistic chance of being elected president to be invited to participate. That is, they had to show evidence of a national organization, national newsworthiness, and national enthusiasm for their candidacies (Hernandez 1995). One indicator of national enthusiasm was a candidate's standing in the public opinion polls. The commission, after judging that Ross Perot's low standing in the polls, along with other evidence, made it unlikely that he could win, excluded him from the debates.

Presidential debates should not be cluttered with numbers of mostly frivolous candidates, but was the decision to exclude Perot appropriate? After all, Perot was on the ballot in all fifty states, he had received 19 percent of the popular vote in 1992, and he had more than $20 million in public funding to finance his 1996 campaign. Although the polls the commission used to exclude Perot showed him with the voting support of only about 5 percent of the American people, other polls showed that more than 70 percent of Americans wanted Perot included in the debates. Moreover, although Perot's 5 percent in the polls at the time the commission made its decision in 1996 was close to his support level at a comparable point in the 1992 election campaign, he ultimately took almost a fifth of the vote in 1992. As Perot learned, using poll standing to exclude a candidate from the presidential debates creates a self-fulfilling prophecy. If a candidate is showing poorly in the polls, excluding that candidate from the most visible event of the presidential campaign can only further erode that candidate's support as the campaign moves into its critical final weeks.

A similar situation occurred in 2000 when the presidential debate commission again decided to use poll standing as one criterion for determining who could participate in the presidential debates. The commission chose a floor of 15 percent in a set of polls conducted shortly after Labor Day. The two most prominent minor-party candidates—Ralph Nader and Pat Buchanan—could not meet that standard and thus were excluded. This situation was particularly frustrating to Buchanan, who, as the nominee of the Reform Party, had received $12 million in public funding based on the Reform Party's performance in the 1996 election.

When and Why Election Predictions Are Wrong

The vast majority of polls are on target. Nevertheless, pollsters have made some notorious mistakes, such as in the *Literary Digest* poll of 1936 (discussed in chapter 4) and the 1948 presidential election polls that indicated that Republican Thomas Dewey would beat Democrat Harry Truman. The bad call in 1948 is widely attributed to the quota method of sampling that the polls employed and, more important, to the fact that polling stopped too far in advance of the election and therefore did not reflect the movement of many Democratic defectors back to Truman. In fact, the last polls showed Dewey with only a five-point lead over Truman, and the trend had been one of a declining Dewey advantage.

National polls have been off target in other important races. In 1980, for example, they failed to predict the magnitude of Reagan's victory. Most polls showed a very tight race, but Reagan beat Carter by ten percentage points. Again the poor predictions were attributed to the fact that many polls did not continue right through to the end of the campaign and thus did not capture the last-minute surge to Reagan by the undecideds and independents. The state-level polls in 1980 were far more accurate in predicting a sizable Reagan victory.

In 1992 the general election presidential polls were quite accurate overall, although critics expressed concerns about the deluge of sometimes conflicting polls and the way the news media reported them. One set of criticisms focused on the tracking polls that Gallup conducted toward the end of the campaign. Those polls, which received substantial media attention (Traugott 1992), generated concerns about the selection of respondents, the method by which undecided voters were allocated to candidates, and most important, a shift in poll analysis from registered voters to likely voters, which created confusion among the media and the public as to how much the gap between Clinton and Bush had actually narrowed.

In 1996 the preelection polls correctly predicted that Clinton would be reelected, but some of them substantially overestimated his margin of victory. Among polls seeking to predict the makeup of the House of Representatives, even the ones conducted just before the election yielded widely varying estimates, with some predicting a sizable Democratic victory, others a smaller Democratic win, and others a narrow GOP victory. Political scientist Everett Carll Ladd described 1996 as a very bad year for pollsters— "an American Waterloo" (1996). Ladd criticized the polls for overstating Clinton's margins and blamed the polls and the news media for contributing to the low voter turnout by dampening interest in the outcome with their predictions of a major Clinton win. Pollsters defended the polls; Newport (1997) and Morin (1997a) found the 1996 polls generally on target.

Perhaps the real problem with election polls is not their accuracy but how they are reported. Too many polls dominate news coverage of the election and contribute to the horse race mentality. Small changes in poll standing often are given too much attention, becoming the subject of breathless news stories when there really is no news. Poll standing, rather than issue stances, often drives coverage of candidates. In the meantime, the subtleties of poll interpretation frequently are lost, particularly those related to the polls' methodological aspects. And news organizations tend to focus on their own polls and ignore those of the competition.

The performance of the polls in 2000 was generally good, with most of the national polls converging toward the end of the campaign to show a very close contest between Bush and Gore. Even so, of eighteen national preelection polls conducted right at the end of the campaign, thirteen indicated a Bush lead, three estimated a tie, and only two had Gore ahead. Gore received 48.6 percent of the popular vote, compared with 48.3 percent for Bush (Traugott 2001). And some of the polls that had Bush ahead showed him with a lead over Gore of 5 percent to 7 percent. Although the national polls generally performed well in 2000, Rademacher and Smith (2001) found that seventy-nine state-level telephone polls were, on average, not as accurate. Probably the worst experience for the pollsters in 2000 (other than the Florida fiasco) was the New Hampshire Republican primary, in which John McCain scored a landslide victory over George W. Bush, when most polls were showing a much closer contest. Part of the problem for pollsters in New Hampshire was that independents could vote in either party's primary, and many of them voted for McCain in the GOP primary. Moreover, as Smith and Hubbard (2000) note, the turnout among the "undeclared" or independents was much higher than normal in 2000.

The performance of the final national preelection polls in 2004 was very good. Traugott (2005) found that most poll estimates were close to the actual results, with thirteen polls showing Bush ahead, five Kerry, and two ties. Many of the final state polls were also quite accurate, particularly in battleground states in the industrial Midwest and Great Lakes region. One point to keep in mind is that when the actual election outcome is very close, say 51 percent Republican to 49 percent Democratic, a poll that indicates a 49 percent Republican to 51 percent Democratic outcome may be "wrong" but it is certainly very accurate.

In 2008, the preelection polls were once again generally on target. An NCPP analysis (2008) showed that the nineteen national presidential polls reported late in the campaign came very close to the actual election outcome. Likewise, the much larger number of state-level polls also performed well, although here there was greater variation in the accuracy of the predictions. Keeter et al. (2009) generally came to the same conclusions about the 2008 national and state preelection polls, although they delved more deeply into the kinds of samples utilized by telephone polls—landline only vs. landline and cell samples—and also examined in greater detail the performance of the polls in battleground states that were key to the presidential outcome. Again, their general conclusion was that the polls performed well. The major embarrassment that the polls endured in 2008 was their inaccurate prediction in the New Hampshire Democratic primary. All of the preelection polls mistakenly predicted an Obama victory over Hillary Clinton, some by a double-digit margin, when in fact Clinton won New Hampshire by about three percentage points. These incorrect predictions were described by many as one of polling's worst modern-day failures, and many pollsters and analysts tried to find a convincing explanation. Many of the usual suspects were brought up, including very-last-minute changes that the polls could not capture, hidden votes for Clinton and/or against Obama, the proportion of independents who chose to vote in the Democratic versus the Republican primary, and the unpredictability of the good citizens of New Hampshire. (See Ramirez [2008], Dilanian [2008], Kohut [2008], Zogby [2008], and Frankovic [2008] for insights and speculation into what went wrong.) It should be noted that these same polls did a fine job predicting the outcome of the New Hampshire Republican primary.

The accuracy of predictions depends on many factors. The rest of this section examines five of them: the timing of preelection polls, the treatment of undecided voters, the estimation of voter turnout, the truthfulness of respondents, and the changing political and economic climate.

Timing of Polls

The closer to the election a preelection poll is conducted, the more accurate its results are likely to be (Felson and Sudman 1975). Late polls can capture the effects of last-minute events and campaign activities that may influence outcomes. By contrast, early polls primarily reflect name recognition and perceptions of incumbents' performance. When voters initially have little information about the candidates, their attitudes are highly likely to change once they acquire some new information about the contenders. For that reason, presidential primary polls often are less accurate than the general election polls. In the primaries, especially the early ones with a large field of candidates, information levels are low and voters' commitments to candidates are weak.

In a comprehensive analysis of the factors affecting the accuracy of preelection polls, Crespi (1988) found that the most important factor was how close to Election Day the preelection poll was conducted. The next-most-important factor was margin of victory, and then either turnout or whether the election was a primary. These findings suggest that polls would be more accurate if they did a better job of identifying likely voters and monitoring trends in voters' preferences in the latter stages of a campaign. This suggestion is directly relevant to the failure of the polls to predict George H. W. Bush's comfortable win in the 1988 New Hampshire Republican primary. Why were most of the polls so wrong? The Gallup Organization explained that it stopped polling too early (by 4 p.m. on Sunday before the Tuesday election) and therefore did not capture late-breaking developments (Grove 1988a). The one poll that correctly predicted Bush's victory was the CBS survey, which involved a tracking poll on the Sunday and Monday before the election (Morin 1988a) and thus reinforces Crespi's advice to poll as close to the election as possible. Clearly, if there is a late-breaking development in a campaign, such as an international crisis or a revelation about scandalous behavior, only polls conducted after those events can capture their impact on citizens' vote choices. Lau's analysis of the accuracy of the 1992 presidential polls found that polls conducted over multiple days were more accurate than overnight polls (1994). Lau also found that tracking polls were more accurate than standard polls and that polls that interviewed on both weekdays and weekends were more accurate than weekday-only polls.

Treatment of Undecided Voters

When respondents claim to be undecided they can mean different things. Some genuinely cannot choose among the candidates because they do not have enough balanced information to make a choice, but that is probably unusual. Others may know very little about one or more of the candidates and therefore be unwilling to make a choice. On the other hand, "undecided" may be a safe answer for those who do not want to reveal their election choices to the interviewer.

Evidence for this third possibility comes via the secret ballot technique that the Gallup Organization has long used. In this procedure respondents are given a ballot by the interviewer, asked to mark their choices, and then requested to drop the folded ballot into a box. Perry (1979) points out that this approach yields an undecided rate that is about one-third to one-fourth as large as that obtained when respondents are asked their vote preference by means of a standard survey item. (Note that the secret ballot technique can only be used with personal interviews.)

Pollsters can simply ignore undecided respondents and tabulate results only for those who have already made up their minds, but that is a highly flawed procedure if the undecideds differ in major ways from the decideds.

Another way of handling the undecideds is to report their numbers but then to assume that they will split in the same way that the decideds already have. Thus if 60 percent of decideds vote Democratic, 60 percent of the undecideds will be allocated to the Democratic Party. This is probably a reasonable rule when both candidates are equally well known and when there is no reason to suspect that anything unusual is going on among the undecideds.

When one candidate is well known and the other is not, however, the treatment of the undecideds is more problematic. In a race between a well-known, longtime incumbent and a relatively unknown challenger, an undecided vote can reflect poorly on the incumbent. In 1978 Ohio state representative Charles Kurfess challenged incumbent governor James Rhodes for the GOP gubernatorial nomination. Rhodes had already served three, four-year terms and was seeking a fourth; he was the well-known warhorse of the Ohio Republican Party. The benchmark survey conducted for the Kurfess campaign showed that respondents favored Rhodes over Kurfess by 66 percent to 6 percent, with 28 percent undecided. The final election results were 67 percent to 33 percent in favor of Rhodes. Without panel data it is impossible to conclude definitively that most of the undecideds moved to support Kurfess, but it seems plausible in this case that the undecided vote was actually a negative comment on the incumbent. In response to another question, the undecideds overwhelmingly preferred a new candidate for governor.

The behavior of undecided voters also partially accounts for the failure of preelection polls to mirror closely the outcomes of two prominent contests in 1989—the races for mayor of New York City and for governor of Virginia. Although polls accurately predicted the winners—David Dinkins in New York and Douglas Wilder in Virginia—the poll estimates of their margins of victory were much too high. Wilder won in Virginia by less than 1 percent, whereas the preelection polls were indicating a double-digit margin. In New York, Dinkins won by about 2 percent, even though the polls had shown him between fourteen and twenty-one points ahead (Balz 1989). The contests received a lot of media coverage because both Dinkins and Wilder would be the first black Americans elected to their respective positions. If, as many pollsters believe, whites who are undecided in a contest between a black and a white candidate vote heavily for the white candidate, then one reason for the polling error in the Dinkins and Wilder contests was the behavior of the heavily white undecided voters. Other factors contributing to the poll discrepancies in the Dinkins and Wilder victories were race-of-interviewer effects, turnout effects, and last minute changes in voter preferences. The fact remains, however, that some white voters gave an "undecided" response to an interviewer querying on a black-versus-white contest even though they may have already decided to support the white candidate.

Estimating Turnout in Elections

Probably the most difficult task pollsters face is estimating which of their respondents will actually vote. If the preferences of voters and nonvoters were identical, that task would not be a problem. But often there are marked differences between the two groups. In the 2010 midterm elections, correctly estimating turnout for Democrats and Republicans was critical to generate accurate election predictions. Most pollsters observed an enthusiasm gap: Republicans were more likely to vote than Democrats and were also firmer in their vote choices. Indeed, in many polls that reported their results based on the entire sample of registered voters and also on the subset of likely voters, there were sharp differences between the predicted outcomes. For example, in its October 18, 2010, report, Gallup found that Republicans led Democrats among registered voters by five percentage points on the generic congressional ballot, an advantage that swelled to eleven and seventeen points among likely voters, depending on turnout. A series of CNN polls on U.S. Senate races also showed Democrats doing better among registered voters than among likely voters. In Colorado, Republican Ken Buck led Democrat Michael Bennet by five points among likely voters but trailed by three points with registered voters. In Wisconsin, Republican Ron Johnson led Democrat Russ Feingold by six points among likely voters but lagged by two points with registered voters. And in Pennsylvania, Republican Pat Toomey led Democrat Joe Sestak by five points among likely voters, but the two candidates were tied among registered voters.

Identifying the likely voters has become even more challenging with the advent of early voting in many states. One might argue that early voting would not change turnout models if the people who did vote early were mainly citizens who otherwise would have voted on Election Day. But what if early voting expands the electorate, perhaps because of major mobilization efforts and ground games? For example, Chris Redfern, the chair of the Ohio Democratic Party in 2010, said that with early voting, he now had thirty-five days rather than the thirteen hours the polls were open on Election Day to stimulate Democratic voters to turn out. Although the Democrats lost all the statewide offices in Ohio in 2010, Redfern believed that the race for governor could not have been as close as it was without early voting.

Over the years, pollsters have used a variety of means to predict whether a person will vote. Utilizing an index, the Gallup Organization has identified a subsample of likely voters from the overall sample (Perry 1979, 320–321). Among the items in the index are the respondents' stated intention to vote, registration status, reported frequency of past voting, awareness of where to vote, interest in politics in general, interest in the particular election, and intensity of candidate preference. Thus in Gallup's final survey for the presidential election in 1976, when all respondents were considered Carter led Ford 48 percent to 43 percent; Eugene McCarthy and others received 4 percent; and undecideds and those who refused to participate amounted to 5 percent. But when the survey considered only likely voters, Carter led 48 percent to 46 percent; the other candidates received 2 percent; and undecideds or those refusing to respond to the poll made up 4 percent. Morin (2001b) notes that the index that the Gallup Organization used to identify likely voters appears to work as well today as it did decades ago.

Other pollsters use similar procedures. For example, Peter Hart has used respondents' reports of registration status, past voting in other races and current intention to vote, interest in the election and estimate of its importance, and awareness of the candidates and where to vote (Goldhaber 1984, 49). In 1998 a CBS News/*New York Times* poll identified likely voters as those who said that they voted in either 1996 or 1994, who said they were paying attention to the current campaign, and who said they would definitely vote in November. Respondents who voted in both 1994 and 1996 were defined as "more likely voters" (Kagay 1998). One interesting result of the CBS News/*New York Times* classification was that the more likely a respondent was to vote, the more that person tended to be pro-Republican. For example, registered voters in the 1998 poll preferred Democratic to Republican congressional candidates by a margin of 45 percent to 37 percent. But among likely voters the Democrats led by only 47 percent to 42 percent, and among the most likely voters Republicans led 48 percent to 44 percent.

After tracking polls did not correctly predict the outcome of the 1988 New Hampshire primary, ABC News/*Washington Post* pollsters changed the way they determined who the likely voters would be (Morin 1988b). In their New Hampshire polling, the ABC News/*Washington Post* pollsters had simply asked self-described registered voters if they were certain to vote, would probably vote, if the chances were 50–50, or if they would probably not vote. Anyone who said that he or she was certain to vote was considered a likely voter. This method produced a sample whose projected turnout rate was twice as high as the real rate because people often say they will vote even when they will not; they want to portray themselves as good citizens. Therefore ABC News/*Washington Post* decided to establish multiple criteria for determining a likely voter. For example, the respondent had to say that he or she was certain to vote and had to have voted in 1986. Other factors also were considered, including strength of commitment to a candidate. This more stringent test of likely voters generated more accurate results but also resulted in more interviews with registered voters being tossed aside when election predictions were made.

A somewhat different approach has been taken by the *Columbus Dispatch,* which uses mailed questionnaires. As discussed in chapter 4, mailed questionnaires have low response rates, and the representativeness of the people who do reply is uncertain. The *Dispatch* partially corrects for these problems by mailing questionnaires to samples selected from lists of registered voters. In 1994 and 1995, the paper used its mailed questionnaires but also commissioned telephone surveys by the Gallup Organization. Overall, the *Dispatch* results were much more accurate than the Gallup telephone polls, most likely because the mail poll did a better job of estimating the likely electorate. Anyone who completes a mailed questionnaire probably has a level of motivation indicative of a likely voter; the Gallup screen for likely voters simply consisted of registered voters who said they were likely to vote.

Visser et al. (1996) conducted an extensive comparative analysis of the performance of the *Dispatch* mail poll and the telephone polls that the University of Akron and the University of Cincinnati conducted in Ohio elections between 1980 and 1994. Overall, the election predictions of the final *Dispatch* poll were much more accurate than those generated by the telephone surveys. Numerous reasons were given for the superiority: a larger sample size, a questionnaire that closely resembled the actual ballot, response categories that minimized undecided answers and eliminated the need to allocate undecided respondents, and sampling and response procedures that produced more representative samples. Thus, contrary to conventional wisdom, mail questionnaires with an average response rate of only 25 percent were more accurate than telephone surveys. Even more surprising, for the final preelection *Dispatch* polls the deadline for the newspaper to receive the mailed surveys was typically the Thursday before Election Day. Therefore no information was gathered over the last weekend before the election, a time when sizable shifts in voter preference might occur, and yet the *Dispatch* polls were still more accurate. The *Dispatch* experience may lead some pollsters to rethink some of the conventional wisdom.

Do Respondents Lie?

Obviously, the accuracy of election predictions will be lessened if respondents lie to pollsters. But what might they lie about? One obvious answer is their

Bob Englehart—*Hartford Courant*

stated intention to vote when they indeed will not vote. One cannot identify likely voters only by asking citizens if they are going to vote, since some respondents will lie and give the correct, socially desirable answer that they will vote. After all, the job of a good American is to vote.

Respondents can also lie about other items, such as their willingness to vote for a candidate of a particular religion, racial or ethnic group, gender, or sexual orientation. In the interview situation, some respondents may feel the need to give what they perceive to be the socially approved response even if they will not vote that way. This phenomenon has occurred in the context of white voters claiming to support African American candidates when they in fact do not. In the 1982 race for governor of California, Los Angeles mayor Tom Bradley, a black Democrat, narrowly lost to a white Republican, despite the preelection polls showing Bradley with a substantial lead. The explanation given for the discrepancy between the poll results and the actual election results was simple: Some white voters would not reveal their opposition to a black candidate. Thus was born the Bradley effect.

The notion of the Bradley effect can be expanded beyond race to any candidate characteristic that might generate hidden opposition. Did Americans in the past lie about their willingness to vote for a Catholic? Would

Americans be fully forthcoming in letting pollsters know their true feelings about voting for a Mormon or a Jew or a woman or a Latino or a gay for president? As it relates to race, the Bradley effect today seems to be very small (Hopkins 2009). There was much discussion in 2008 prior to the presidential election as to whether there would be a Bradley effect with respect to the Obama candidacy. Some observers said no, that the United States had changed and that race was not as salient a factor as it was twenty years earlier. Other observers argued that Obama needed to remain above 50 percent in the polls to actually win the popular vote, since undecideds might break against him because of his race and some white Democratic voters might be lying to pollsters about their willingness to vote for the black Democratic candidate. (For differing views on this topic, see Altman (2008), Barth (2008), Carroll (2008), Fulbright (2008), Greener (2008), Holmes (2008), Levin (2008), Morrison (2008), Novak (2008), and Silver (2008).) The fact that the preelection polls were so congruent with the actual vote totals suggests that there was no noteworthy Bradley effect in 2008. Keeter et al. (2009) conducted a more sophisticated and complex analysis that also suggested that whatever Bradley effect there was in 2008 was quite modest.

The Changing Political and Economic Climate

Surveys predict best when there is a normal voter turnout pattern, as is demonstrated by the polls of 1982. Those polls performed poorly because they consistently underestimated the Democratic turnout, which was higher than expected that year because of the deepening economic recession and effective efforts by labor unions and black organizations to mobilize participation by their members. Moreover, although voter turnout is usually low among the unemployed, the 1982 election may have been atypical because many of the newly unemployed had been regular voters, and they participated at a higher-than-expected rate (Rothenberg 1983, 8).

The 1982 contest that probably did the most damage to the polls' reputation was the Illinois gubernatorial election. Most polls had predicted that incumbent Republican governor James Thompson would score a fifteen-to-twenty-point victory over Democrat Adlai Stevenson III. But when the votes were tabulated, Thompson won by less than 0.2 percent.

Kohut (1983) and Day and Becker (1984) tested numerous hypotheses about the inaccuracy of the 1982 Illinois polls. They ruled out some, such as last-minute shifts in preference that the polls missed; polls were conducted to the very end of the campaign, and they still showed Thompson winning by a large margin. A poor estimate of the likely voters also was ruled out. Instead, the polls' poor performance seems to have been caused mainly by an upsurge in straight-ticket voting among Democrats, including some who preferred Thompson to Stevenson but still cast a straight Democratic vote. In Chicago the Democratic organization had devoted its resources to a "Punch 10" (that is, vote straight Democratic) media campaign, an effort that was particularly effective in black areas, where it was part of an overall anti-Reagan theme (Kohut 1983, 42; Day and Becker 1984, 613). Thus a good part of the Illinois poll debacle stemmed from political organization and mobilization, developments that are difficult to anticipate and assess by means of a poll.

Another example of inaccuracy occurred in the 1994 midterm elections, in which the Republican victory was more sweeping than had been indicated by the polls conducted weeks before the elections. Perhaps part of the discrepancy was attributable to the difficulty of estimating the likely Democratic and Republican turnout, but this time events in the ten days before the elections also may have affected the results. Extensive and visible campaigning by President Clinton, for example, may have served to nationalize many local contests, to the advantage of the GOP. The polls conducted right before Election Day were largely on target in predicting the Republican sweep, as many races broke in favor of the GOP over the final weekend of the campaign. A similar situation occurred in the 2002 midterm congressional elections, in which the Election Day results evidenced greater Republican success than had been expected based on polls conducted weeks earlier. Some attribute the GOP's strong performance to effective and extensive campaigning by President Bush and the greater ability of the Republican Party to frame the key issues of the election.

In the 2006 midterm elections, the final results reflected what many of the preelection polls were indicating: a solid Democratic victory in the U.S. House of Representatives. A whole variety of indicators, such as the generic congressional ballot question, congressional approval ratings, presidential approval ratings, attitudes about Iraq, concerns about the economy, views on issues such as health care and corruption, and many others, all suggested that the Democrats would regain control of the House. Yet even in the last week of the election, there was much speculation about how late changes in the political climate would affect the outcome. Would the president's campaigning and the famed GOP seventy-two-hour effort save the Republican majority? Would John Kerry's muffed joke hurt the Democrats? Would television news stories and pictures of an increasingly violent Iraq hurt the Republicans? How would Americans react to these late developments? In the event of a Democratic wave, would the way that congressional district boundaries had been drawn protect many Republican seats? In 2010 the generic congressional ballot, approval ratings of Congress, approval ratings of incumbent members of Congress, concerns about the economy, the deficit, health care reform, and other issues all converged to suggest that the GOP would regain control of the U.S. House of Representatives and dramatically reduce the Democratic advantage in the U.S. Senate. Both outcomes occurred.

How Preelection Polls Affect Voters

Speculation about how polls affect voters has been widespread and contradictory. Some observers argue that polls that show one candidate ahead of another encourage supporters of the trailing candidate to change their preference and climb on board the winning candidate's bandwagon. Others emphasize underdog effects: sympathetic voters, they claim, rally around the candidate the polls show to be losing. Little strong evidence supports either view. The bandwagon effect would require that leading candidates consistently increase their margin, and the underdog effect predicts that the losing candidate will inexorably gain on the leader. These kinds of simple effects have not shown up consistently.

An experimental study by de Bock (1976) found some evidence that reports of disheartening poll results weakened support and motivation to turn out among a candidate's adherents. However, this finding seems to have been influenced by the experimental design itself, in which exposure to the negative polls was much more direct than would be the case in the real world. Other experimental studies have shown that polls can encourage support for the underdog, although the effects are not strong (Marsh 1984).

A 1985 ABC News/*Washington Post* poll attempted to address the effects of polls on voter choice. The survey asked a sample of Americans whether they knew whom the polls had favored in the 1984 election and whether the polls had influenced their voting behavior (Sussman 1985d). Seventy-eight percent correctly knew that the polls had picked Reagan to win, 7 percent said Mondale, and 15 percent did not know or remember what the polls had said. Among the 78 percent who knew the polls had predicted a Reagan victory, 4 percent said it helped them decide for Reagan, 4 percent said it helped them decide for Mondale, and 93 percent said it had no effect. Sussman concluded that the preelection polls could not have had any significant impact on the vote split because the pro-Mondale and pro-Reagan effects almost canceled each other out.

Anyone using Sussman's study, however, should weigh three factors. First, asking people to recall their views seven months after the election is risky—people simply forget. Second, Sussman's procedure required people to remember explicitly that the polls had influenced them; polls can

You Can't Fool Us...

© Jeff Danziger, New York Times Syndicate.

influence voters even though they may not be aware of it. Third, some people might not be willing to admit that the polls affected their vote lest they appear to be making decisions on inappropriate grounds. Despite these reservations, Sussman's conclusion seems plausible in general and certainly so for the 1984 election.

Bandwagon and underdog effects can and do occur, but their magnitude is small and probably inconsequential. Polls may affect voters indirectly through their impact on campaign contributors, campaign workers, and media coverage. In addition to affecting voting behavior, polls can influence public opinion itself, a topic addressed in chapter 9. For example, if people become aware of changes in public opinion on an issue, that information may lead them to support the position favored by the trend. Or if they learn that their views are not shared by their fellow citizens, they may become unwilling to express their views. The very act of polling people can sensitize them to politics and campaigns in general and can encourage them to seek out information or become more involved. Given the prominence of polls in elections and in political discourse in general, it is important for citizens to understand both the positive and the manipulative uses made of polls, regardless of the original intent.

Conclusion

By and large, election polls in the United States are very accurate, particularly those conducted and sponsored by reputable media and polling organizations. In nations where the history of polling and free elections is much shorter, the track record of polls is far less impressive. For example, in December 1993, in the first multiparty election ever held in Russia, the pollsters' performance was abysmal. Shlapentokh (1994) recounts that the pollsters failed to predict the victorious party and even the order in which the parties would finish. In some countries polling is problematic for both technical and cultural reasons. For example, it may be very difficult to pick a good sample: telephone ownership may not be widespread, and other information about residential units, especially in rural areas, may be flawed. Citizens in countries with traditions of totalitarian governments and repression may be wary about being interviewed by strangers and therefore may not participate in polling or give answers that reflect their true views. As one Russian analyst commented about the difficulties of polling in the former Soviet Union, "You are talking about sampling 30,000 villages and more than 1,000 cities. You must go to places that have for decades despised authority and then ask people their most personal fears about the future. And they are supposed to tell people they have never met what is on their mind" (Specter 1996).

Fortunately, these technical and cultural problems are far less prevalent in the United States, and the track record of American election polls is impressive. Of greater concern is how the polling enterprise affects the behavior of citizens in a democratic nation. We return to the issue of how the polls affect citizens and society in the last chapter.

Exercises

1. First examine the national-level, preelection polls conducted between Labor Day and Election Day by two different polling organizations in the 2004 or 2008 presidential election. Note changes in the relative standings of the Democratic and Republican candidates and the minor party candidates over this time period. Try to link specific campaign occurrences to changes in the candidates' poll standings. Then compare how similar or dissimilar the results of the two polling organizations were over the period from Labor Day to Election Day.

   Next, pick two states and follow the state-level polls for the same time period. Pick one state in which the presidential contest was very close and a second state in which the contest was lopsided. Trace the fluctuations in the poll results in both states. How does sampling error affect your description of how the presidential contest was unfolding in each of the states you selected?

2. Pollsters often query Americans about what they think is the most important problem facing the nation and which political party can better address that problem. Find one polling organization that has asked these types of questions and trace the responses of the American people between early 2005 and 2010. How did citizens' responses change over that time? What do the patterns you uncovered suggest to you about possible Democratic and Republican campaign strategies and messages in presidential and congressional elections?

8 Analyzing and Interpreting Polls

Thus far we have considered how public opinion surveys are conducted, how they are reported in the media, and how they influence elections and campaigns. This chapter focuses on the end products of public opinion surveys—the analysis and interpretation of poll data.

Interpreting a poll is more an art than a science, even though statistical analysis of poll data is central to the enterprise. An investigator examining poll results has tremendous leeway in deciding which items to analyze, which sample subsets or breakdowns to present, and how to interpret the statistical results. Take as an example a poll with three items that measure attitudes toward stem cell research. The investigator may construct an index from these three items, as discussed in chapter 3. Or the investigator may emphasize the results from one question, perhaps because of space and time constraints and the desire to keep matters simple or because those particular results best support the analyst's own policy preferences. Another possibility is to examine the results from the entire sample and ignore subgroups whose responses deviate from the overall pattern. Again, time and space limitations or the investigator's own preferences may influence the choices. Finally, two investigators may interpret identical poll results in sharply different ways depending on the perspectives and values they bring to their data analysis: the glass may be half full or half empty.

The analysis and interpretation of poll data entail a high degree of subjectivity and judgment. Subjectivity in this context does not mean deliberate bias or distortion but simply professional judgments about the importance and relevance of information. Certainly, news organizations generally interpret their polls in an unbiased fashion. But biases can slip in—sometimes unintentionally, sometimes deliberately—when, for example, an organization

FRANK & ERNEST: © Thaves/Dist. By United Feature Syndicate, Inc.

has sponsored a poll to promote a particular position. Because this final phase of polling is likely to have the most direct influence on public opinion, this chapter presents several case studies to illustrate the more subjective aspects of analyzing and interpreting poll results.

Choosing Items to Analyze

Many public opinion surveys deal with multifaceted, complex issues. For example, a researcher querying Americans about their attitudes toward tax reform might find initially that they overwhelmingly favor a fairer tax system. But if respondents are asked about specific aspects of tax reform, their answers may reflect high levels of confusion, indifference, or opposition. And depending on which items the researcher chooses to emphasize, the report might convey support, indifference, or opposition toward tax reform. U.S. foreign policy in the Middle East is another highly complex subject that can elicit divergent reactions from Americans, depending on which aspects of the policy they are questioned about.

Health care reform (discussed in chapter 6, pages 147-150) also is a very complex topic that requires multiple questions to capture the many facets of the issue. Some of the specific items discussed in chapter 6 show strong support for aspects of health care reform; others show substantial opposition. Any poorly chosen subset of these items might present a distorted picture of where Americans stand on the issue. This is particularly worrisome for a topic such as health care reform, where many Americans do not closely follow the issue and may have major gaps in their information.

Moreover, when citizens have incomplete information, the introduction of new information and arguments can dramatically alter preferences, as demonstrated by Blumenthal (2009b) in a discussion of the "individual mandate" feature of the health care debate. A Kaiser Family Foundation Health Tracking Poll asked Americans about the individual mandate:

"Would you favor or oppose requiring all Americans to have health insurance, either from their employer or from another source, with financial help for those who can't afford it?" Sixty-six percent favored the requirement and 31 percent opposed. Then the supporters were asked: "What if you heard that this could mean that some people would be required to buy health insurance that they find too expensive or did not want?" These erstwhile supporters now opposed the individual mandate by a margin of 73 percent to 21 percent. Likewise, the initial opponents of the individual mandate were asked: "What if you heard that without such a requirement, insurance companies would still be allowed to deny coverage to people who are sick?" Now the initial opponents to the individual mandate moved to a favorable position by a margin of 71 percent to 23 percent. Note how dramatically the distribution of opinions changed because of the follow-up questions: Initial supporters overwhelmingly moved to opposition, and initial opponents moved heavily to support. This kind of movement suggests attitudes on health care reform that are not fully developed and further suggests the need to delve more deeply by employing multiple questions to study the issue.

Some surveys go into great depth on a topic through multiple items constructed to measure its various facets. The problem for an investigator in this case again becomes deciding which results to report. Moreover, even though an extensive analysis is conducted, the news media might publicize only an abbreviated version of it, so that the consumer of the poll results is at the mercy of how accurately the media portray the overall study. Groups or organizations that sponsor polls to demonstrate support for a particular position or policy option often disseminate results in a selective fashion that enables them to put the organization and its policies in a favorable light.

In contrast with in-depth surveys on a topic, *omnibus surveys* cover many subjects superficially in a single survey. Here the problem for an investigator becomes ensuring that the few questions directed to a specific topic really do justice to that topic's substance and complexity. It is left to the consumers of both kinds of polls to judge whether they are receiving the central information on a topic, or whether other poll items might yield different results.

The issue of prayer in public schools is a good example of how public opinion polling can be incomplete and potentially misleading. Typically pollsters ask respondents whether they support a constitutional amendment that would permit voluntary prayer in public schools. In response, more than three-fourths of Americans say they would favor such an amendment. But this question misses the mark. Voluntary prayer by individuals is in no way prohibited; the real issue is *organized* voluntary prayer. Yet many pollsters do not include items that tap this aspect of the voluntary prayer issue. Will there be a common prayer? If so, who will compose it? Will someone lead the class in prayer? If so, who? Under what circumstances and when will the prayer be uttered? What about students who do not wish to participate or who prefer a different prayer?

The difficulty with both the in-depth poll and the omnibus survey is that the full set of items used to study a particular topic is usually not reported, and thus the consumer cannot make informed judgments about whether the conclusions of the survey are valid. Sometimes the sponsors of a survey will provide the complete report on request, and increasingly sponsors are providing the entire survey and results on their Web sites. But most often, the typical consumer of public opinion polls will not do the extra work necessary to become more informed about the poll and its results and, instead, simply relies on media coverage, press releases, and the like. Recognizing this, individuals should take a skeptical view of claims by a corporate executive or an elected officeholder, or even a friend, that the polls demonstrate public support for or opposition to a particular position. The first question to ask is, what is the evidence cited to support the claim? From there, one might examine the question wording, the response alternatives, the screening for nonattitudes, and the treatment of "don't know" responses. Then one might attempt the more difficult task of assessing whether the questions used to study the topic at hand were really optimal. Might other questions have been used? What aspects of the topic were not addressed? Finally, one might ponder whether different interpretations could be imposed on the data and whether alternative explanations could account for the reported patterns.

When people cite poll results, they may be tempted to seize on those that support their position and ignore those that do not. The problem is that one or two items cannot capture the full complexity of most issues. For example, Gallup polls conducted in early May 2003 illustrate how important the selective use and analysis of survey items could be in generating rather different impressions on the issue of gay rights. Fortunately, the Gallup Organization asked a range of questions and presented the results of all of them in a fair and unbiased fashion (Newport 2003a; 2003b). Among the questions Gallup asked were the following four:

Q. Do you think homosexual relations between consenting adults should or should not be legal?

Should	60%
Should not	35%
No opinion	5%

Q. Do you feel that homosexuality should be considered an acceptable alternative lifestyle or not?

Should	54%
Should not	43%
No opinion	3%

Q. Would you favor or oppose a law that would allow homosexual couples to legally form civil unions, giving them some of the legal rights of married couples?

Favor	49%
Oppose	49%
No opinion	2%

Q. As you may know, there has been considerable discussion in the news regarding the rights of homosexual men and women. In general, do you think homosexuals should or should not have equal rights in terms of job opportunities?

Should	88%
Should not	9%
No opinion	1%

If one focused on the second and third items, one might describe American public opinion as sharply split on gay rights. If one emphasized the first and last items, one would conclude that a substantial majority of Americans favor gay rights. Clearly, people promoting an agenda on the issue could easily select the items that favored their position. However, the Gallup Organization recognized that the attitudes toward homosexuality and gay rights are multifaceted, requiring multiple items to capture the complexity of public opinion.

The issue of government funding of faith-based initiatives further illustrates the importance of item selection and analysis in appreciating the complexity of popular opinion. A poll conducted by the Pew Forum on Religion and Public Life and the Pew Research Center for People and the Press in March 2001 found that 75 percent of Americans favored government funding of faith-based initiatives that provide social services, while 21 percent opposed the idea (Goodstein 2001; Morin 2001a). But support dropped dramatically when specific religious groups were mentioned as recipients of public money. Catholic and Protestant churches and Jewish synagogues still received substantial support at 62, 61 and 58 percent respectively, but Mormon churches, Muslim mosques, and Buddhist temples enjoyed the support of only 51, 38, and 38 percent of Americans. In addition, respondents expressed concerns about religions' using public dollars to proselytize, about excessive government involvement with religious organizations, and about the fundamental issue of separation of church and state. Moreover, 78 percent of the respondents said that religious organizations that use government funds to provide social services should not be allowed to hire only people who share their religious beliefs. Thus, although there is widespread support—75 percent—for faith-based initiatives, there are important conditions and restrictions on that support.

Additional examples of the importance of item selection are provided by the polls taken to gauge Americans' attitudes about the Iraqi invasion of Kuwait in 1990, the war with Iraq in 2003, and the war against terrorism in the post–September 11 era. Early in the first Persian Gulf crisis, various survey organizations, using different questions, asked Americans how they felt about taking military action against Iraq. Not surprisingly, the organizations obtained different results:

Q. Do you favor or oppose direct U.S. military action against Iraq at this time? (Gallup, August 3–4, 1990)

Favor	23%
Oppose	68%
Don't know/refused	9%

Q. Do you agree or disagree that the U.S. should take all actions necessary, including the use of military force, to make sure that Iraq withdraws its forces from Kuwait? (ABC News/*Washington Post,* August 8, 1990)

Agree	66%
Disagree	33%
Don't know	1%

Q. Would you approve or disapprove of using U.S. troops to force the Iraqis to leave Kuwait? (Gallup, August 9–12, 1990; quoted in *Public Perspective,* September/October 1990, 13)

Approve	64%
Disapprove	36%

Q. I'm going to mention some things that may or may not happen in the Middle East and for each one, please tell me whether the U.S. should or should not take military action in connection with it. . . . If Iraq refuses to withdraw from Kuwait? (NBC News/*Wall Street Journal,* August 18–19, 1990; quoted in *Public Perspective,* September/October 1990, 13)

No military action	51%
Military action	49%

Note that the responses indicate varying levels of support for military action, even though most of the questions were asked within two weeks of each other.

The first question shows the most opposition to military action. This is easily explained: The question concerns military action *at this time,* and many Americans may have seen such a step as premature until other means had been tried.

The next two questions indicate majority support for military action, and the final item shows a very divided American populace. It is clear which survey items proponents and opponents of military action would cite to support their arguments.

Throughout the Persian Gulf crisis, public opinion was highly supportive of President George H. W. Bush's policies; only in the period between October and December 1990 did support for the president's handling of the situation drop below 60 percent. For example, a November 1990 CBS News/*New York Times* poll showed the following patterns of response:

Q. Do you approve or disapprove of the way George Bush is handling Iraq's invasion of Kuwait?

Approve	50%
Disapprove	41%
Don't know/NA	8%

An ABC News/*Washington Post*/poll in mid-November asked:

Q. Do you approve or disapprove of the way George Bush is handling the situation caused by Iraq's invasion of Kuwait?

Approve	59%
Disapprove	36%
Don't know/NA	5%

Some opponents of the military buildup tried to use these and similar polls to demonstrate that support for the president's policies was decreasing—earlier polls had indicated support levels in the 60–70 percent range. Fortunately, the *Washington Post* poll cited above asked respondents who disapproved of Bush's policy whether the president was moving too slowly or too quickly. It turned out that 44 percent of the disapprovers said "too slowly" and 37 percent "too quickly." Thus a plurality of the disapprovers preferred more rapid action against Iraq—a result that provided little support for those critics of the president's policies who were arguing against a military solution.

In August 2003, the Gallup Organization (Newport 2003d) queried Americans about their views on aspects of American involvement in Iraq. Among the items in the survey were the following:

Q. How would you say things are going for the U.S. in Iraq now that the major fighting has ended—very well, moderately well, moderately badly, or very badly?

Very/moderately well	50%
Very/moderately badly	49%

Q. All in all, do you think the situation in Iraq was worth going to war over, or not?

Worth going to war	63%
Not worth going to war	35%

Q. Do you approve or disapprove of the way that George W. Bush is handling the situation with Iraq?

Approve	57%
Disapprove	41%

Q. Do you think the Bush administration does—or does not—have a clear plan for handling the situation in Iraq?

Does	44%
Does not	54%
No opinion	2%

Q. Which comes closest to your view about what the U.S. should now do about the number of U.S. troops in Iraq—the U.S. should send more troops to Iraq, the U.S. should keep the number of troops as it is now, the U.S. should begin to withdraw some troops from Iraq, or the U.S. should withdraw all of its troops from Iraq?

Send more troops	15%
Keep as it is now	36%
Withdraw some troops	32%
Withdraw all troops	14%

Fortunately, we have all of the above items to capture the complexity of American public opinion about the situation in Iraq. But clearly very different portraits of public opinion could be generated if one focused selectively on only some of the items. For example, someone hostile to the Bush administration might focus on the fourth item, which indicates that a majority of the American people believed that the Bush administration did not have a clear plan for handling the situation in Iraq. A proponent of the Bush administration might focus on the second and third questions, which show that healthy majorities of Americans thought it was worthwhile to go to war with Iraq and approved the president's handling of the situation. Another observer might emphasize the first and last items and write that Americans were sharply divided on Iraq.

In September 2006, a poll of 1,150 Iraqi adults was conducted for WorldPublicOpinion.org by the Program on International Policy Attitudes (PIPA) at the University of Maryland. Among the many questions asked Iraqis were the following four items:

Q. Do you think that the new Iraqi system of government grants the central government too much power, too little power, or about the right amount of power?

Too much	37%
About right	26%
Too little	35%

Q. Please tell me if you have a very favorable, somewhat favorable, somewhat unfavorable, or very unfavorable opinion of:

	Very favorable	Somewhat favorable	Somewhat unfavorable	Very unfavorable
Osama Bin Laden	1%	7%	16%	77%
Al Qaeda	2%	5%	12%	82%

Q. Do you strongly approve, approve somewhat, disapprove somewhat, or strongly disapprove of the following:

	Strongly approve	Approve somewhat	Disapprove somewhat	Strongly disapprove
Attacks on U.S.-led forces in Iraq	27%	34%	23%	16%

Q. Which of the following would you like the Iraqi government to ask the U.S.-led forces to do?

Withdraw all U.S.-led forces within six months	37%
Gradually withdraw U.S.-led forces according to a one-year timeline	34%
Gradually withdraw U.S.-led forces according to a two-year timeline	20%
Only reduce U.S.-led forces as the security situation improves in Iraq	9%

Imagine that someone was an advocate, rather than an opponent, of American involvement in Iraq and wanted to cite Iraqi public opinion in support of his or her stance. Proponents of American involvement might cite the first two questions, pointing out that 61 percent (26 + 35) favor the Iraqi government having at least as much power as it does, while overwhelming majorities of Iraqis are very unfavorable to Osama bin Laden and al-Qaida.

Opponents of American policy, on the other hand, would likely point to the last two items that show that 61 percent (27 + 34) of Iraqis approve of attacks on U.S.-led forces and 71 percent (37 + 34) would like American

forces out of Iraq within a year. Clearly, one can paint very different portraits of Iraqi public opinion depending upon which survey items one
emphasizes.

A Fox News/Opinion Dynamics poll in July 2003 included a number
of questions about how safe Americans felt since the terrorist attacks of
September 11, 2001 (*The Polling Report,* August 11, 2003):

Q. How surprised are you that there has not been another terrorist attack in the
United States since the 9/11 attacks?

Very surprised	21%
Somewhat surprised	30%
Not very surprised	27%
Not at all surprised	19%
Not sure	3%

Q. How confident are you that U.S. intelligence agencies have now improved their
procedures and will be able to prevent attacks like the 9/11 attacks in the
future?

Very confident	17%
Somewhat confident	45%
Not very confident	20%
Not at all confident	13%
Not sure	5%

Q. Do you think another major terrorist attack in the United States will happen
within the next three months, within the next sixth months, in the next one to
two years, more than two years from now, or never?

Within the next three months	4%
Within the next six month	10%
In the next one to two years	31%
More than two years from now	17%
Never	16%
Not sure	22%

Q. Do you think there are members of the Al Qaeda terrorist group in the United
States today?

Yes	92%
No	4%
Not sure	4%

Q. Do you think America is doing enough to secure the country's borders?

Yes	35%
No	57%
Not sure	8%

How safe and secure do Americans actually feel? Again, emphasizing different questions will produce different portraits of public opinion. For example, 62 percent of Americans (17 + 45) are either very or somewhat confident that U.S. intelligence agencies will be able to prevent future attacks, but 62 percent (4 + 10 + 31 + 17) believe there will be another major terrorist attack in the United States. Americans are split on whether or not they are surprised by the absence of another terrorist strike since September 11, but they are almost unanimous in their belief that al-Qaida members are in the United States. The lesson of this and the previous examples is clear: Constructing an interpretation around any single survey item can generate a misleading description of public opinion. And sometimes advocates of particular positions do that deliberately, using survey results selectively and misleadingly to advance their cause.

An ABC News/*Washington Post* poll conducted in June 2006 included the following items about prisoners being held at Guantanamo Bay by the United States:

Q. Do you support or oppose the federal government holding suspected terrorists without trial at the U.S. military prison in Guantanamo Bay, Cuba?

Support	57%
Oppose	37%
Unsure	5%

Q. Some people say that these prisoners should be given prisoner-of-war rights or charged with a crime so they can defend themselves at a trial. Others say POW status or criminal laws don't apply to suspected terrorists because of the risk if they were released. What's your opinion? Do you think the prisoners at Guantanamo should be given POW status or charged with a crime, or should be held without charges indefinitely?

POW status/charged	71%
Held without charges	25%
Unsure	4%

Q. How confident are you that the United States is adequately protecting the rights of prisoners being held at Guantanamo: very confident, somewhat confident, not too confident, or not confident at all?

Very confident	21%
Somewhat confident	45%
Not too confident	17%
Not confident at all	14%
Unsure	2%

Q. Do you think holding prisoners at the Guantanamo Bay military prison has or has not damaged the United States' image in the rest of the world?

Has	62%
Has not	35%
Unsure	3%

Q. Do you think holding prisoners at the Guantanamo Bay military prison has or has not made the United States safer from terrorism?

Has	51%
Has not	45%
Unsure	4%

Imagine members of Congress arguing about American policy at Guantanamo. Proponents of the policy are likely to cite the 57 percent of Americans in favor of the policy, but opponents will cite the 71 percent of Americans who think that prisoners should be given POW status or charged with a crime. Proponents are likely to claim that 66 percent (21 + 45) of Americans feel at least somewhat confident that the rights of prisoners are adequately protected, while opponents will cite the 62 percent of Americans who believe that our Guantanamo policy has damaged the image of the United States in the rest of the world. Again, the selective use of particular items can present a very misleading description of American public opinion.

In the political debate surrounding tax cuts in 2001 and 2002 people often cited poll results to justify various positions. And certainly, all other things being equal, Americans would prefer to have lower taxes, a position that Republican tax cut advocates routinely cited. In the first round of tax cuts in 2001, the Bush administration claimed that the projected multi-trillion-dollar surplus would allow the United States to have tax cuts, pay down the national debt, and shore up Social Security and Medicare. But even under those circumstances, tax cuts were not a high priority for Americans. For example, a February 2001 CBS poll asked Americans the following question:

Q. Some lawmakers are saying that there will be a budget surplus in the coming years. If that happens and you had to choose among the following things, how would you like the money to be used: (1) to cut income taxes, (2) to pay down the national debt, (3) to preserve programs like Medicare and Social Security, or (4) something else?

Cut income taxes	19%
Pay down debt	13%
Medicare/Social Security	48%
Something else	7%
Combination (volunteered)	12%
Don't know	1%

As the economy weakened and projected surpluses turned into actual deficits, opponents of the various actual and proposed rounds of tax cuts regularly cited poll results that showed that when tax cuts were paired against other public policy objectives, the desire for tax cuts declined markedly. For example, an NPR/Kaiser Family Foundation/Kennedy School of Government poll asked Americans in February and March 2003:

Q. What's more important to you, having the government provide needed services or cutting taxes?

Provide needed services	66%
Cut taxes	31%
Don't know	2%

In some ways this is a flawed question, since "needed services" could mean starkly different things to different respondents. But the question is representative of the typical pattern of responses obtained when the question of services versus tax cuts is presented to Americans. In a similar vein, a *Washington Post*/ABC News poll conducted in late summer 2003 found that about 60 percent of Americans were unhappy about the president's request to Congress to provide another $87 billion for the reconstruction of postwar Iraq and Afghanistan (although about the same proportion of the American public favored staying in Iraq). But when asked how the $87 billion should be generated, a plurality (41 percent) called for the repeal of recently passed tax cuts.

The obvious point of the tax cut example is that an accurate portrayal of American public opinion must take into account not simply a preference for lower taxes but also the trade-offs that might be involved in any tax cut, particularly when the federal budget is under great strain. Clearly, to capture the complexity and conditional nature of citizens' views, multiple items must be used. And when that is done, then the results of the multiple items should be made public, even if partisans on either side of the issue would prefer that only the results that support their position become public.

One of the anomalies of the 1996 and 2006 elections was the substantial number of Americans who were worried about the health of the economy at a time when many objective indicators suggested the economy was performing very well. Part of the answer to this puzzle was Americans' ignorance and misinformation about the country's economic health. For example, even though unemployment was substantially lower in 1996 than in 1991, 33 percent of Americans thought that it was higher, and 28 percent thought it was the same. The average estimate of the unemployment rate was 20.6 percent, when in reality it was just over 5 percent. Americans' perceptions of inflation and the deficit were similar; in each case people thought that it was much worse than it actually was. It is no wonder that many Americans expressed feelings of economic insecurity during good economic times: they were not aware of how strongly the economy was performing (Morin and Berry 1996).

Sometimes it is tempting to speculate broadly about citizens' opinions and policy preferences based on their responses to particular survey items. In many cases, the speculations and projections would be incorrect, but only additional polling questions would confirm the mistake. For example, in 1999 a survey conducted for CNN/*USA Today* by the Gallup Organization asked Americans, "Do you support the 'don't ask, don't tell' policy on homosexuality in the military?" Fifty percent of the respondents said they supported the policy, and 46 percent opposed it, suggesting a sharply divided citizenry with only the barest majority in favor of letting gays serve in the military. Fortunately, the survey posed a follow-up question to the 46 percent who opposed "don't ask, don't tell": "Do you oppose it because you think homosexuals should be able to serve openly in the military, or because you believe homosexuals should not be able to serve in the military under any circumstances?" In response to this question, the 46 percent broke down into 35 percent who said that gays should be able to serve openly, 8 percent who said they should never be able to serve, and 3 percent who cited no reason for their stance. Inclusion of the second item revealed a portrait of American public opinion that is much more supportive of gays serving in the military.

A similar pattern emerged in a February 2010 Ipsos/McClatchy poll on health care reform. When asked whether they favored or opposed "the health care reform proposals presently being discussed," 41 percent of Americans said they favored them and 47 percent opposed. With only this item, critics of health care reform might claim that a plurality of Americans do not want health care reform. But a follow-up question asked of the initial opponents to health care reform showed that the situation was more complicated. "Is [your opposition] because you favor health care reform overall but think the current proposals don't go far enough to reform health care; OR you oppose health care reform overall and think the current proposals go too far in reforming health care?" Of these initial opponents, 37 percent said they favored reform but did not believe that the proposals went far enough, while 54 percent opposed reform and thought the proposals went too far. Here is a case where more than a third of the opponents would move to support if the reform proposals were stronger, certainly not what critics of health care reform wanted to hear. Of course, if the proposed reforms were strengthened, some of the initial supporters would be converted to opponents. This example again illustrates the problems inherent in accurately portraying American public opinion on an issue as complicated as health care reform.

SALLY FORTH © 1989 KING FEATURES SYNDICATE

Two polls on abortion demonstrate that while support for the use of abortion may have weakened in recent years, one cannot conclude that citizens are therefore more likely to favor legally restricting it. A 2000 *Los Angeles Times* poll found that more than half of the respondents thought abortion should be either totally illegal or legal only in cases of rape, incest, or when the mother's life was in danger (Rubin 2000). Yet more than two-thirds said the decision to have an abortion should be left to the woman and her doctor. Even among the 57 percent of respondents who believed abortion to be murder, more than half agreed that the decision to have an abortion should be left to the woman. A 1998 *Columbus Dispatch* poll of Ohioans obtained similar results (Rowland 1998). Only 27 percent of Ohioans believed that abortion should be generally available; 15 percent said that it should be available but under stricter limits; 43 percent said that abortion should be against the law except in cases involving rape, incest, and the life of the mother; and 15 percent believed that abortion should not be permitted at all. Moreover, 51 percent of the respondents believed that abortion was an act of murder. These results might suggest that Ohioans would support government action to limit or prohibit abortions, but that was not the case. Ohioans were asked whether they agreed or disagreed with the following statement: "Even in cases where I might think abortion is the wrong thing to do, I don't think the government has any business preventing a woman from having an abortion." Fully 66 percent of respondents agreed with this statement, and only 27 percent disagreed. The lesson here is that one cannot presume to know citizens' policy prescriptions based on their opinions on an issue. Rather, one has to ask specific questions about both issue opinions and policy preferences. Some citizens do not like abortion but are unwilling to impose their views on others. Likewise, some citizens may reject gun ownership for themselves, but that does not mean that they would prevent their fellow citizens from owning guns. Some may oppose mercy killings and doctor-assisted suicides, but that does not mean that they support stiff criminal penalties to punish such actions.

The final example in this section focuses on how the news media select what citizens learn about a poll, even when the complete poll and analyses are readily available. *Sex in America: A Definitive Survey,* by Robert T. Michael and others, was published in 1994, along with a more specialized and comprehensive volume, *The Social Organization of Sexuality: Sexual Practices in the United States,* by Edward O. Laumann, Michael, and John H. Gagnon. Both books are based on an extensive questionnaire administered by the National Opinion Research Center to 3,432 scientifically selected respondents, a genuine public opinion survey on sexual behavior, unlike the sex pseudopolls discussed in chapter 1.

Because of the importance of the subject matter and because sex sells, media coverage of the survey was widespread. How various news organizations reported the story indicates how much leeway the media have in selecting which findings to emphasize and therefore determining what citizens learned about the research. For example, the *New York Times* ran a front-page story on October 7, 1994, titled "Sex in America: Faithfulness in Marriage Thrives After All." Less-prominent stories appeared in subsequent issues, including one on October 18, 1994, inaccurately titled "Gay Survey Raises a New Question."

Two of the three major newsmagazines featured the sex survey on the covers of their October 17, 1994, issues. The *Time* cover simply read, "Sex in America: Surprising News from the Most Important Survey since the Kinsey Report." The *U.S. News and World Report* cover was more risqué, showing a partially clad man and woman in bed; it read, "Sex in America: A Massive New Survey, the Most Authoritative Ever, Reveals What We Do behind the Bedroom Door." In contrast, *Newsweek* simply ran a two-page story with the lead, "Not Frenzied, but Fulfilled. Sex: Relax. If you do it—with your mate—around twice a week, according to a major new study, you basically wrote the book of love."

Other magazines and newspapers also reported on the survey in ways geared to their readership. The November issue of *Glamour* featured the survey on its cover with the teaser, "Who's doing it? And how? MAJOR U.S. SEX SURVEY." The story that followed was written by the authors of the book. The cover of the November 15, 1994, issue of *The Advocate* read, "What That Sex Survey Really Means," and the story focused largely on what the survey had to say about the number of gays and lesbians in the population. The lead stated, "10%: Reality or Myth? There's little authoritative information about gays and lesbians in the landmark study

Sex in America—but what there is will cause big trouble." Finally, the *Chronicle of Higher Education,* a weekly newspaper geared to college and university personnel, in its October 17, 1994, issue headlined its story, "The Sex Lives of Americans. Survey That Had Been Target of Conservative Attacks Produces Few Startling Results."

Both books about the survey contain a vast amount of information and a large number of results and findings. Although most of the media coverage cited above was accurate in reporting the actual survey results, it also was selective in focusing on the more titillating parts of the survey, an unsurprising outcome given the need to satisfy their readers.

Examining Trends with Polling Data

Researchers often use polling data to describe and analyze trends. To study trends, a researcher must ensure that items relating to the topic under investigation are included in multiple surveys conducted at different times. Ideally, the items should be identically worded. But even when they are, serious problems of comparability can make trend analysis difficult. Identically worded items may not mean the same thing or provide the same stimulus to respondents over time because social and political changes in society have altered the meaning of the questions. For example, consider this question:

Q. Some say that the civil rights people have been trying to push too fast. Others feel they haven't pushed fast enough. How about you? Do you think that civil rights leaders are trying to push too fast, are going too slowly, or are they moving at about the right speed?

The responses to this item can be greatly influenced by the goals and agenda of the civil rights leadership at the time of the survey. A finding that more Americans think that the civil rights leaders are moving too fast or too slowly may reflect not a change in attitude from past views about civil rights activism but a change in the civil rights agenda itself. In this case, follow-up questions designed to measure specific components of the civil rights agenda are needed to help define the trend.

As another example of the importance of context in assessing the significance of a trend, consider the following question:

Q. How much of the time do you think you can trust government in Washington to do what is right—just about always, most of the time, or only some of the time?

Responses to this question over time had shown a substantial decline in trust from the mid 1960s to 1980, a leveling off in the 1980s, an increase in trust in the 1990s, and a sharp increase in trust after the terrorist attacks of September 2001. But what did this post-9/11 spike in trust really mean? Both Langer (2002) and Bishop (2002) argue that the meaning of the question changed after the terrorist attack, that citizens were now responding to a question that implicitly asked how much they trusted the federal government in matters of defense and national security, whereas in the past they had answered the question in the context of social and domestic programs. Indeed, as the events of 9/11 became more distant and politics in Washington returned to "normal," trust in government once again declined.

In addition to changes in the political environment, there are other obstacles to achieving comparability over time. For example, even if the wording of an item were to remain the same, its placement within the questionnaire could change, and that could alter its meaning (see chapter 3). Likewise, the definition of the sampling frame and the procedures used to achieve completed interviews could change. In short, comparability entails much more than simply wording questions identically. Unfortunately, consumers of poll results seldom receive the information that enables them to judge whether items are truly comparable over time.

Two studies demonstrate the advantages and disadvantages of using identical items over time. Abramson (1990) complained that the biennial National Election Studies conducted by the Survey Research Center at the University of Michigan, Ann Arbor, were losing their longitudinal comparability as new questions were added to the surveys and old ones removed. Baumgartner and Walker (1988), by contrast, complained that the use of the same standard question over time to assess the level of group membership in the United States had systematically underestimated the extent of such activity. They argued that new measures of group membership should be employed, which of course would make comparisons between past and present surveys more problematic. Although both the old and the new measures can be included in a survey, it becomes very costly if the survey must cover many other topics.

Two other studies show how variations in question wording can make the assessment of attitude change over time difficult. Borrelli, Lockerbie, and Niemi (1989) found that polls measuring Americans' political party loyalties in 1980 and in 1984 varied widely in their results. They attributed the differences to three factors: whether the poll sampled voters only; whether the poll emphasized "today," or the present, in inquiring about citizens' partisanship; and whether the poll was conducted close to Election Day, which would tend to give the advantage to the party ahead in the presidential contest. The implication of this research for assessing changes in party identification over time is evident: to conclude that either of the two polls showed that genuine partisan change had occurred, other possible sources of observed differences, such as modifications in the wording of questions, must be ruled out. In a study of support for aid to the Nicaraguan contras between 1983 and 1986, Lockerbie and Borrelli (1990) argue that much of the observed change in American public opinion was not genuine. Instead, it was attributable to changes in the wording of the questions used to measure support for the contras.

Smith's (1993) critique of three major national studies of anti-Semitism conducted in 1964, 1981, and 1992 is an informative case study of how longitudinal comparisons may be undermined by methodological differences across surveys. The 1981 and 1992 studies were ostensibly designed to build on the 1964 effort, thereby facilitating an analysis of trends in anti-Semitism. But, as Smith notes, longitudinal comparisons among the three studies were problematic because of differences in sample definition and interview mode, changes in question order and question wording, and insufficient information to evaluate the quality of the sample and the design execution. In examining an eleven-item anti-Semitism scale, however, Smith did find six items highly comparable over time that indicated a decline in anti-Semitic attitudes.

Trends in presidential popularity or approval are probably the most analyzed and reported of all standard polling items. This question has been asked for decades, which enables comparisons of presidential approval across administrations and analyses of subsets of Americans' views, especially broken down by political party affiliation and self-reported ideological preference. When one examines presidential approval scores, one should be examining the overall trends as well as major bumps and departures from these trends. These bumps may be due to a dramatic event, perhaps a foreign policy crisis where Americans rally around the president or a domestic blunder that damages the credibility of the presidential administration. As Election Day draws near, the media give greater attention to presidential popularity as a harbinger of the likely election outcome. Certainly in the 2010 midterm elections, many prognosticators cited the fact that President Barack Obama's less-than-50-percent approval rating was another omen of the likely defeat the Democrats would suffer in 2010.

In addition to presidential popularity, pollsters and analysts often want to describe and explain changing American attitudes on a variety of public policy issues. One such cluster of issues deals with the situation of gay and lesbian Americans and focuses on such topics as gays and lesbians serving in the military, gay civil unions and gay marriage, gay and lesbian adoption, and gay rights in the workforce. In the past two decades, polls have generally found growing support for gay rights in these areas. For example, Pew polls found that between 1999 and 2006, support for allowing gays to adopt rose from 38 percent to 46 percent of Americans, while opposition declined from 57 percent to 48 percent, still leaving a slight plurality of Americans opposed to gay adoption. With respect to gays serving openly in the military, support rose from 52 percent in 1994 to 60 percent in 2006, while opposition dropped to 32 percent from its previous level of 45 percent. Other surveys have yielded similar patterns. For example, American National Election Studies data showed support for gay adoption almost doubling from 1992 to 2008, going from 26 percent up to 51 percent. And support for gays in the military went from about 56 percent in 1992 to 71 percent in 2008.

One question that arises is what are the processes by which Americans have become more supportive of gay rights? Is it because individual Americans are changing their views on these issues, or is it because more hostile older generations are gradually being replaced in the American population by more sympathetic younger generations? The answer, of course, is that both processes are happening. Indirect evidence for this is provided in the following Pew results presented by age groups:

Age group	Gay and Lesbian Adoption				Gays in the Military			
	Favor (%)		Oppose (%)		Favor (%)		Oppose (%)	
	1999	2006	1999	2006	1994	2006	1994	2006
18–29	49	58	46	38	56	72	43	23
30–49	44	47	51	46	56	62	42	30
50–64	30	44	66	49	47	59	50	35
65 and older	21	32	75	62	41	47	50	39

Note that between 1994/1999 and 2006, all age cohorts became more supportive of gay adoption and gays in the military. Note also that for both issues, the youngest (18–29) cohort was the most supportive of progay policies in both years, while the 65-and-older respondents were the most hostile. One plausible conclusion from these numbers is that as the oldest Americans depart the scene and are replaced by younger citizens, support for progay policies will continue to grow. The fact that all age cohorts became more gay supportive suggests, but does not prove, that at the individual level some attitudes were changing in a progay direction. The most direct way to demonstrate this would be to have panel surveys (see chapter 7) that would trace the opinions of the same individuals over time. But panel surveys are costly and time consuming and therefore not as common as cross-sectional surveys based on different samples of citizens interviewed over time. But if one does have multiple cross-sectional surveys done over time that include some identical questions and also measure the actual age of the respondents, then it is possible to conduct cohort analysis where one follows the attitudes of groups of respondents over time.

Imagine that one had polls conducted every five years between 1985 and 2010 on gay-related issues that also measured the actual age of the respondents. Then one could define age cohorts in 1985 and follow those same cohorts over time. For example, one might define one age cohort in 1985 as citizens between 18 and 29, a second age cohort of citizens between 30 and 39 and so on. In the 1990 poll the 18–29 cohort would now be between 23 and 34 years old and in 1995 between 28 and 39 years old, and so forth. Or one could start with the 2010 survey, place every citizen in a cohort, and work backward in time. The key point here is that following age cohorts of citizens over time allows one to draw some inferences about individual-level attitude change among the members of the respective cohorts and thereby enhances our understanding of the processes that produce the trends we observe.

Examining Subsets of Respondents

There is no necessary reason for public opinion on an issue to be uniform across subgroups. Indeed, on many issues there are reasons to expect just the opposite. That is why a fuller understanding of American public opinion is gained by taking a closer look at the views of relevant subgroups of the sample. In doing so, however, one should note that dividing the sample into subsets increases the sampling error and lowers the reliability of the sample estimates. For example, a sample of 1,600 Americans might be queried about their attitudes on abortion. After the overall pattern is observed, the researcher might wish to break down the sample by religion—yielding 1,150 Protestant, 400 Catholic, and 50 Jewish respondents—to determine whether religious affiliation is associated with specific attitudes toward abortion. The researcher then might observe that Catholics on the whole are the most opposed to abortion. To find out which Catholics are most likely to oppose abortion, she might further divide the 400 Catholics into young and old Catholics, or regular church attendees and nonregular attendees, or into four categories of young Catholic churchgoers, old Catholic churchgoers, young Catholic nonattenders, and old Catholic nonattenders. The more such breakdowns are done, the quicker the sample size in any particular category plummets, perhaps leaving insufficient cases in some categories to draw solid conclusions. But such breakdowns often yield noteworthy findings. For example, a Gallup report (Newport 2005) revealed sharp differences on social issues among Catholics, depending on their frequency of church attendance. For example, only 20 percent of Catholics who attended church weekly viewed abortion as morally acceptable, compared with 54 percent among Catholics who seldom or never attended church. Likewise, 35 percent of regular church attenders viewed homosexual behavior as morally acceptable, compared with 63 percent of Catholics who seldom or never attended church.

Examples are plentiful of the advantages of delving more deeply into poll data on subsets of respondents. An ABC News/*Washington Post* poll conducted in February 1986 showed major differences in the attitudes of men and women toward pornography; an examination of only the total sample would have missed these important divergences. For example, in response to the question "Do you think laws against pornography in this country are too strict, not strict enough, or just about right?" 10 percent of the men said the laws were too strict, 41 percent said they were not strict enough, and 47 percent said they were about right. Among women, only 2 percent said the laws were too strict, a sizable 72 percent said they were not strict enough, and 23 percent thought they were about right (Sussman 1986, 37).

Polls showed dramatic differences by race in opinions about the O. J. Simpson case, with blacks more convinced of Simpson's innocence and more likely to believe that he could not get a fair trial. For example, in a Field poll of Californians (*U.S. News and World Report,* August 1, 1994) only 35 percent of black respondents believed that Simpson could get a fair trial, compared with 55 percent of whites. Also, 62 percent of whites thought Simpson was "very likely or somewhat likely" to be guilty of murder, compared with only 38 percent of blacks. Comparable results were found in a national *Time*/CNN poll (*Time,* August 1, 1994): 66 percent of whites thought Simpson got a fair preliminary hearing, compared with only 31 percent of black respondents, and 77 percent of the white respondents thought the case against Simpson was "very strong" or "fairly strong," compared with 45 percent for blacks. A *Newsweek* poll (August 1, 1994) revealed that 60 percent of blacks believed that Simpson was set up (20 percent attributing the setup to the police); only 23 percent of whites believed in such a conspiracy. When asked whether Simpson had been treated better or worse than the average white murder suspect, whites said better by an overwhelming 52 percent to 5 percent margin, and blacks said worse by a 30 percent to 19 percent margin. These various reactions to the Simpson case startled many Americans, who could not understand how their compatriots of another race could see the situation so differently.

Sometimes the opinions of Americans differ by age. For example, consider the topic of physician-assisted suicide. A number of studies have shown that the older the age group, the greater the opposition to physician-assisted suicide (Rosenbaum, 1997; Moore 2005). Another area in which age makes a difference is opinions about whether or not homosexual relations between consenting adults should be legal. A May 2003 Gallup Poll showed that among 18-to-29-year-old Americans, 66 percent thought homosexual relations should be legal; 33 percent disagreed. But among Americans 65 years and older, 39 percent believed that homosexual relations should be legal, while 55 percent were opposed (Newport 2003a). There were also age differences in support for going to war with Iraq. According to a *Washington Post*/ABC News poll, only 49 percent of Americans aged 65 or over favored going to war, compared with 60 percent of 18-to-34-year-olds and 67 percent of 35-to-44-year-olds. Indeed, Morin and Deane (2003) note that public opinion polling has often shown older citizens less supportive of going to war.

Two state-level polls on gun ownership and gun rights also demonstrate the importance of examining subsets of respondents. A 1999 Field poll asked Californians, "Which is more important—to protect the right of Americans to own guns, or to impose greater control on gun ownership?" Overall, 64 percent of Californians said it was more important to control gun ownership; 30 percent opted to protect the rights of gun owners. But an examination of responses by the respondent's party affiliation brought sharp differences to light. Democrats cited controlling gun ownership over protecting the right to own guns by a margin of 79 percent to 16 percent. But 49 percent of Republicans thought protecting the right to own guns was more important, with 45 percent opting for greater regulation of gun ownership. Similarly, a 1999 poll conducted for the *Columbus Dispatch* revealed sharp differences by gender in response to the question "Which one do you think is more important: to protect the right of Americans to own guns or to control gun ownership?" (Rowland 1999). Men divided evenly on this item, but 70 percent of female respondents thought controlling gun ownership was more important, compared with only 21 percent who gave higher priority to protecting the right to own guns. The *Dispatch* survey also reinforces an earlier point: One cannot assume how respondents stand on particular issues based on their positions on other issues. Small-to-sizable majorities of Ohioans supported a variety of gun control and gun safety measures. Ninety percent favored a mandatory waiting period to allow background checks; 70 percent favored registering handguns with the government; 86 percent favored child safety locks; 85 percent favored requiring handgun owners to attend a course on gun safety; and 53 percent favored banning gun shows where guns are bought and sold without much supervision and regulation. But 53 percent would favor legislation (with various safeguards) that would permit adults to carry concealed weapons.

In many instances, the categories used for creating subgroups are already established or self-evident. For example, if one is interested in gender or racial differences, the categories of male and female or white and black are straightforward candidates for investigation. Other breakdowns require more thought. For example, what divisions might be used to examine the effects of age? Young, middle-aged, and old? If so, what actual ages correspond to those categories? Is middle age 35 to 65, 40 to 60, or what? Or should more than three categories of age be defined? In samples selected to study the effects of religion, the typical breakdown is Protestant, Catholic, and Jewish. But this simple threefold division might overlook some interesting variations—that is, some Protestants are evangelical, some are fundamentalist, and others are in the so-called mainline denominations. Moreover, because most blacks are Protestants, comparisons of Catholics and Protestants that do not also control for race may be misleading. The threefold division also overlooks a growing number of Muslims in the United States.

Creating subsets by ideology is another common approach to analyzing public opinion. The ideological categories used most often are liberal, moderate, and conservative, and typically respondents are assigned to these categories based on their answers to this question: "Generally speaking, do you think of yourself as a liberal, moderate, or conservative?" But do people really assign common meanings to these terms? Do these terms oversimplify reality? Journalist Kevin Phillips (1981) cited the work of political scientists Stuart A. Lilie and William S. Maddox, who argue that the traditional liberal-moderate-conservative breakdown is inadequate for analytical purposes. Instead, they propose a fourfold classification of liberal, conservative, populist, and libertarian, based on two underlying dimensions: whether one supports or opposes government intervention in the economy and whether one supports or opposes expansion of individual behavioral liberties and sexual equality. They define liberals as those who support both government intervention in the economy and expansion of personal liberties, conservatives as those who oppose both, libertarians as citizens who favor expanding personal liberties but oppose government intervention in the economy, and populists as persons who favor government economic intervention but oppose the expansion of personal liberties. According to one poll, populists make up 24 percent of the electorate, conservatives 18 percent, liberals 16 percent, and libertarians 13 percent. The rest of the electorate is not readily classifiable or is unfamiliar with ideological terminology.

The more elaborate breakdown of ideologies may be helpful to those seeking to better understand public opinion, but the traditional categories still dominate political discourse. Even so, citizens who oppose government programs that affect the marketplace but support pro-choice court decisions on abortion and proposed gay rights statutes cannot be easily labeled liberals or conservatives, because they appear to be conservative on economic issues and liberal on lifestyle issues. Perhaps, then, they are best classified as libertarians.

Sometimes, the analytically interesting subsets are based on respondents' knowledge and awareness levels. For example, opinions about the future of Social Security and Medicare are related to citizens' knowledge about the two programs (Pianin and Brossard 1997). In one poll, the more people knew about Social Security and Medicare, the more likely they were to believe that the programs were in crisis and that major government action was needed. For example, among highly knowledgeable respondents, 88 percent believed that Social Security either was in crisis or had major problems; only 70 percent of respondents with little knowledge agreed. Likewise, 89 percent of the highly knowledgeable respondents believed Social Security would go bankrupt if Congress did nothing, compared with only 61 percent of the less-informed respondents.

This finding raises some interesting normative issues about public opinion polls. As mentioned in chapter 1, the methodology of public opinion polls is very democratic. All citizens have a nearly equal chance to be selected for a sample and have their views counted; all respondents are weighted equally (or nearly so) in the typical data analysis. Yet except in the voting booth all citizens do not have equal influence in shaping public policy. The distribution of political resources, whether financial or informational, is not uniform across the population. Polls themselves become a means to influence public policy, as various decision makers cite poll results to legitimize their policies. But should the views of all poll respondents be counted equally? An elitist critic might argue that the most informed segments of the population should be given the greatest weight, but this stance would meet with great resistance among those with a more egalitarian perspective. We will return to the role of the polls in a democratic political system in the last chapter.

Interpreting Poll Results

After all is said and done, sometimes reactions to poll results and their subsequent interpretation are functions of one's own underlying values and beliefs. For example, if a poll showed that 75 percent of Americans would allow their own children to attend school with a child suffering from AIDS, while 25 percent would not, what would be the reaction to this finding? Some people might be shocked and depressed to discover that almost one-fourth of Americans could be so mean-spirited toward AIDS victims, when the scientific evidence shows that AIDS is not a disease transmitted by casual contact. Others might be reassured and relieved that three-fourths of Americans are sufficiently enlightened or tolerant to allow their children to attend school with children who have AIDS. Some people might feel dismay: How could 75 percent of Americans foolishly allow their children to go to school with a child who has AIDS when there is no absolute guarantee that AIDS cannot be transmitted casually?

Or what if a public opinion survey showed that 90 percent of white Americans would vote for a black person for president of the United States, but 10 percent would not. How might this response be interpreted? One might feel positive about how much racial attitudes have changed in the United States. A different perspective would decry the fact that in this supposedly tolerant and enlightened era, 10 percent of white survey respondents could not bring themselves to say they would vote for a qualified black candidate.

In neither of the examples just given can a single correct meaning be assigned to the data. Instead, the interpretation favored will be a function of the interpreter's individual values, beliefs, and purposes in analyzing the survey. This observation is demonstrated in an analysis of two national surveys on gun control, one sponsored by the National Rifle Association (NRA) and conducted by Decision/Making/Information, Inc., and the other sponsored by the Center for the Study and Prevention of Handgun Violence and conducted by Cambridge Reports, Inc. (pollster Patrick Caddell's firm). Although the statistical results from both surveys were comparable, the two reports arrived at substantially different conclusions. The NRA's analysis concluded,

> Majorities of American voters believe that we do *not* need more laws governing the possession and use of firearms and that more firearms laws would *not* result in a decrease in the crime rate. (Wright 1981, 25)

By contrast, the center's report stated:

> It is clear that the vast majority of the public (both those who live with handguns and those who do not) want handgun licensing and registration. . . .
> The American public wants some form of handgun control legislation. (Wright 1981, 25)

Wright carefully analyzed the evidence cited in support of each conclusion and found that "the major difference between the two reports is not in the findings, but in what is said about or concluded about the findings: what aspects of the evidence are emphasized or de-emphasized, what interpretation is given to a finding, and what implications are drawn from the findings about the need, or lack thereof, for stricter weapons controls"

(Wright 1981, 38). In essence, it was the interpretation of the data that generated the difference in the recommendations.

Two polls on tax reform provide another example of how poll data can be selectively interpreted and reported (Sussman 1985a). The first, sponsored by the insurance industry, was conducted by pollster Burns Roper. Its main conclusion, announced at a press conference, was that 77 percent of the American public "said that workers should not be taxed on employee benefits," and only 15 percent supported such a tax, a conclusion very reassuring to the insurance industry. However, Roper included other items in the poll that the insurance industry chose not to emphasize. As Sussman points out, the 77 percent opposed to the taxing of fringe benefits were then asked, "Would you still oppose counting the value of employee benefits as taxable income for employees if the additional tax revenues went directly to the reduction of federal budget deficits and not into new spending?" Twenty-six percent were no longer opposed to taxing fringe benefits under this condition, bringing the overall opposition down to 51 percent of the sample.

A second follow-up question asked, "Would you still oppose counting the value of employee benefits as taxable income for employees if the additional tax revenues permitted an overall reduction of tax rates for individuals?" (that feature was part of the Treasury Department's initial tax proposals). Now only 33 percent of the sample were opposed to taxing fringes, 50 percent supported it, and 17 percent were undecided. Thus, depending on which results are used, anyone reporting this poll could show a majority of citizens supportive of, or opposed to, taxing fringe benefits.

The other poll that Sussman analyzed also tapped people's reactions to the Treasury Department's tax proposal. One poll item read:

Q. The Treasury Department has proposed changing the tax system. Three tax brackets would be created, but most current deductions from income would be eliminated. Non-federal income taxes and property taxes would not be deductible, and many deductions would be limited. Do you favor or oppose this proposal? (Sussman 1985a)

SALLY FORTH © 1989 KING FEATURES SYNDICATE

Not surprisingly, 57 percent opposed the Treasury plan, and only 27 percent supported it. But as Sussman points out, the question was highly selective and leading because it focused on changes in the tax system that hurt the taxpayer. For example, nowhere does it inform the respondent that a key part of the Treasury plan was to reduce existing tax rates, so that 80 percent of Americans would be paying either the same amount in taxes or less than they were paying before. This survey was obviously designed to obtain a set of results compatible with its sponsor's policy objectives.

In August 2003, Zogby International, working with the *American Enterprise* magazine, conducted a survey of Iraqi public opinion that was asserted to be scientific. Within a week after Zogby released the survey, on September 10, the National Council on Public Polls' Polling Review Board issued a critique of the poll, claiming that it was not a scientific probability sample but instead simply a convenience sample, in which Iraqis were interviewed in only four cities (excluding Baghdad) in public places such as shopping areas and coffeehouses.

Whatever the merits of the sampling procedure, it is the interpretation of this poll that is most noteworthy. At the time of the poll, domestic criticism of President Bush's planning for postwar Iraq was growing in intensity. More and more Americans believed that matters were not going well in Iraq despite the conclusion of the formal war. American soldiers in Iraq were regularly being attacked, and it appeared that many Iraqis were angry at American policies and the American presence. When the results of the poll were made public, supporters of the Bush administration claimed that they demonstrated that American policies in Iraq were going much better than the news media had been reporting. Indeed, Karl Zinsmeister, editor in chief of the *American Enterprise,* concluded his analysis of the poll with the admonition, "We're making headway in a benighted part of the world, America. Hang in there" (Zinsmeister 2003).

Perhaps Zinsmeister was correct. But one would be worried about the accuracy of poll results that did not include respondents from the Baghdad area. More important, some of the interpretations given to the responses may be unduly optimistic. For example, in his article Zinsmeister wrote, "Iraqis are optimistic. Seven out of ten say they expect both their country and their personal lives will be better five years from now." A skeptic might respond that given the current situation in Iraq, of course Iraqis thought things would be better in five years; they certainly could not get much worse. Another item in the poll asked Iraqis:

Q. If you were asked to name one foreign country you would like Iraq to model its new government on, which one of the following countries would you choose?

Syria	11.9%
Saudi Arabia	17.4%
United States	23.3%
Iran	3.1%
Egypt	7.1%
Other	15.4%
None	21.9%

In reporting these results, Zinsmeister only considered Iraqis who selected one of the five countries specifically listed in the question and wrote that "the most popular model by far was the U.S. The U.S. was preferred as a model by 37 percent (23.3/(11.9 + 17.4 + 23.3 + 3.1 + 7.1)) of Iraqis. . . ." But another way to look at these figures is to say that 23.3 percent chose the United States, or, even more pessimistically, that when Iraqis were given the opportunity to cite the United States as a model for the new Iraqi government, 76.7 percent of them chose an alternative other than the United States.

Zinsmeister was also optimistic that Iraq would not turn into a fundamentalist Islamic republic. He wrote:

Perhaps the strongest indication that an Islamic government won't be part of Iraq's future: The nation is thoroughly secularized. We asked how often our respondents had attended the Friday prayer over the previous month. Fully 43 percent said "Never." It's time to scratch Khomeini II from the Iraq critics' list of morbid fears.

Here Zinsmeister has clearly made a huge leap from the results of one survey question to the conclusion that there is no danger of an Islamic republic's being established. Another question asked whether Iraq should have an Islamic government or whether the government should let everyone practice their own religion. About 33 percent preferred an Islamic government, while 60 percent favored letting people practice their own religion. This question shows that one-third of Iraqis want an Islamic government, but it is not at all clear that letting people practice their own religion rules out an Islamic government.

It is obvious that Zinsmeister is using the poll results to encourage Americans to stay the course in Iraq. He makes very clear to the reader that he is writing as an advocate, as well as how he is using and manipulating the polling data. But two other articles about the poll, one in the *Christian Science Monitor* (Hughes 2003) and the other in the *Financial Times* of England (Dinmore 2003), illustrate how very different spins can be given to the same data. The *Financial Times* story was somewhat negative, with the headline "Opinion Poll Underlines Iraqi Distrust of America." In contrast, the *Christian Science Monitor* story was much more upbeat about

Iraqi attitudes toward the United States. At one point Hughes wrote, "Two-thirds of those polled urged that U.S. and British troops should remain for at least another year." This is somewhat misleading since the actual question asked of Iraqis was, "Given a choice, would you like to see the American and British forces leave Iraq in six months, one year, or two years or more?" Thirty-one percent wanted them to leave in six months, and a total of 65.5 percent in a year. Clearly, this is not two-thirds of Iraqis urging that U.S. and British troops stay at least another year, but two-thirds of Iraqis wanting American and British forces to leave within a year.

When Polls Conflict: Some Final Thoughts

Sometimes consumers of public opinion polls are perplexed when different polls conducted on the same topic at approximately the same time yield divergent results. This is particularly the case for presidential election trial heat surveys, when multiple surveys conducted in close temporal proximity to each other occasionally show rather discrepant results. For example, in the 1984 election, polls conducted at comparable times yielded highly dissimilar results. A Harris poll had Reagan leading Mondale by nine percentage points, an ABC News/*Washington Post* poll had Reagan ahead by twelve points, a CBS News/*New York Times* survey had Reagan leading by thirteen points, a *Los Angeles Times* poll gave Reagan a seventeen-point lead, and an NBC News poll had the president ahead by twenty-five points (Oreskes 1984). In September 1988 seven different polls on presidential preference were released within a three-day period with results ranging from Bush ahead by eight points to a Dukakis lead of six points (Morin 1988c). In 1992 ten national polls conducted in the latter part of August showed Clinton with leads over Bush ranging from five to nineteen percentage points (Elving 1992). In 1996 the final preelection polls showed Clinton leading Dole by margins ranging from seven to eighteen percentage points. In 2000 six polls released on October 26 showed outcomes ranging from a Bush lead of thirteen percentage points to a Gore lead of two percentage points. The final preelection polls in 2004 and 2008 showed a narrower range of outcomes. How can polls on an ostensibly straightforward topic such as presidential vote preference differ so widely? Many reasons can be cited, some obvious and others subtler in their effects.

There is a substantial body of literature that addresses the sources of poll discrepancies in particular election years (Lipset 1980; Lewis and Schneider 1982; Dolnick 1984; Traugott 1987; Voss, Gelman, and King 1995). Zukin (2004) provides a readily understandable overview of factors that help explain why different election polls conducted at about the same time may arrive at different results. Zukin first points out that discrepant results may simply be due to sampling error in the various surveys. Results that appear to be different might actually fall within the same interval when the sampling error is applied to the percentage point estimates. Using Zukin's example, if a poll with a four percentage point margin of error shows Bush ahead of Kerry by 48 to 43, Bush's true level of support could range from 44 percent to 52 percent (at a certain level of confidence), while Kerry's true percentage could range from 39 percent to 47 percent. Thus, Bush could be ahead by as much as thirteen points (52 percent to 39 percent) or behind by three points (44 percent to 47 percent). Zukin notes that sampling error can account for many of the disparities we see across polls.

Zukin then considers a number of technical decisions that pollsters must make that could help explain variations across different polls. For example, he notes that pollsters may use different sampling frames and different methods for selecting the actual respondents to be interviewed. There may also be differences in the timing of competing polls, just as there might be differences in field procedures, question wording and question order, and weighting methods. Different polling organizations may have different methods for identifying likely voters. There may be differences in how interviews are conducted, what kinds of callback techniques are employed, and whether efforts are made to convert refusals to participants.

Presidential polling discrepancies are probably easier to understand and explain than divergent results on issue and policy questions, particularly when these divergent results come from polls conducted during approximately the same time period. In addition to all of the factors listed above as explanations for discrepant election polling, one must give even greater attention to the potential effects of question wording and question context as well as the treatment of nonattitudes and the possible consequences of differential response rates. Because poll consumers are likely unaware of the methodological and design differences among competing surveys, they often find it difficult to decide which poll results are the most compelling and how to reconcile conflicting results. I often advise friends, when they encounter disparate polls on the same topic, to take an average of the results across the polls to come up with the best estimate. But this advice only works when one is dealing with reputable polls; one would not incorporate unscientific polls with self-selected samples into my suggested averaging process. When multiple polls on the same topic yield similar findings, citizens view those results with greater confidence. And when there is only one survey on a topic, citizens must hope that the substantive results obtained are genuine and not simply the product of methodological choices made in the polling process. In short, because at times it is difficult to separate the substantive interpretation of the polling data from the procedures that were used to collect the data in the first place, citizens will find it even more challenging to be informed consumers of polls.

Exercises

1. Review the survey examples in this book. Pick one example and construct two very different interpretations of the same results. That is, write two very different commentaries about the identical set of results.
2. Assume that the job approval rating of President Obama was 45 percent in September 2010. How would you report this result? What commentary might you offer? In thinking about the various issues affecting the context of this result, you may want to consult a national newspaper from that month. How might one judge whether that approval level is high or low? What kinds of comparisons might be helpful in making that judgment?

9 Polling and Democracy

It's very clear
The polls are here to stay;
Not for a year,
But ever and a day.

The interviews and the questionnaires
And the pollsters that we know
Aren't just passing fancies—
Oh, my goodness, no!

The media
Love polls in every way.
It matters not
If polls have scant to say.

In time statistics may numb you,
Results may stun you.
Wait for another day,
For—the polls are here to stay.

—With apologies to George Gershwin

Public opinion polling is a contemporary manifestation of classical democratic theory; it attests to the ability of the rational and wise citizen to make informed judgments on the major issues of the day. Polling makes it possible for political organizations to demonstrate that public opinion is on their side as they promote their ends. News organizations also are enamored of polling, in part because polls seem to elevate the citizen (and thus the media audience) into a more prominent political role; in effect, the polls transform the amorphous citizenry into a unified actor in the political process. Poll results that are not supportive of government actions provide the news media with stories of conflict between the government and the people, just as points of contention between the president and the Congress or between the House and the Senate do.

As the technology of polling has been refined, upgraded, and made more available, many different kinds of groups, for-profit and nonprofit, public and private, have gained the ability to sponsor and conduct polls. Organizations can readily hire pollsters for surveys that will promote their aims, or if they want to be absolutely sure that the poll results will be favorable, they can conduct their own surveys. Such self-serving polls are replete with loaded questions, skewed samples, and faulty interpretations, as, for example, those done by the Tobacco Institute and the Michigan Tobacco and Candy Distributors and Vendors Association to try to head off higher cigarette taxes and antismoking legislation back in the 1980s (Perlstadt and Holmes 1987; Morin 1989a).

One way the technology of polling has changed is that today there are cheaper and quicker options available to conduct a public opinion poll, especially Internet polling and automated telephone polling with prerecorded scripts. These less expensive options make it likely that the number of polls conducted will grow dramatically, which in turn raises the question of how sound and valid these polls will be. Internet polls and automated phone polls, when conducted with the appropriate rigor and safeguards, can be very useful methods to ascertain public opinion. But they can also be carried out in a less rigorous and flawed fashion, particularly as it relates to the representativeness of the obtained sample. Today, too many flawed polls receive media coverage, thereby giving these polls implied validation. This in turn means that the consumers of polls have to be even more careful and insightful in their evaluation and critique of poll results.

The major news organizations have invested heavily in their own polling operations, adding to the proliferation of surveys. When the presidential candidates' debates take place, for example, a news organization that failed to conduct and report a poll on the winner would be accused of providing incomplete news coverage. The unseemly contest among the media to be the first to "call" the outcomes of particular elections illustrates how the pressures of competition and ratings promote the widespread use of polls. The media operate under the assumption that public reactions to major news events are meaningful and that public opinion polls enhance the news value of a story.

How to Evaluate Polls: A Summary

Polls are a significant way for citizens to participate in society and to become informed about the relationship between the decisions of government and the opinions of the citizenry. As more organizations conduct polls and disseminate their results, whether to inform or to sway public opinion, citizens should be wary consumers, sensitive to the factors that can affect poll results. Gaining such sensitivity does not require familiarity with statistics or survey research experience. Consumers need only treat polls with a healthy skepticism and keep in mind the following questions and points as tools to evaluate poll results.

First, poll consumers should ask whether a public opinion survey is measuring genuine opinions or nonattitudes. Are the respondents likely to be informed and have genuine opinions about the topic? Or is the focus so esoteric that their responses reflect the social pressures of the interview situation, pressures that cause respondents to provide answers even when they have no real views on the subject at hand? As Neuman argued, there is often not a clear demarcation between attitudes and nonattitudes. Neuman coined the term *quasi-attitude* to designate something between an attitude and a nonattitude and points out that citizens' responses to survey questions are "a mixture of carefully thought-out, stable opinions, halfhearted opinions, misunderstandings, and purely random responses" (1986, 184).

Another question to consider is, Have the researchers made any effort to screen out respondents who lack genuine attitudes on the topic? Unfortunately, reports frequently omit information about screening questions and their effects—that is, often one cannot tell what proportion of the total sample answered a particular item and what proportion was screened out. To do a better job of reporting this information, news organizations should, at minimum, provide the number of respondents who answered a particular question when they report on a poll. If that number is substantially smaller than the total sample size, they should explain the discrepancy.

When screening information is not presented, citizens are forced to form impressionistic judgments about whether the measurement of nonattitudes has been a problem in the survey. Some issues of public policy that have been hotly contested by political elites, even issues such as tax reform, may not be of much interest to many Americans and thus may be highly susceptible to the measurement of nonattitudes.

Citizens are in a better position to evaluate the potential effects of question wording than the presence of nonattitudes. Because the media usually provide the actual wording of questions, readers (or viewers) can judge whether any words or phrases in the questions are blatantly loaded, whether the alternatives are presented in a fair and balanced fashion, and whether a question accurately reflects the topic under study. If a report of a survey omits question wording, particularly items dealing with controversial issues, the consumer should be wary and ask why.

Question wording is just one reason a complete questionnaire should be made available with a survey report. The questionnaire also is helpful when a survey contains many questions on a topic but the results are reported for only one or two. Without the complete questionnaire, a poll consumer is unable to assess whether the selective release of results has created any misleading impressions.

Another reason to examine the entire questionnaire is to assess the potential effects of question order. This is seldom possible because press releases (other than those issued by news organizations) and news stories rarely include the complete survey form. Nevertheless, citizens should be aware that the way earlier questions are asked could affect responses to subsequent ones. This is a subtle phenomenon for which most citizens have little intuitive feel, yet the strategic placement of questions is one of the most effective ways to "doctor" a survey. While each individual question may be balanced and fair, their order could stimulate the specific responses preferred by the sponsor of the survey. One clue that this problem exists is the refusal of an organization, such as a political campaign team, to release the entire poll results.

The next question consumers should address is sampling. Although it is the most mysterious aspect of polling for most poll consumers, sampling is probably the least important to understand in detail. Sampling error is *not* where polls typically go astray. Reputable pollsters pick good samples and typically report sampling error and confidence levels, so that citizens can form independent judgments about the significance of results. To make sure that a sample properly reflects the aims of a poll, a poll consumer should pay close attention to how the sample is defined. And certainly the consumer should confirm that the sample is a scientifically selected probability sample rather than a self-selected sample or some inappropriate convenience sample.

One aspect of sampling that citizens should not overlook is the proportion of the total sample to which a particular finding applies. For a variety of reasons, such as the use of screening questions or the need to study analytically interesting subsets of the original sample, the proportion of respondents on which a result is based may be substantially smaller than the overall sample. Thus one should know not only the sampling error of the total sample but also the sampling error of the subsets.

It is almost impossible for citizens to evaluate the effects of interviewing on poll results because reports usually provide too little information about the interviewing process beyond the method of interviewing (for example, telephone or personal) and the dates of the interviews. The poll consumer normally assumes that an interview was performed competently, undoubtedly a safe assumption with reputable polling firms. But consumers should note that an interviewer bent on generating biased responses has many opportunities to achieve that end while asking questions. The best way for the poll consumer to gain some sense of potential interviewer effects is to be a poll respondent and carefully observe the performance of the interviewer—an opportunity that may or may not come one's way.

The final questions to ask when evaluating a poll relate to the end products, analyses and interpretation. Most citizens do not have access to raw poll data and must rely on the analyses and interpretations of news organizations and other sources. But do these sources of information have a vested interest in a particular poll outcome? If so, consumers should scrutinize poll results even more carefully. For example, a poll sponsored by the insurance industry purporting to demonstrate that the liability insurance crisis is due to the rapacious behavior of trial lawyers should be viewed with greater skepticism than a similar poll sponsored by an organization with a less-direct interest in the outcome. Likewise, election poll results released by a candidate should be viewed more cautiously than those released by a respected news organization.

After evaluating the source of a poll, the consumer then faces the more difficult task of ascertaining whether the pollster's conclusions follow from the data. This task is problematic because often, as noted earlier, only a portion of the relevant evidence is presented in a news story or press release. Or a poll may have included many items on a particular topic, yet the report may present only some of them. Without knowledge of the total questionnaire, one can only hope that the analyst has reported a representative set of results or speculate on how different items on the same topic might have yielded different results. Likewise, reports might include results from the entire sample but not important variations in the responses of subsets of the sample. Without direct access to the data, the citizen is left to ponder how the overall results might differ for subsets of respondents.

Interpretation of a poll is not an objective enterprise; different analysts examining the same polling data may come to different conclusions. Although that may occur for a variety of reasons, an obvious one is that analysts bring different values and perspectives to their task. Often there are no objective standards, for example, for what constitutes a high or low level of support on an issue; it may indeed be partly cloudy or partly sunny depending on one's perspective. Thus poll consumers should ask themselves whether they would necessarily come to the same conclusions on the basis of the data presented. Just that a poll is sponsored by a prestigious organization and conducted by a reputable firm does not mean that consumers have to defer automatically to the substantive conclusions drawn. If a poll is conducted by an organization with an obvious vested interest in the results, that warrants an independent judgment by the consumer.

Polls and Their Effect on the Political System

Do polls promote or hinder citizens' influence in their society? Is the overall effect of polls on the political system positive or negative? These questions continue to be vigorously debated. Writing in 1940, Cherington argued that polls enhanced the public's influence because they provide a way for the voices of a representative cross-section of Americans to be heard; no longer would the views of a tiny segment of the population be the only ones to gain prominence. Meyer (1940) argued further that polls provide information about the preferences of the citizenry that enable political leaders to resist the pressures of narrow groups pushing their own agendas in the name of the broader public.

These arguments are still valid today, yet the limitations inherent in polls as a mode of citizen influence must be recognized. First, as discussed in chapter 1, the United States is a representative democracy that comprises, in addition to elected representatives, a wide variety of organized groups trying to promote their own interests. Any assumption that the results of public opinion polls can be translated directly into public policy is naive. It might not be desirable for public opinion polls to be routinely translated into public policy. Polls at times may tap only the most ephemeral and transitory of opinions. Little deliberation and thought may have gone into the responses the public offered. And certainly the rich complexities of issues can never be captured in a public opinion poll as effectively as they are in a legislative debate or a committee hearing.

Second, even if the public's views as reflected in the polls are well formed, polling often demonstrates that there is no majority view on an issue; opinion may be split in many different ways. Moreover, automatically opting for the majority or plurality position would call into question such cherished values as the protection of minority rights. One can envisage situations in which the unqualified use of public opinion polls might threaten rather than enhance representative democracy and related values.

Third, a focus on poll results ignores the processes by which the public's opinions are formed and modified. For example, one factor that shapes popular opinion is the behavior of political elites. When the White House orchestrates a massive public relations campaign, with a nationally televised presidential address, highly publicized presidential travels, and the submission of a legislative package to Congress, it is not surprising to see public opinion shift in the direction the White House intends. Public opinion is not always an independent expression of the public's views; it can be an opinion that has been manipulated, at least in part, by elites.

Sometimes the president may take the lead on an unpopular issue, as typically occurs during an international crisis. After the president delivers a major address to the nation, public opinion polls usually indicate an upsurge of support for the president's actions, emerging from feelings of patriotism and a desire for national unity in times of crisis. Such was the case with the Persian Gulf crisis that arose in 1990, the terrorist attacks on American soil in 2001, and the war with Iraq in 2003.

*"The latest poll shows your approval rating
holding steady at a hundred per cent."*

At other times the president may scramble to catch up with, and then shape, public opinion. That happened in summer and fall 1986 in response to Americans' heightened concern about the drug abuse problem. After the tragic deaths of famous athletes and increased media coverage of the drug crisis, a plurality of Americans cited drugs as the nation's most important problem in a CBS News/*New York Times* poll conducted in August 1986 (Clymer 1986b). Congress, particularly House Democrats, trying to get out in front on this issue, proposed a major antidrug offensive. The White House responded by taking the initiative from Congress: President Ronald Reagan offered his own proposals, and he and the first lady gave an unprecedented joint address on national television. Major new legislation was passed to address the drug problem. In 1989 President George Bush declared a war on drugs and named a drug "czar" to coordinate federal initiatives. The president announced many antidrug proposals, which, according to the polls, were supported overwhelmingly by Americans even though they felt strongly that Bush's plan did not go far enough.

What do these examples say about citizen influence? Certainly, the drug example suggests the potency of popular opinion on issues that arouse the public. But even there the salience of the issue was very much a function of the behavior of the news media and the political elites who brought it to the fore; the public responded to the issue but did not create it. The adoption of antidrug measures into law suggests that aroused public opinion spurs government policy initiatives. But when the media and political leaders stop talking about an issue, it becomes less salient and recedes from popular consciousness, and citizens may have a misguided feeling that somehow the problem has been resolved.

Sometimes political elites may misinterpret (deliberately or unintentionally) what the polls are actually saying. Unfortunately, political leaders sometimes fail to recognize the limitations and circumstances of poll responses and automatically construe supportive poll results as ringing endorsements of a broad policy agenda. The tendency of Americans to rally around the leadership of the president during an international crisis should not be blindly interpreted as a popular mandate for particular policies.

Ginsberg (1986) has argued that polling weakens the influence of public opinion in a democratic society. He asserts that there are many ways besides participating in a poll for citizens to express their opinions, such as demonstrations and protests, letter-writing campaigns, and interest group activities. But because polling is deemed to be scientific and representative of the broad public, it has dominated the other types of expression.

According to Ginsberg, four fundamental changes in the nature of public opinion are attributable to the increased frequency of polling: First, responding to a public opinion survey is an easier form of expression than writing a letter or participating in a protest—activities usually undertaken by citizens who are intensely committed to their positions. Anyone can respond to a poll question, whether or not their feelings about an issue are strong. Thus in a public opinion poll the intense opinions of a small minority can be submerged by the indifferent views of the sizable majority. Indeed, government leaders may try to dismiss the views of dissidents by citing polls that indicate that most Americans do not support the dissidents' position.

Second, polling changes public opinion from a behavior, such as letter writing or demonstrating, to an *attitude,* as revealed in a verbal response to a poll question. Ginsberg argues that public opinion expressed through polls is less threatening to political elites than are opinions expressed through behavioral mechanisms. Moreover, polls can inform leaders about dissidents' attitudes before they become behaviors. The information on attitudes gives government a kind of early warning as well as an opportunity to change attitudes either by seeking remedies to problems or by relying on public relations techniques to manipulate opinions.

Third, polls convert public opinion from a characteristic of groups to an attribute of individuals. This factor enables public officials to ignore group leaders and instead attend directly to the opinions of citizens. Unfortunately, this attention may effectively weaken individuals' political power because organized activity, not individual activity, is the key to citizen influence in the United States. If government leaders are able to use the polls as an excuse to ignore group preferences, then citizen influence will be lessened.

Finally, polling reduces citizens' opportunities to set the political agenda. The topics of public opinion polls are those selected by the polls' sponsors rather than by the citizenry. Therefore, citizens lose control over the agenda of issues, and the agenda as revealed through the polls may differ in major ways from the issues that really matter to people.

Ginsberg's conclusion is that polling makes public opinion safer and less threatening for government. Opinions expressed through the polls place fewer demands and constraints on decision makers and provide political leaders with an enhanced ability "to anticipate, regulate, and manipulate popular attitudes" (Ginsberg 1986, 85). In short, Ginsberg's thesis is that the advent and growth of public opinion polling have been detrimental to citizen influence.

Ginsberg has raised some important issues about the dangers inherent in the proliferation of public opinion polls, even if one does not agree with all of his conclusions. Clearly, citizens must be on guard against allowing public opinion to become synonymous with the results of public opinion polls. Public opinion manifests itself in many ways, including those Ginsberg mentioned—protests, letter-writing campaigns, direct personal contact with decision makers—and many others. Political elites recognize the potential costs of ignoring these alternative forms of political expression, but it is critical that the media also recognize that polls are not the only legitimate expression of public opinion. Citizens, too, must avoid allowing a passive activity such as responding to a poll to replace more active modes of political participation.

Although there is evidence that direct electoral participation has declined in the United States, other group-based activities are on the rise. And if groups have the resources, they can use polls to promote their agenda when it differs from that of the political elites. Contrary to Ginsberg's assertion, polls need not make public opinion a property of individuals rather than groups. Polls can identify clusters of citizens (often defined by demographic characteristics) who do not share the prevailing views of the citizenry at large. For example, public opinion polls on the ultimate outcome of the 2000 presidential election showed sharp differences between white and black Americans on the perceived legitimacy of the Bush victory and the overall fairness of the legal and election process. Whether Ginsberg's concerns are overstated or not, the polls are playing a growing role in American political life, in campaigns, in governance, and in popular discourse.

Bartels (2003) takes a different view of the role of public opinion polls in democratic governance. He argues that public opinion polls do not and cannot provide political leaders with directions about what policy options to pursue because, while the polls measure citizens' attitudes, they do not measure the public's preferences on public policies. Bartels argues that responses to policy questions in a poll can vary so dramatically, depending on the wording of the questions, the context in which they are placed, and the choices that are offered, that they provide leaders with little real guidance about how they should govern. Althaus (2003) makes a similar point. Recognizing the limits of surveys and survey respondents, he argues that polls are best used to determine the problems citizens care most about rather than the solutions to those problems. If citizens have limited information about the intricacies and details of public policies, then it is better to use polls to assess citizens' policy aspirations and goals rather than their opinions about how specifically to solve problems. In this formulation, the role of the citizen as reflected in public opinion polls is to communicate broad objectives to decision makers, but it is left to elites to determine how to accomplish those objectives.

Observers have been concerned about the effect of polls not only on citizens' political clout but also on the performance of elected officeholders. More than sixty years ago Bernays (1945) warned that polls would dominate the political leadership and that decision makers would slavishly follow the polls to please the people and maintain popularity. The polls might even paralyze political leaders, preventing them from taking unpopular positions and from trying to educate the public on controversial issues. Political observers like Bernays still contemptuously deride politicians who figuratively always keep the polls in their pockets, lacking the courage to act on their own convictions no matter what the polls say.

Some officeholders do blindly follow the polls, but today those who abuse, manipulate, and misinterpret polls are of greater concern. In particular, presidents have increasingly tried to manage public opinion. For example, Altschuler (1986) describes how President Lyndon Johnson tried to take the offensive when his poll ratings began to decline. To convince key elites that he was still strong, Johnson attacked the public polls, selectively leaked private polls, and tried to influence poll results and poll reporting by cultivating the acquaintance of the pollsters. Likewise, the Nixon administration tried to manipulate the Gallup and Harris polling organizations by influencing how they carried out and reported their national polls (Jacobs and Shapiro 1995–1996). In-house polling was a central part of the skillful public relations efforts of the Reagan presidency (Blumenthal 1981). Writing about the Reagan administration, Beal and Hinckley (1984) argued that polls became more important after the presidential election than before it; indeed, polls were a much more important tool of governing than was commonly recognized. Likewise, polling was central to the operation of the Clinton White House and prominent in the George W. Bush White House. Jacobs and Shapiro (1995) have shown how the polling operations of the Kennedy, Johnson, and especially the Nixon presidencies served as precursors for the contemporary White House use of polls. Shapiro and Jacobs (2002) examine how presidents utilize polls to manipulate public opinion and thereby make themselves less responsive to the popular will. Certainly no one would deny the president and other elected officials their pollsters. But the measure of an incumbent's performance should not simply be the degree of success achieved in shaping public opinion in particular ways.

Although much of the research looks at how presidents try to shape public opinion, there is a growing literature on how polls may influence the choices and decisions of presidential administrations. Two recent studies, one on the Nixon administration (Druckman and Jacobs 2006) and the other on the Reagan administration (Murray 2006), suggest that presidential administrations did more than simply try to manipulate public opinion and the attendant opinion poll results. Examining the private polls commissioned by the Nixon and Reagan administrations, as well as archival materials and other data sources, both studies found evidence of responsiveness to public opinion on issues that were salient and important to the mass public. But on less-important issues, presidents had more freedom to take stances likely to please core supporters and other groups rather than the broad public. At minimum, these studies suggest some presidential responsiveness to polls on key issues; in some situations, the polls may indeed be an instrument of citizen influence.

Another example of the impact of polls on elite behavior occurred in the 2006 midterm elections. Although candidates for office always pay attention to the polls and how they are doing in them, in 2006 one could observe directly how candidates, especially Republicans, strategically altered their campaign behaviors. As the media publicized the results of public opinion polls showing Americans increasingly opposed to the Iraq war, more disapproving of President Bush's performance on Iraq, and more likely to vote Democratic, many Republican incumbents modified their positions on Iraq or changed their campaign tactics. Some Republicans distanced themselves from the Bush administration's Iraq policy, others expressed no confidence in Secretary of Defense Donald Rumsfeld (who resigned the day after the election), and others did not want the president to campaign for them in their districts. Certainly the results of the polls and the heavy media attention accorded them helped change the conduct of the 2006 elections.

One final effect of polls on the political system merits consideration: their contribution to political discourse. One might ask whether contemporary policy debates are becoming too poll-driven. For example, the 2009–2010 debate on health care reform and the attendant media coverage were very much influenced by the polls, with some commentary suggesting that the policies ultimately adopted should reflect citizens' preferences as revealed by the polls. Normally it would certainly be reasonable to assert that policies should reflect the public's opinions. But what if opinions have been excessively influenced by a political battle waged by proponents and opponents of health care reform that relied on distortion, half-truths, scare tactics, and the like? What if actors external to the Congress such as industry groups, trade associations, labor unions, and other entities waged misleading campaigns for and against health care reform utilizing every tactic possible, including television and radio ads, direct mail, newspaper op-eds, robo calls, and phone banking? The opponents of health care reform were very skillful in raising the nonissue of death panels, while the proponents certainly worked hard to demonize the insurance industry. As the debate wore on, pollsters would ask about these charges and countercharges and the media would subsequently report these poll results. Eventually, the substantive debate on health care reform would become enmeshed in the more peripheral issues, lessening the quality of the debate and oftentimes trivializing it. Manipulating polls and exploiting them to advance a cause are certainly not new developments in American politics; advocates on any issue would want to be able to claim that the people were with them. But the health care debate takes this to new heights (depths) and raises the specter that this may be the wave of the future. If the goal is to win at all costs, then anything goes. And polls, which can be excellent tools for uncovering the preferences of Americans, may become tools to obfuscate and distort issues and manipulate the American public.

Polls may also affect political discourse in more subtle ways. In particular, Americans' awareness of the attitudes of their fellow citizens, learned through the polls, may alter their opinions and subsequent behaviors. This phenomenon has been explained in terms of the theories of the spiral of silence and pluralistic ignorance.

The spiral of silence thesis, developed by Noelle-Neumann (1974, 1977), argues that individuals desire to be respected and popular. To accomplish this, they become sensitive to prevailing opinions and how they are changing. If, on the one hand, individuals observe that their opinions seem to be in the minority and are losing support, they are less likely to express them publicly. Consequently, such opinions will seem to the individuals who hold them to be weaker than they actually are. On the other hand, if people perceive that their views are popular and on the ascendant, they are more likely to discuss them openly. Such opinions then gain more adherents and seem stronger than they actually are. Thus one opinion becomes established as dominant, while the other recedes to the background. "Pluralistic ignorance" refers to people's misperceptions of what other individuals and groups believe (O'Gorman 1975; O'Gorman and Garry 1976–1977). Those misperceptions affect their own views and their willingness to express them. Lang and Lang (1984) linked the notions of pluralistic ignorance and the spiral of silence in a discussion of American racial attitudes in the 1960s:

> Typical of pluralistic ignorance has been the unwillingness of many whites to acknowledge their own antiblack prejudice, which they believe to contradict an accepted cultural ideal. As a way of justifying their own behavior, these whites often attribute such prejudice to other whites by saying "I wouldn't mind having a black neighbor except that my neighbors wouldn't stand for it."
>
> But what if such fears about their neighbors' reactions proved unjustified? What if polls showed an expressed readiness for a range of desegregation measures that these whites do not believe others are prepared to accept? Such a finding contrary to prevailing belief would be controversial. Where the real opinion lies may be less important than the change in perception of the climate of opinion. A definitive poll finding can destroy the premise that underlies the justification for behavior clearly at variance with professed ideals. In these circumstances a spiral of silence about the real opinion fosters a climate inhospitable to segregationist sentiment and drives it underground. (141)

As this example illustrates, public opinion polls provide citizens with a mechanism for knowing what their fellow citizens think and believe. This is especially important for people who interact mostly with like-minded individuals and may therefore have little sense of the diversity of opinion that may exist on an issue. If the polls can accurately measure the underlying beliefs and values of the citizenry, then people no longer have to be at the mercy of unrepresentative views that they mistakenly believe are those of the majority. The polls can tell people a lot about themselves as part of

Peanuts: © 2010 Peanuts Worldwide LLC., distributed by UFS, Inc.

American society, and that self-knowledge may foster a healthier and more open political debate. That being said, it also is possible that what they learn from polls about the views of their fellow citizens may surprise, shock, offend, and even divide them. Certainly it was shocking to learn from public opinion polls that substantial numbers of Americans believed that weapons of mass destruction had been found in Iraq after the war, when they had not; that weapons of mass destruction had been used against American soldiers during the war with Iraq, when they had not; and that Iraq and Saddam Hussein had worked with al-Qaida on the September 11 terrorist attacks, when no proof of such a link had yet been found. How Americans came to those beliefs is beyond our task in this book. But learning about them from public opinion polls helps us to better understand the preferences that Americans did hold regarding various aspects of U.S. policy toward Iraq. When polls inform us that some Americans mistakenly believe that President Obama is a Muslim or that he was not born in the United States, or both, it helps us understand some of the vitriol in contemporary American politics.

Conclusion

As the *Peanuts* cartoon makes clear, Americans have ambivalent feelings about polls. Citizens resent the polls when surveys become too intrusive and seem to be telling them what they will be doing even before they do it. Yet Americans are also fascinated by what the polls tell them about themselves. They are suspicious because they seldom are respondents in a poll, yet they readily cite the surveys conducted by reputable and even disreputable pollsters. They complain about the pervasiveness of polls, yet they are apt to raise questions that only polls can answer.

Perhaps this ambivalence arises out of people's uncertainty about just what goes into a poll. Polls are called scientific, yet citizens know that the polls are sometimes wrong. Politicians on one day swear by the polls; the next day they swear at them. Americans are in a better position to evaluate polls if they understand the factors that can affect poll results. Thus the aim of this book has been to remove the mystery from public opinion research, so that citizens can master the polls rather than be mastered by them.

Exercise

1. Write an essay about the role of public opinion polls in a democratic political system. How might leaders use public opinion polls? Should leaders follow their own views or the views of the public as expressed in the polls? Are there conditions under which you would argue that leaders should ignore the polls and popular preferences and instead do what they believe to be right? Discuss such conditions. Are there conditions under which leaders should follow the polls even when they disagree with the poll results? Discuss such conditions. Finally, what ways other than public opinion polls might there be to measure and assess public opinion? Do you believe that these other ways of assessing public opinion are better or worse than using polls? Why do you believe this?

Web Sites

Media

Print

www.ap.org	Associated Press
www.latimes.com	*Los Angeles Times*
www.nationaljournal.com	*National Journal*
www.nytimes.com	*New York Times*
www.upi.com	United Press International
www.usatoday.com	*USA Today*
www.wsj.com	*Wall Street Journal*
www.washingtonpost.com	*Washington Post*

Television

www.abcnews.com	ABC
www.cbsnews.com	CBS
www.cnn.com	CNN
www.foxnews.com	FOX
www.msnbc.com	NBC

Organizations

www.aapor.org	American Association for Public Opinion Research
www.amstat.org	American Statistical Association
www.casro.org	Council of American Survey Research Organizations
www.census.gov	U.S. Census Bureau

eagletonpoll.rutgers.edu	Eagleton Center for Public Interest Polling
ec.europa.eu/public_opinion/ index_en.htm	Eurobarometers (Web site for the Public Opinion Analysis sector of the European Commission)
www.electionstudies.org	American National Election Studies
www.epi.org	Economic Policy Institute
www.field.com	Field Research Corporation
www.gallup.com	Gallup Organization
www.harrisinteractive.com	Harris Interactive
www.icpsr.umich.edu	Inter-University Consortium for Political and Social Research
www.ipr.uc.edu/OhioPoll/ OhioPoll.html	The Ohio Poll
www.knowledgenetworks.com	Knowledge Networks, Inc.
www.maristpoll.marist.edu	Marist Institute for Public Opinion
www.marketingpower.com	American Marketing Association
www.mra-net.org/ga/	Marketing Research Association[1]
www.ncpp.org	National Council on Public Polls
www.norc.uchicago.edu	NORC—National Opinion Research Center
www.people-press.org	Pew Research Center for the People and the Press
www.pipa.org	The Program on International Policy Attitudes (PIPA)
www.pollingreport.com	The Polling Report
www.quinnipiac.edu	Quinnipiac University Polling Institute
www.ropercenter.uconn.edu	Roper Center
www.rasmussenreports.com	Rasmussen Reports
survey.rgs.uky.edu/nnsp/	National Network of State Polls
www.surveyusa.com	SurveyUSA
www.worldopinion.com	World Opinion
www.zogby.com	Zogby International

Political Sites

www.dailykos.com	Daily Kos
FiveThirtyEight.com	Five Thirty Eight—Nate Silver's Political Calculus
www.huffingtonpost.com/ news/pollster	HuffPost Pollster

www.politico.com	Politico
www.realclearpolitics.com	Real Clear Politics
www.vote-smart.org	Project Vote Smart[2]

---

1. CMOR merged with MRA in 2008

2. This was only active for 2000 and 2004 campaigns

References

Abramowitz, Alan I. 2006. "Just Weight! The Case for Dynamic Party Identification Weighting." *PS: Political Science and Politics* 39 (July): 473–475.

Abramson, Paul R. 1990. "The Decline of Overtime Comparability in the National Election Studies." *Public Opinion Quarterly* 54 (Summer): 177–190.

Abramson, Paul R., Brian D. Silver, and Barbara Anderson. 1987. "The Effects of Question Order in Attitude Surveys: The Case of the SRC/CPS Citizen Duty Items." *American Journal of Political Science* 31 (November): 900–908.

Akron Beacon Journal. 1994. "Foreign Poll-icy" (editorial), 8 May, A14.

Aldrich, John H., Richard Niemi, George Rabinowitz, and David Rohde. 1982. "The Measurement of Public Opinion about Public Policy: A Report on Some New Issue Question Formats." *American Journal of Political Science* 26 (May): 391–414.

Althaus, Scott L. 2003. *Collective Preferences in Democratic Politics: Opinion Surveys and the Will of the People.* New York: Cambridge University Press.

Altman, Alex. 2008. "The Bradley Effect." *Time,* October 17. www.time.com/time/nation/article/0,8599,1851287,00.html.

Altschuler, Bruce E. 1986. "Lyndon Johnson and the Public Polls." *Public Opinion Quarterly* 50 (Fall): 285–299.

Alvarez, Lizette. 1998. "After Polling, GOP Offers a Patients' Bill." *New York Times,* July 16, A1.

Alvarez, R. Michael, and John Brehm. 2002. *Hard Choices, Easy Answers.* Princeton: Princeton University Press.

American Association for Public Opinion Research (AAPOR). 1997a. *Best Practices for Survey and Public Opinion Research and Survey Practices AAPOR Condemns,* May.

———. 1997b. "Major Opinion Research Association Finds Pollster Frank Luntz Violated Ethics Code," press release, April 23.

———. 2005. *Code of Professional Ethics and Practices.* www.aapor.org., revised version.

———. 2007. "AAPOR Statements on 'Push Polls,'" press release. www.aapor.org.

———. 2009. "Standard Definitions: Final Disposition of Case Codes and Outcome Rates for Surveys."

Anderson, Barbara A., Brian D. Silver, and Paul R. Abramson. 1988. "The Effects of the Race of the Interviewer on Race-Related Attitudes of Black Respondents in SRC/CPS National Election Studies." *Public Opinion Quarterly* 52 (Fall): 289–324.

Ansolabehere, Stephen, and Brian F. Schaffner. 2010. "Residential Mobility, Family Structure, and the Cell-Only Population." *Public Opinion Quarterly* 74 (Summer): 244–259.

Aquilino, William S. 1994. "Interview Mode Effects in Surveys of Drug and Alcohol Use." *Public Opinion Quarterly* 58 (Summer): 210–240.

Aquilino, William S., and Leonard A. Losciuto. 1990. "Effects of Interview Mode on Self-Reported Drug Use." *Public Opinion Quarterly* 54 (Fall): 362–395.

Asher, Herbert B. 1974a. "The Reliability of the Political Efficacy Items." *Political Methodology* 1 (May): 45–72.

———. 1974b. "Some Consequences of Measurement Error in Survey Data." *American Journal of Political Science* 18 (May): 469–485.

———. 1974c. "Some Problems in the Use of Multiple Indicators." Paper presented at the Conference on Design and Measurement Standards for Research in Political Science, Delevan, Wis., May 13–15.

———. 1992. *Presidential Elections and American Politics,* 5th ed. Pacific Grove, Calif.: Brooks/Cole.

Associated Press. 2003. "Media Group in Deal to Conduct Exit Polls." February 4.

Bacon, Perry, Jr.. 2010. "Rep. Ryan Pushes Budget Reform, and His Party Winces." *Washington Post*, August 2, A1.

Baker, Peter, and Dan Balz. 2005. "Bush Words Reflect Public Opinion Strategy." *Washington Post,* June 30, A1.

Balz, Dan. 1989. "About Those Predictions We Made Last Tuesday . . ." *Washington Post* National Weekly Edition, November 13–19, 38.

Bardes, Barbara A., and Robert W. Oldendick. 2003. *Public Opinion: Measuring the American Mind,* 2nd ed. Belmont, Calif.: Thompson/Wadsworth.

Barnes, James A. 1993. "Polls Apart." *National Journal* 25 (July10): 1750–1754.

Bartels, Larry M. 2003. "Is 'Popular Rule' Possible? Polls, Political Psychology, and Democracy." *Brookings Review* 21 (Summer): 12–15.

Barth, William K. 2008. "Will Obama Beat the Bradley Effect?" *Jerusalem Post*, October 18.

Battaglia, Michael P., Michael W. Link, Martin R. Frankel, Larry Osborn, and Ali H. Mokdad. 2008. "An Evaluation of Respondent Selection Methods for Household Mail Surveys." *Public Opinion Quarterly* 72 (Fall): 459-469.

Bauman, Sandra, and Susan Herbst. 1994. "Managing Perceptions of Public Opinion: Candidates' and Journalists' Reactions to the 1992 Polls." *Political Communication* 11: 133–144.

Baumgartner, Frank R., and Jack L. Walker. 1988. "Survey Research and Membership in Voluntary Associations." *American Journal of Political Science* 32 (November): 908–928.

Beal, Richard S., and Ronald H. Hinckley. 1984. "Presidential Decision Making and Opinion Polls." *Annals of the American Academy of Political and Social Science* 472 (March): 72–84.

Benson, John M. 2001. "Heard Enough: When Is an Opinion Really an Opinion?" *Public Perspective* 12 (September/October): 40–41.

Berinsky, Adam J. 2004. *Silent Voices: Public Opinion and Political Participation in America*. Princeton: Princeton University Press.

Bernays, Edward L. 1945. "Attitude Polls—Servants or Masters?" *Public Opinion Quarterly* 9 (Fall): 264–268.

Bernick, E. Lee, and David J. Pratto. 1994. "Improving the Quality of Information in Mail Surveys: Use of Special Mailings." *Social Science Quarterly* 75 (March): 212–219.

Bierma, Nathan. 2002. "The Pollsters Are Calling, but Who Is Answering?" *Chicago Tribune* Online Edition, September 24.

Bishop, George F. 1987. "Experiments with the Middle Response Alternative in Survey Questions." *Public Opinion Quarterly* 51 (Summer): 220–232.

———. 1990. "Issue Involvement and Response Effects in Public Opinion Surveys." *Public Opinion Quarterly* 54 (Summer): 209–218.

———. 2002. "Illusion of Change: Sometimes It's Not the Same Old Question." *Public Perspective* 13 (May/June): 38–41.

———. 2005. *The Illusion of Public Opinion: Fact and Artifact in American Public Opinion Polls*. Lanham, Md.: Rowman and Littlefield.

Bishop, George, and David Moore. 2009. "1st Annual: 2009 Top Ten 'Dubious Polling' Awards." www.stinkyjournalism.org, January 29.

Bishop, George F., Robert W. Oldendick, and Alfred J. Tuchfarber. 1980. "Pseudo-Opinions on Public Affairs." *Public Opinion Quarterly* 44 (Summer): 198–209.

———. 1982. "Political Information Processing: Question Order and Context Effects." *Political Behavior* 4: 177–200.

Black, Joan S. 1991. "Presidential Address: Trashing the Polls." *Public Opinion Quarterly* 55 (Fall): 474–481.

Blais, Andre, Neil Nevitte, Elisabeth Gidengil, and Richard Nadeau. 2000. "Do People Have Feelings toward Leaders about Whom They Say They Know Nothing?" *Public Opinion Quarterly* 64 (Winter): 452–463.

Blumberg, Stephen J., and Julian V. Luke. 2007. "Coverage Bias in Traditional Telephone Surveys of Low-Income and Young Adults." *Public Opinion Quarterly* 71 (Special Issue): 734–749.

Blumenthal, Mark. 2009a. "The Public Opinion: No "Perfect" Poll." www.pollster.com, August 27.

———. 2009b. "Polling on the Individual Mandate." www.pollster.com, December 15.

Blumenthal, Sidney. 1981. "Marketing the President." *New York Times Magazine*, September 13, 110–118.

Borrelli, Stephen, Brad Lockerbie, and Richard G. Niemi. 1989. "Why the Democrat-Republican Partisan Gap Varies from Poll to Poll." *Public Opinion Quarterly* 51 (Spring): 115–119.

Brener, Nancy D., et al. 2006. "The Association of Survey Setting and Mode with Self-Reported Health Risk Behaviors among High School Students." *Public Opinion Quarterly* 70 (Fall): 354–374.

Brennan, Mike, and Jan Charbonneau. 2009. "Improving Mail Survey Response Rates Using Chocolate and Replacement Questionnaires." *Public Opinion Quarterly* 73 (Summer): 368–378

Broder, David S. 1984. "The Needless Exit-Polls Battle." *Washington Post* National Weekly Edition, January 2, 4.

Brodie, Mollyann, Lisa Ferraro Parmelee, April Brackett, and Drew Altman. 2001. "Polling and Democracy." *Public Perspective* 12 (July/August): 10–24.

Broh, C. Anthony. 1980. "Horse-Race Journalism: Reporting the Polls in the 1976 Presidential Election." *Public Opinion Quarterly* 44 (Winter): 514–529.

Brynaert, Rob. 2010. *"Scary" Harris Poll: 24% of Republicans Think Obama "May Be the Antichrist."* www.rawstory.com, March 25.

Budiansky, Stephen. 1995. "Consulting the Oracle." *U.S. News and World Report*, December 4, 52.

Busch, Ronald J., and Joel A. Lieske. 1985. "Does Time of Voting Affect Exit Poll Results?" *Public Opinion Quarterly* 49 (Spring): 94–104.

Campbell, Bruce A. 1981. "Race-of-Interviewer Effects among Southern Adolescents." *Public Opinion Quarterly* 45 (Summer): 231–244.

Carroll, Jason. 2008. "Will Obama Suffer from the 'Bradley Effect'?" *CNNPolitics*, October 13. articles.cc.com/2008-10-13/politics/obama.bradley.effect_1_bradley-effect-bradley-campaign-exit-polls?_s=PM:POLITICS

Carter, Bill. 1996. "Three Networks Admit Error in Arizona Race Reports." *New York Times*, February 29, A9.

Chang, Linchiat, and Jon A. Krosnick. 2010. "Comparing Oral Interviewing with Self-Administered Computerized Questionnaires." *Public Opinion Quarterly* 74 (Spring): 154–167.

Cherington, Paul T. 1940. "Opinion Polls as the Voice of Democracy." *Public Opinion Quarterly* 4 (June): 236–238.

Christian, Leah Melani, and Don A. Dillman. 2004. "The Influence of Graphical and Symbolic Language Manipulations on Responses to Self-Administered Questions." *Public Opinion Quarterly* 68 (Spring): 57–80.

Christian, Leah, Scott Keeter, Kristen Purcell, and Aaron Smith. 2010. "Assessing the Cell Phone Challenge." Washington, D.C.: Pew Research Center.

Clymer, Adam. 1986a. "One Issue That Seems to Defy a Yes or No." *New York Times*, February 23, 22-E.

———. 1986b. "Public Found Ready to Sacrifice in Drug Fight." *New York Times*, September 2, D16.

———. 1996. "Phony Polls That Sling Mud Raise Questions over Ethics." *New York Times*, May 20, A1.

Columbus Dispatch. 2010. "How the Dispatch Poll Was Conducted." October 31, A8.

Converse, Jean M. 1976–1977. "Predicting No Opinion in the Polls." *Public Opinion Quarterly* 40 (Winter): 515–530.

Converse, Philip E. 1970. "Attitudes and Nonattitudes: Continuation of a Dialogue." In *The Quantitative Analysis of Social Problems*, edited by Edward Tufte, 168–189. Reading, Mass.: Addison-Wesley.

Coombs, Clyde H., and Lolagene C. Coombs. 1976–1977. " 'Don't Know': Item Ambiguity or Respondent Uncertainty?" *Public Opinion Quarterly* 40 (Winter): 497–514.

Cotter, Patrick R., Jeffrey Cohen, and Philip B. Coulter. 1982. "Race-of-Interviewer Effects on Telephone Interviews." *Public Opinion Quarterly* 46 (Summer): 278–284.

Couper, Mick P. 2000. "Web Surveys: A Review of Issues and Approaches." *Public Opinion Quarterly* 64 (Winter): 464–494.

Couper, Mick P., Frederick G. Conrad, and Roger Tourangeau. 2007. "Visual Context Effects in Web Surveys." *Public Opinion Quarterly* 71 (Special Issue): 623–634.

Couper, Mick P., and Peter V. Miller. 2008. "Web Survey Methods: Introduction." *Public Opinion Quarterly* 72 (December): 831–835.

Crane, Misti. 2010. "Doctors Wary of Changes in Healthcare." *Columbus Dispatch*, July 18.

Crespi, Irving. 1980. "Polls as Journalism." *Public Opinion Quarterly* 44 (Winter): 462–476.

———. 1988. *Pre-election Polling: Sources of Accuracy and Error*. New York: Russell Sage Foundation.

Crossley, Archibald M., and Helen M. Crossley. 1969. "Polling in 1968." *Public Opinion Quarterly* 33 (Spring): 1–16.

Curtin, Michael. 1986a. "Celeste Leading Rhodes 48% to 43%, with Kucinich Trailing." *Columbus Dispatch*, August 10, 1-A.

———. 1986b. "Here Is How Poll Was Taken." *Columbus Dispatch*, August 10, 8-E.

Curtin, Richard, Stanley Presser, and Eleanor Singer. 2000. "The Effects of Response Rate Changes on the Index of Consumer Sentiment." *Public Opinion Quarterly* 64 (Winter): 413–428.

———. 2005. "Changes in Telephone Survey Nonresponse over the Past Quarter Century." *Public Opinion Quarterly* 69 (Spring): 87–98.

Davis, Darren W. 1997. "The Direction of Race of Interviewer Effects among African-Americans: Donning the Black Mask." *American Journal of Political Science* 41 (January): 309–322.

Davis, Darren W., and Brian D. Silver. 2003. "Stereotype Threat and Race of Interviewer Effects in a Survey on Political Knowledge." *American Journal of Political Science* 47 (January): 33–45.

Day, Richard, and Kurt M. Becker. 1984. "Preelection Polling in the 1982 Illinois Gubernatorial Contest." *Public Opinion Quarterly* 48 (Fall): 606–614.

de Bock, Harold. 1976. "Influence of In-State Election Poll Reports on Candidate Preference in 1972." *Journalism Quarterly* 53 (Autumn): 457–462.

Delli Carpini, Michael X. 1984. "Scooping the Voters? The Consequences of the Networks' Early Call of the 1980 Presidential Race." *Journal of Politics* 46 (August): 866–885.

Delli Carpini, Michael X., and Scott Keeter. 1991. "Stability and Change in the U.S. Public's Knowledge of Politics." *Public Opinion Quarterly* 55 (Winter): 583–612.

———. 1996. *What Americans Know about Politics and Why It Matters*. New Haven: Yale University Press.

Dilanian, Ken. 2008. "Pollsters Struggle to Explain Clinton Win." *USA Today*, January 9.

Dinmore, Guy. 2003. "Opinion Poll Underlines Iraqi Distrust of America." *Financial Times*, September 11, 11.

Dolnick, Edward. 1984. "Pollsters Are Asking: What's Wrong." *Columbus Dispatch*, August 19, C1.

Dran, Ellen M., and Anne Hildreth. 1995. "What the Public Thinks about How We Know What It Is Thinking." *International Journal of Public Opinion Research* 7 (2): 128–144.

Drew, Christopher R. 2006. "Automated Telemarketing Tactic Steers Voters Toward Republicans." *New York Times*, November 6, A1, A16.

Druckman, James N., and Lawrence R. Jacobs. 2006. "Lumpers and Splitters: The Public Opinion Information that Politicians Collect and Use." *Public Opinion Quarterly* 70 (Winter): 453–476.

Durand, Claire. 2008. "Assessing the Usefulness of a New Measure of Interviewer Performance in Telephone Surveys." *Public Opinion Quarterly* 72 (Winter): 741–752.

Durrant, Gabriele B., Robert M. Groves, Laura Staetsky, and Fiona Steele. 2010. "Effects of Interviewer Attitudes and Behaviors on Refusal in Household Surveys." *Public Opinion Quarterly* 74 (Spring): 1–36.

Edison Media Research and Mitofsky International. 2005. "Evaluation of Edison/ Mitofsky Election System 2004." Report prepared for the National Election Pool.

Ehlen, John, and Patrick Ehlen. 2007. "Cellular-Only Substitution in the United States as Lifestyle Adaptation: Implications for Telephone Survey Coverage." *Public Opinion Quarterly* 71 (Special Issue): 717–733.

Elliott, Philip. 2007. "Telephone Push Poll Raises Questions about Mitt Romney and His Mormon Faith." *Deseret News*, November 16.

Elving, Ronald D. 1989. "Proliferation of Opinion Data Sparks Debate over Use." *Congressional Quarterly Weekly Report,* August 19, 2187–2192.

———. 1992. "Polls Confound and Confuse in This Topsy-Turvy Year." *Congressional Quarterly Weekly Report,* September 12, 2725–2727.

Epstein, Joan Faith, Peggy Ripley Barker, and Larry A. Kroutil. 2001. "Mode Effects in Self-Reported Mental Health Data." *Public Opinion Quarterly* 65 (Winter): 529–549.

Epstein, Laurily, and Gerald Strom. 1984. "Survey Research and Election Night Projections." *Public Opinion* 7 (February/March): 48–50.

Erikson, Robert S. 1976. "The Relationship between Public Opinion and State Policy: A New Look Based on Some Forgotten Data." *American Journal of Political Science* 20 (February): 25–36.

Fahimi, Mansour, Dale Kulp, and J. Michael Brick. 2009. "A Reassessment of List-Assisted RDD Methodology." *Public Opinion Quarterly* 73 (Winter): 751–760.

Faulkenberry, G. David, and Robert Mason. 1978. "Characteristics of Nonopinion and No Opinion Response Groups." *Public Opinion Quarterly* 42 (Winter): 533–543.

Felson, Marcus, and Seymour Sudman. 1975. "The Accuracy of Presidential Preference Primary Polls." *Public Opinion Quarterly* 39 (Summer): 232–236.

Finkel, Steven E., Thomas M. Guterbock, and Marian J. Borg. 1991. "Race-of-Interviewer Effects in a Preelection Poll: Virginia 1989." *Public Opinion Quarterly* 55 (Fall): 313–330.

Fishkin, James. 1992. "A Response to Traugott." *Public Perspective* 3 (May/June): 29–30.

———. 1996. "Bringing Deliberation to Democracy." *Public Perspective* 7 (December/ January): 1–4.

———. 2009. "Town Halls by Invitation." *New York Times*, August 16, A9.

Fishkin, James S., Robert C. Luskin, and Henry E. Brady. 2003. "Informed Public Opinion about Foreign Policy: The Uses of Deliberative Polling." *Brookings Review* 21 (Summer): 16–19.

Fitzgerald, Michael R., Patra Rule, and Claudia Bryant. 1998. "Polls, Politics and the TV News: A Longitudinal Study of the Uses of Public Opinion Polling on the Evening News Broadcasts." Paper presented at the annual meeting of the American Political Science Association, Boston.

Fowler, Floyd Jackson, Jr. 1992. "How Unclear Terms Affect Survey Data." *Public Opinion Quarterly* 56 (Summer): 218–231.

Fox, Richard J., Melvin R. Crask, and Jonghoon Kim. 1988. "Mail Survey Response Rate: A Meta-Analysis of Selected Techniques for Inducing Response." *Public Opinion Quarterly* 52 (Winter): 467–491.

Frankovic, Kathleen. 2008. "N.H. Polls: What Went Wrong?" www.cbsnews.com, January 14.

Frey, James H. 1983. *Survey Research by Telephone.* Beverly Hills, Calif.: Sage.

Fricker, Scott, et al. 2005. "An Experimental Comparison of Web and Telephone Surveys." *Public Opinion Quarterly* 69 (Fall): 370–392.

Fulbright, Leslie, 2008. "Many Think 'Bradley Effect' Won't Hurt Obama." *SFgate,* October 21. articles.sfgate.com/2008-10-21/news/17137368_1_bradley-effect-bradley-s-loss-pollsters

Galesic, Merta, and Michael Bosnjak. 2009. "Effects of Questionnaire Length on Participation and Indicators of Response Quality in a Web Survey." *Public Opinion Quarterly* 73 (Summer):349–360.

Gallup, George. 1947. "The Quintamensional Plan of Question Design." *Public Opinion Quarterly* 11 (Fall): 385–393.

———. 1965–1966. "Polls and the Political Process—Past, Present, and Future." *Public Opinion Quarterly* 29 (Winter): 544–549.

Galtung, Johan. 1969. *Theory and Methods of Social Research.* New York: Columbia University Press.

Gawiser, Sheldon R., and G. Evans Witt. 2006. *Twenty Questions a Journalist Should Ask about Poll Results,* 3rd ed. National Council on Public Polls, www.ncpp.org/qajsa.htm. Retrieved August 26.

Genesys News. 1996. "Unlisted Numbers: What's *Really* Important?" Spring, 1–2.

Genesys Q & A. 1997. "Number Portability." January.

Gilens, Martin. 2001. "Political Ignorance and Collective Policy Preferences." *American Political Science Review* 95 (June): 379–396.

Gilljam, Mikael, and Donald Granberg. 1993. "Should We Take Don't Know for an Answer?" *Public Opinion Quarterly* 57 (Fall): 348–357.

Ginsberg, Benjamin. 1986. *The Captive Public: How Mass Opinion Promotes State Power.* New York: Basic Books.

Goldhaber, Gerald M. 1984. "A Pollster's Sampler." *Public Opinion* 7 (June/July): 47–50, 53.

Goodstein Laurie. 2001. "Support for Religion-Based Plan Is Hedged." *New York Times,* April 11, A12.

Goyder, John. 1985. "Face-to-Face Interviews and Mailed Questionnaires: The Net Difference in Response Rate." *Public Opinion Quarterly* 49 (Summer): 234–252.

Greenberg, Anna, and Douglas Rivers. 2001. "Pioneer Days, The Promise of Online Polling." *Public Perspective* 12 (March/April): 40–41.

Greenberg, Daniel S. 1980. "The Plague of Polling." *Washington Post,* September 16, A17.

Greener, Bill. 2008. "Why Obama Has to Stay above 50 percent." *Salon.com*, October 27. www.salon.com/opinion/feature/2008/10/27undecideds/

Grove, Lloyd. 1988a. "New Hampshire Confounded Most Pollsters." *Washington Post,* February 18, A1.

———. 1988b. "Focus Groups: Politicians' Version of Taste-Testing." *Washington Post,* July 6, A5.

Groves, Robert M. 2006. "Nonresponse Rates and Nonresponse Bias in Household Surveys." *Public Opinion Quarterly* 70 (Special Issue): 646–675.

Hallett, Joe. 2006. "Blackwell also Had Problem Worker." *Columbus Dispatch,* October 24, 1.

Hargrove, Thomas, and Guido H. Stempel III. 2006. "Was 9/11 an 'Inside Job'?" http://tinyurl.com/9zb9n.

Harker, Kathryn. 1998. "Asking about Income: A Preliminary Experiment." *National Network of State Polls Newsletter* 33 (Summer).

Harmon, Amy. 1998. "Underreporting Found on Male Teen-Ager Sex." *New York Times,* May 8, A14.

Harris, John F. 2001a. "Presidency by Poll." *Washington Post* National Weekly Edition, January 8–14, 9.

———. 2001b. "Campaign Promises Aside, It's Politics as Usual." *Washington Post* National Weekly Edition, July 2–8, 11.

Harwood Group. 1993. "Meaningful Chaos: How People Form Relationships with Public Concerns." A report prepared for the Kettering Foundation, Dayton, Ohio.

Harwood, Richard. 1992. "The 'Bumps' and the Reality Are Polls Apart." *Cleveland Plain Dealer,* August 29, 4C.

Hatchett, S., and H. Schuman. 1975–1976. "White Respondents and Race-of-Interviewer Effects." *Public Opinion Quarterly* 39 (Winter): 523–528.

Heerwegh, Dirk. 2005. "Effects of Personal Salutations in E-mail Invitations to Participate in a Web Survey." *Public Opinion Quarterly* 69 (Winter): 588–598.

Heerwegh, Dirk, and Geert Loosveldt. 2008. "Face-to-Face versus Web Surveying in a High-Internet-Coverage Population." *Public Opinion Quarterly* 72 (December): 836–846.

Heerwegh, Dirk, Tim Vanhove, Koen Matthijs, and Geert Loosveldt. 2005. "The Effects of Personalization on Response Rates and Data Quality in Web Surveys." *International Journal of Social Research Methodology: Theory and Practice* 8 (April): 85–99,

Hembroft, Larry A., Debra Rusz, Ann Rafferty, Harry McGee, and Nathaniel Ehrlich. 2005. "The Cost-Effectiveness of Alternative Advance Mailings in a Telephone Survey." *Public Opinion Quarterly* 69 (Summer): 232–245.

Herbers, John. 1982. "Polls Find Conflict in Views on Aid and Public Welfare." *New York Times,* February 14, 19.

Hernandez, Debra Gersh. 1995. "Formats Recommended for Presidential Debates." Abridged from *Editor and Publisher,* November 18.

Hernandez, Raymond. 2009. " 'Survey' Telephone Calls Attack Bloomberg Rival." *New York Times,* April 7, A21.

Holbrook, Allyson L., Melanie C. Green, and Jon A. Krosnick. 2003. "Telephone versus Face-to-Face Interviewing of National Probability Samples with Long Questionnaires." *Public Opinion Quarterly* 67 (Spring): 79–125.

Holbrook, Allyson L., and Jon A. Krosnick. 2010. "Social Desirability Bias in Voter Turnout Reports: Tests Using the Item Count Technique." *Public Opinion Quarterly* 74 (Spring): 37–67.

Holmes, Stephen A. 2008. "Pollsters Debate 'Bradley Effect.'" *Washington Post,* October 12, A06.

Hopkins, Daniel J. 2009. "No More Wilder Effect, Never a Whitman Effect: When and Why Polls Mislead about Black and Female Candidates." *The Journal of Politics* 71 (July):769–781.

Howe, Peter J. 2003. "Technology and Innovation: for Many, Caller ID Frustrates: Service Often Doesn't Work as Advertised." *Boston Globe,* May 5.

Huddy, Leonie, and John Bracciodieta. 1992. "The Effects of Interviewer Gender on the Survey Response." Paper presented at the annual meeting of the American Political Science Association, Chicago.

Hughes, John. 2003. "What Do Iraqis Want? And When Can They Get It?" *Christian Science Monitor,* September 17, 9.

Hyman, Herbert H., and Paul B. Sheatsley. 1950. "The Current Status of American Public Opinion." In *The Teaching of Contemporary Affairs,* edited by J. C. Payne, 11–34. Twenty-First Yearbook of the National Council of Social Studies. Washington, D.C.: National Council of Social Studies, National Education Association.

Jackson, John. 1983. "Election Night Reporting and Voter Turnout." *American Journal of Political Science* 27 (November): 615–635.

Jackson, John, and William McGee. 1981. "Election Reporting and Voter Turnout." Report of the Center for Political Studies, University of Michigan, Ann Arbor.

Jacobs, Lawrence R., and Robert Y. Shapiro. 1995. "The Rise of Presidential Polling: The Nixon White House in Historical Perspective." *Public Opinion Quarterly* 59 (Summer): 163–195.

———. 1995–1996. "Presidential Manipulation of Polls and Public Opinion: The Nixon Administration and the Pollsters." *Political Science Quarterly* 110 (Winter): 519–538.

Jacobson, Lou. 2006. "Polls Apart: Upstart Firms May Be Gaining on Old-Line Pollsters." *Roll Call,* September 27.

James, Jeannine M., and Richard Bolstein. 1990. "The Effect of Monetary Incentives and Follow-up Mailings on the Response Rate Quality in Mail Surveys." *Public Opinion Quarterly* 54 (Fall): 346–361.

Johnson, Timothy P. 1989. "Obtaining Reports of Sensitive Behavior: A Comparison of Substance Use Reports from Telephone and Face-to-Face Interviews." *Social Science Quarterly* 70 (March): 174–183.

Kagay, Michael. 1998. "Stalking the Elusive Likely Voter." *New York Times,* October 18, 5.

———. 1999. "A Sample of a Sample." *New York Times,* November 9. www.nytimes.com/library/ national/110499poll-watch.html.

Kagay, Michael R., with Janet Elder. 1992. "Numbers Are No Problem for Pollsters. Words Are." *New York Times,* August 9.

Kane, Emily W., and Laura J. Macaulay. 1993. "Interview Gender and Gender Attitudes." *Public Opinion Quarterly* 57 (Spring): 1–28.

Keene, Karlyn H., and Victoria A. Sackett. 1981. "An Editors' Report on the Yankelovich, Skelly and White 'Mushiness Index.'" *Public Opinion* 4 (April/May): 50–51.

Keeter, Scott. 2006a. *The Cell Phone Challenge to Survey Research.* Washington, D.C.: Pew Research Center for the People and the Press.

———. 2006b. "The Impact of Cell Phone Noncoverage Bias on Polling in the 2004 Presidential Election." *Public Opinion Quarterly* 70 (Spring): 88–98.

Keeter, Scott, Jocelyn Kiley, Leah Christian, and Michael Dimock. 2009. "Perils of Polling in Election '08." Washington, D.C.: Pew Research Center for the People and the Press.

Keeter, Scott, Carolyn Miller, Andrew Kohut, Robert M. Groves, and Stanley Presser. 2000. "Consequences of Reducing Nonresponse in a National Telephone Survey." *Public Opinion Quarterly* 64 (Summer): 125–148.

Kennedy, Kelli. 2008. "Jewish Voters Report Calls Disparaging Obama." *Boston Globe,* September 16.

Kifner, John. 1994. "Pollster Finds Error on Holocaust Doubts." *New York Times,* May 20, A6.

Kinder, Donald R., and Lynn M. Sanders. 1986. "Survey Questions and Political Culture: The Case of Whites' Response to Affirmative Action for Blacks." Paper presented at the annual meeting of the American Political Science Association, Washington, D.C., August 28–31.

Koch, Nadine S. 1985. "Perceptions of Public Opinion Polls." PhD diss., Ohio State University.

Kohut, Andrew. 1983. "Illinois Politics Confound the Polls." *Public Opinion* 5 (December/January): 42–43.

———. 1993. "The Vocal Minority in American Politics." *Times Mirror* Center for the People and the Press, Washington, D.C., July 16.

———. 2008. "Getting It Wrong." *New York Times,* January 10.

Kolbert, Elizabeth. 1995. "Public Opinion Polls Swerve with the Turns of a Phrase." *New York Times,* June 5, A1, C11.

Kreuter, Frauke, Stanley Presser, and Roger Tourangeau. 2008. "Social Desirability Bias in CATI, IVR, and Web Surveys." *Public Opinion Quarterly* 72 (December): 847–865.

Krosnick, Jon A. 1989. "Question Wording and Reports of Survey Results: The Case of Louis Harris and Associates and Aetna Life and Casualty." *Public Opinion Quarterly* 53 (Spring): 107–113.

Krosnick, Jon A., and Duane F. Alwin. 1987. "An Evaluation of a Cognitive Theory of Response-Order Effects in Survey Measurement." *Public Opinion Quarterly* 51 (Summer): 201–219.

Krosnick, Jon A., and Matthew K. Berent. 1993. "Comparisons of Party Identification and Policy Preferences: The Impact of Survey Question Format." *American Journal of Political Science* 37 (August): 941–964.

Krysan, Maria, Howard Schuman, Lesli Jo Scott, and Paul Beatty. 1994. "Response Rates and Response Content in Mail Surveys versus Face-to-Face Surveys." *Public Opinion Quarterly* 58 (Fall): 410–430.

Kurtz, Howard. 2002. "A Slow News Night." *Washington Post* National Weekly Edition, November 11–17, 34.

Ladd, Everett Carll. 1980. "Polling and the Press: The Clash of Institutional Imperatives." *Public Opinion Quarterly* 44 (Winter): 574–584.

———. 1994. "The Holocaust Poll Error: A Modern Cautionary Tale." *Public Perspective* 5 (July/August): 3–5.

———. 1996. "The Election Polls: An American Waterloo." *Chronicle of Higher Education,* November 22, A52.

Lang, Kurt, and Gladys Engel Lang. 1984. "The Impact of Polls on Public Opinion." *Annals of the American Academy of Political and Social Science* 472 (March): 130–142.

Langer, Gary. 2000. "Under the Hood." *Public Perspective* 11 (September/October): 8–9.

———. 2002. "Touchpoint: Responsible Polling in the Wake of 9/11." *Public Perspective* 13 (March/April): 14–16.

————. 2003. "About Response Rates: Some Unresolved Questions." *Public Perspectives* 16 (May/June): 16–18.

————. 2006. "The Numbers Game: ABC News' Guide to Polls and Public Opinion." ABC News, September 1.

Langer, Gary, and Daniel Merkle. 2006. "ABC News' Polling Methodology and Standards: The Nuts and Bolts of Our Public Opinion Surveys." ABC News, September 1.

Lardner, George, Jr. 1985. "A Majority of the People Are against the 'Star Wars' Defense Plan." *Washington Post* National Weekly Edition, September 9, 37.

Larson, Stephanie Greco. 2003. "Misunderstanding Margin of Error: Network News Coverage of Polls during the 2000 General Election." *Harvard International Journal of Press/Politics* 8 (1): 66–80.

Lau, Richard R. 1994. "An Analysis of the Accuracy of 'Trial Heat' Polls during the 1992 Presidential Election." *Public Opinion Quarterly* 58 (Spring): 2–20.

Laumann, Edward O., Robert T. Michael, and John H. Gagnon. 1994. *The Social Organization of Sexuality: Sexual Practices in the United States.* Chicago: University of Chicago Press.

Lavrakas, Paul J. 1987. *Telephone Survey Methods: Sampling, Selection, and Supervision.* Newberry Park, Calif.: Sage.

Lever, Janet. 1994. "Sexual Revelations." *The Advocate,* August 23, 15–24.

Levin, Blair. 2008 "What Bradley Effect?" *New York Times*, October 20. www.nytimes. com/2008/10/20opinion/20levin.html?_r=1&pagewanted=print.

Lewis, I. A., and William Schneider. 1982. "Is the Public Lying to the Pollsters?" *Public Opinion* 5 (April/May): 42–47.

Lightman, David. 2007. "Mysterious 'Push Poll' Attacks Romney's Religion." www. mcclatchydc.com, November 16.

Link, Michael W., Michael P. Battaglia, Martin R. Frankel, Larry Osborn, and Ali H. Mokdad. 2008. "A Comparison of Address-Based Sampling (ABS) versus Random-Digit Dialing (RDD) for General Population Surveys." *Public Opinion Quarterly* 72 (Spring): 6–27.

Link, Michael W., and Ali Mokdad. 2005. "Advance Letters as a Means of Improving Respondent Cooperation in Random Digit Dial Studies: A Multistate Experiment." *Public Opinion Quarterly* 69 (Winter): 572–587.

Lipset, Seymour Martin. 1980. "Different Polls, Different Results in 1980 Politics." *Public Opinion* 3 (August/September): 19–20, 60.

Lockerbie, Brad, and Stephen A. Borrelli. 1990. "Question Wording and Public Support for Contra Aid, 1983–1986." *Public Opinion Quarterly* 54 (Summer): 195–208.

Malhotra, Neil, Jon A. Krosnick, and Randall K. Thomas. 2009. "Optimal Design of Branching Questions to Measure Bipolar Constructs." *Public Opinion Quarterly* 73 (Summer):304–324.

Margolis, Michael. 1984. "Public Opinion, Polling, and Political Behavior." *Annals of the American Academy of Political and Social Science* 472 (March): 61–71.

Marimow, Ann E. 2006. "Last-Minute Push Polls Send Some Voters over the Edge." *Washington Post,* November 3, B4.

Marsh, Catherine. 1984. "Do Polls Affect What People Think?" In *Surveying Subjective Phenomena,* edited by Charles F. Turner and Elizabeth Martin, 565–591. New York: Russell Sage Foundation.

Marshall, Aaron. 2010. "Most Ohioans Support Medical Marijuana, Pollsters Say, but State Lawmakers Shy Away." *Cleveland Plain Dealer*, April 11.

Martin, Elizabeth. 1999. "Who Knows Who Lives Here? Within-Household Disagreements as a Source of Survey Coverage Error." *Public Opinion Quarterly* 63 (Summer): 220–236.

———. 2010. "Can a Deadline and Compressed Mailing Schedule Improve Mail Response to the Decennial Census?" *Public Opinion Quarterly* 73 (Fall): 361–367.

Martin, Jonathan. 2007. "Apparent Pro-Huckabee Third-Party Group Floods Iowa with Negative Calls." www.politico.com, December 3.

Marton, Krisztina, and Lowndes F. Stephens. 2001. "The New York Times' Conformity to AAPOR Standards of Disclosure for the Reporting of Public Opinion Polls." *Journalism and Mass Communication Quarterly*, 78(3): 484–502.

Meislin, Richard J. 1987. "Racial Divisions Seen in Poll on Howard Beach Attack." *New York Times,* January 8, 16.

Merkle, Daniel M. 1996. "The National Issues Convention Deliberative Poll." *Public Opinion Quarterly* 60 (Winter): 588–619.

Merkle, Daniel M. and Gary Langer. 2008. "How Too Little Can Give You a Little Too Much." *Public Opinion Quarterly* 72 (Spring): 114–124.

Messer, Benjamin L., and Don A. Dillman. 2010. "Using Address Based Sampling to Survey the General Public by Mail vs. 'Web plus Mail' ". Paper prepared for The National Science Foundation Division of Science Resource Statistics, March 3.

Meyer, Eugene. 1940. "A Newspaper Publisher Looks at the Polls." *Public Opinion Quarterly* 4 (June): 238–240.

Michael, Robert T., John H. Gagnon, Edward O. Laumann, and Gina Kolata. 1994. *Sex in America: A Definitive Survey.* Boston: Little, Brown.

Michaels, Stuart, and Alain Giami. 1999. "The Polls—Review: Sexual Acts and Sexual Relationships: Asking about Sex in Surveys." *Public Opinion Quarterly* 63 (Fall): 401–420.

Miller, M. Mark, and Robert Hurd. 1982. "Conformity to AAPOR Standards in Newspaper Reporting of Public Opinion Polls." *Public Opinion Quarterly* 46 (Summer): 243–249.

Mills, Kim I. 1993. "Cheers' Fans Wanted to See Sam Malone Single." *Akron Beacon Journal,* May 2, A13.

Mitofsky, Warren J. 1992. "What Went Wrong with Exit Polling in New Hampshire." *Public Perspective* 3 (March/April): 17.

———. 1996. "It's Not Deliberative and It's Not a Poll." *Public Perspective* 7 (December/ January): 4–6.

———. 1999. "Pollsters.com." *Public Perspective* 10 (June/July): 24–26.

———. 2001. "Fool Me Twice." *Public Perspective* 12 (May/June): 35–38

Moore, David W. 2005. "Three in Four Americans Support Euthanasia." Gallup Organization, Gallup News Service, May 17, 1–5.

———. 2009. "Why Pollsters Manipulate Public Opinion." www.pollster.com, January 23.

Moore, David W., and Frank Newport. 1994. "Misreading the Public: The Case of the Holocaust Poll." *Public Perspective* 5 (March/April): 28–29.

Morin, Richard. 1988a. "What Went Wrong?" *Washington Post* National Weekly Edition, February 22–28, 37.

————. 1988b. "Tracking a Formula for Success." *Washington Post* National Weekly Edition, April 25–May 1, 37.

————. 1988c. "Behind the Numbers: Confessions of a Pollster." *Washington Post,* October 16, C1, C4.

————. 1989a. "Where There's a Smoking Poll, There's Smoke." *Washington Post* National Weekly Edition, January 30–February 5, 37.

————. 1989b. "The Answer May Depend on Who Asked the Question." *Washington Post* National Weekly Edition, November 6–21, 38.

————. 1990. "Women Asking Women about Men Asking Women about Men." *Washington Post* National Weekly Edition, January 15–21, 37.

————. 1992a. "Another Contribution to SLOPpy Journalism." *Washington Post* National Weekly Edition, February 10–16, 37.

————. 1992b. "This Time in New Hampshire, A Somewhat More Graceful Exit." *Washington Post* National Weekly Edition, February 24–March 1, 37.

————. 1992c. "Surveying the Surveyors." *Washington Post* National Weekly Edition, March 2–8, 37.

————. 1992d. "Polling '92: Who's on First." *Washington Post,* June 6, A1.

————. 1992e. "Putting the Focus on Presidents and Peanut Butter." *Washington Post* National Weekly Edition, October 19–25, 37.

————. 1993a. "Getting a Handle on the Religious Right." *Washington Post* National Weekly Edition, April 5–11, 37.

————. 1993b. "Economics: A Puzzle to Many." *Washington Post* National Weekly Edition, May 31–June 6, 37.

————. 1993c. "Wrong about the Religious Right." *Washington Post* National Weekly Edition, November 1–7, 37.

————. 1993d. "Ask and You Might Deceive." *Washington Post* National Weekly Edition, December 6–12, 37.

————. 1994a. "Public Enemy No. 1: Crime." *Washington Post* National Weekly Edition, January 24–30, 37.

————. 1994b. "The Answer Depends on the Question." *Washington Post* National Weekly Edition, March 21–27, 37.

————. 1994c. "From Confusing Questions, Confusing Answers." *Washington Post* National Weekly Edition, July 18–24, 37.

————. 1995a. "What Informed Public Opinion?" *Washington Post* National Weekly Edition, June 26–July 2, 34.

————. 1995b. "How Perceptions of Race Can Affect Poll Results." *Washington Post* National Weekly Edition, June 26–July 2, 34.

————. 1995c. "Medicare Changes Get a Jaundiced Look." *Washington Post* National Weekly Edition, July 10–16, 37.

————. 1996a. "What Nature Never Intended." *Washington Post* National Weekly Edition, July 8–14, 34.

————. 1996b. "Taking the Pulse on Pulse-Takers," *Washington Post* National Weekly Edition, September 23–29, 37.

————. 1997a. "Right on the Money." *Washington Post* National Weekly Edition, March 3, 3.

————. 1997b. "Getting Behind a Bigger NATO." *Washington Post* National Weekly Edition, March 24, 35.

———. 1997c. "Public Policy Surveys: Lite and Less Filling." *Washington Post* National Weekly Edition, November 10, 35.

———. 1998a. "The Pollsters' Greatest Enemy: Themselves." *Washington Post* National Weekly Edition, February 23, 35.

———. 1998b. "Missing the Story on Bosnia." *Washington Post* National Weekly Edition, April 27, 35.

———. 1999a. "It's All in the Wording." *Washington Post* National Weekly Edition, January 18, 21.

———. 1999b. "Believe Them, or Not." *Washington Post* National Weekly Edition, July 12, 34.

———. 2001a. "Thou Shalt Not Fund . . ." *Washington Post* National Weekly Edition, April 16–22, 34.

———. 2001b. "Who Goes to the Polls?" *Washington Post* National Weekly Edition, June 4–10, 34.

———. 2002. "That Magic Touch." *Washington Post* National Weekly Edition, November 18–24, 34.

———. 2004. "Surveying the Damage." *Washington Post,* November 21, B1.

Morin, Richard, and John M. Berry. 1996. "Economic Anxieties." *Washington Post* National Weekly Edition, November 4–10, 6–7.

Morin, Richard, and Claudia Deane. 2000. "What's Up with Gallup?" *Washington Post* National Weekly Edition, October 16, 34.

———. 2003. "Reasonable Doubt: Older People Are Less Inclined to Support Invading Iraq." *Washington Post* National Weekly Edition, March 10–16, 34.

Morrison, Patt. 2008. "The 'Bradley Effect' in 2008." *Los Angeles Times,* October 2. www.latimes.com/news/opinion/opinionla/la-oe-morrison2-2008oct02,0, 261322,print.column.

Moskowitz, Joel M. 2004. "Assessment of Cigarette Smoking and Smoking Susceptibility among Youth: Telephone Computer-Assisted Self-Interviews *versus* Computer-Assisted Telephone Interviews." *Public Opinion Quarterly* 68 (Winter): 565–587.

Munro, Ralph, and Curtis B. Gans. 1988. "Let's Say No to Exit Polls." *New York Times,* November 4, 27.

Murray, Shoon Kathleen. 2006. "Private Polls and Presidential Policymaking: Reagan as a Facilitator of Change." *Public Opinion Quarterly* 70 (Winter): 477–498.

Murray, Shoon Kathleen, and Peter Howard. 2002. "Variation in White House Polling Operations, Carter to Clinton." *Public Opinion Quarterly* 66 (Winter): 527–558.

Nagourney, Adam. 2002. "Cellphones and Caller ID Are Making It Harder for Pollsters to Pick a Winner." *New York Times,* November 5, A20.

National Council on Public Polls (NCPP). 1995. "A Press Warning from the National Council on Public Polls." Press release, May 22.

———. 2000. "Errors Associated with 'Instant' and Overnight Polls." Press release issued by NCPP Polling Review Board, August 14. www.ncpp.org/presspost.htm.

———. 2003. "Poll of Iraq." Polling Review Board, September 15. www.ncpp.org.

———. n.d. "Principles of Disclosure." www.ncpp.org.

———"NCPP Analysis of Final Presidential Pre-Election Polls, 2008." www.ncpp.org, December 18.

National Council on Public Polls, Polling Review Board. 2006. "Statement about Internet Polls." www.ncpp.org/internet.htm.

Neblo, Michael A., Kevin M. Esterling, Ryan P. Kennedy, David M.J. Lazer, and Anand E. Sokhey. 2010. "Who Wants to Deliberate—And Why?" *American Political Science Review* 104 (August): 566–583.

Neuman, W. Russell. 1986. *The Paradox of Mass Politics: Knowledge and Opinion in the American Electorate*. Cambridge: Harvard University Press.

Newport, Frank. 1997. "The Pre-election Polls Performed Well in '96." *Public Perspective* 8 (December/January): 50–51.

———. 2003a. "Six out of Ten Americans Say Homosexual Relations Should Be Recognized as Legal." Gallup Organization, Gallup News Service, May 15.

———. 2003b. "Six in Ten Americans Agree That Gay Sex Should Be Legal." Gallup Organization, Gallup News Service, June 27, 1–6.

———. 2003c. "Public Shifts to More Conservative Stance on Gay Rights." Gallup Organization, Gallup News Service, July 30, 1–6.

———. 2003d. "Americans Maintain Support for U.S. Presence in Iraq." Gallup Organization, Gallup News Service, August 28, 1–13.

———. 2005. "U.S. Catholics Vary Widely on Moral Issues." Gallup Organization, Gallup News Service, April 8, 1–5.

———. 2006. "Where Do Americans Stand on the Wiretapping Issue?" Gallup Organization, Gallup News Service, February 24, 1–5.

New York Times. 2010. "How the Poll Was Conducted." October 28, A18.

Noelle-Neumann, Elisabeth. 1974. "The Spiral of Silence: A Theory of Public Opinion." *Journal of Communication* 24 (Spring): 43–51.

———. 1977. "Turbulence in the Climate of Opinion: Methodological Applications of the Spiral of Silence Theory." *Public Opinion Quarterly* 41 (Summer): 143–158.

Norpoth, Helmut, and Milton Lodge. 1985. "The Difference between Attitudes and Nonattitudes in the Mass Public: Just Measurement?" *American Journal of Political Science* 29 (May): 291–307.

Novak, Robert. 2008. "The Bradley Effect?" *Real Clear Politics*, February 11. www.realclearpolitics.com/articles/2008/02/the_bradley_effect.html.

O'Gorman, Hubert J. 1975. "Pluralistic Ignorance and White Estimates of White Support for Racial Segregation." *Public Opinion Quarterly* 39 (Fall): 313–330.

O'Gorman, Hubert J., and Stephen L. Garry. 1976–1977. "Pluralistic Ignorance— A Replication and Extension." *Public Opinion Quarterly* 40 (Winter): 449–458.

Olson, Kristen, and Andy Peytchev. 2007. "Effect of Interviewer Experience on Interview Pace and Interviewer Attitudes." *Public Opinion Quarterly* 71 (Summer): 273–286.

O'Neill, Harry W. 1997. "An Honorable Profession, Warts and All." Comments delivered on the occasion of receiving the 1997 Award for Outstanding Achievement, New York Chapter, American Association for Public Opinion Research, June 18, 1997, www.mediastudies.org/ho.html, August 6, 2000.

Oreskes, Michael. 1984. "Pollsters Offer Reasons for Disparity in Results." *New York Times*, October 20, A8.

———. 1990. "Drug War Underlines Fickleness of Public." *New York Times*, September 6, A22.

Orton, Barry. 1982. "Phony Polls: The Pollster's Nemesis." *Public Opinion* 5 (June/July): 56–60.

Page, Benjamin I., and Robert Y. Shapiro. 1983. "Effects of Public Opinion on Policy." *American Political Science Review* 77 (March): 175–190.

———. 1992. *The Rational Public: Fifty Years of Trends in Americans' Policy Preferences.* Chicago: University of Chicago Press.

Paletz, David L., Jonathan Y. Short, Helen Baker, Barbara Cookman Campbell, Richard J. Cooper, and Rochelle M. Oeslander. 1980. "Polls in the Media: Content, Credibility, and Consequences." *Public Opinion Quarterly* 44 (Winter): 495–513.

Pascale, Joanne, Marc I. Roemer, and Dean Michael Resnick. 2009. "Medicaid Underreporting in the CPS: Results from a Record Check Study." *Public Opinion Quarterly* 73 (Fall): 497–520.

Patterson, Thomas E. 2005. "Of Polls, Mountains: U.S. Journalists and Their Use of Election Surveys." *Public Opinion Quarterly* 69 (Special Issue): 716–724.

Payne, Stanley L. 1951. *The Art of Asking Questions.* Princeton: Princeton University Press.

Perlmutter, David D. 2002. "Americans Are Long on Opinions." *Columbus Dispatch,* May 1, A7.

Perlstadt, Harry, and Russell E. Holmes. 1987. "The Role of Public Opinion Polling in Health Legislation." *American Journal of Public Health* 77 (May): 612–614.

Perry, Paul. 1979. "Certain Problems in Election Survey Methodology." *Public Opinion Quarterly* 43 (Fall): 312–325.

Peterson, Robert A. 1984. "Asking the Age Question: A Research Note." *Public Opinion Quarterly* 48 (Spring): 379–383.

Petrolia, Daniel R., and Sanjoy Bhattacharjee. 2009. "Revisiting Incentive Effects: Evidence from a Random-Sample Mail Survey on Consumer Preferences for Fuel Ethanol." *Public Opinion Quarterly* 73 (Fall): 537–550.

Peytchev, Andy. 2009. "Survey Breakoff." *Public Opinion Quarterly* 73 (Spring): 74–97.

Phillips, Kevin P. 1976. "Polls Used to Reflect Electability." *Columbus Dispatch,* July 19, B2.

———. 1981. "Polls Are Too Broad in Analysis Divisions." *Columbus Dispatch,* September 8, B3.

Pianin, Eric, and Mario Brossard. 1997. "Hands off Social Security and Medicare." *Washington Post* National Weekly Edition, April 7, 35.

Piekarski, Linda B. 1989. "Choosing between Directory Listed and Random Digit Dialing in Light of New Demographic Findings." Paper presented at the AAPOR Conference, St. Petersburg, Fla.

Piekarski, Linda, Gwen Kaplan, and Jessica Prestgaard. 1999. "Telephony and Telephone Sampling: The Dynamics of Change." www.worldopinion.com/latenews. taf?f=d&news=3966, December 26, 1999.

Plissner, Martin. 2003. "An * for 2002?" *Public Perspective* 14 (January/February): 4–6.

Presser, Stanley, et al. 2004. "Methods for Testing and Evaluating Survey Questions." *Public Opinion Quarterly* 68 (Spring): 109–130.

Presser, Stanley, and Howard Schuman. 1980. "The Measurement of a Middle Position in Attitude Surveys." *Public Opinion Quarterly* 44 (Spring): 70–85.

Prior, Markus. 2009. "The Immensely Inflated News Audience: Assessing Bias in Self-Reported News Exposure." *Public Opinion Quarterly* 73 (Spring): 130–143.

Public Opinion Quarterly. 1987. Fiftieth Anniversary Issue. 51, supplement (Winter): S1–S191.

Rademacher, Eric W., and Andrew E. Smith. 2001. "Poll Call." *Public Perspective* 12 (March/April): 36–37.

Rainie, Lee. 2010. "Internet, Broadband, and Cell Phone Statistics." Washington, D.C.: Pew Research Center for the People and the Press.

Ramirez, Jessica. 2008. "So Right, Yet So Wrong." www.newsweek.com, January 10.

Rao, Kumar, Olena Kaminska, and Allan L. McCutcheon. 2010. "Recruiting Probability Samples for a Multi-Mode Research Panel with Internet and Mail Components." *Public Opinion Quarterly* 74 (Spring): 68–84

Reese, Stephen D., Wayne A. Danielson, Pamela J. Shoemaker, Tsan-Kuo Chang, and Huei-Ling Hsu. 1986. "Ethnicity-of-Interviewer Effects among Mexican Americans and Anglos." *Public Opinion Quarterly* 50 (Winter): 563–572.

Robinson, Michael J., and Margaret A. Sheehan. 1983. *Over the Wire and on TV: CBS and UPI in Campaign '80.* New York: Russell Sage Foundation.

Romer, Daniel, Kate Kenski, Paul Waldman, Christopher Adasiewicz, and Kathleen Hall. 2004. *Capturing Campaign Dynamics: The National Annenberg Election Survey.* New York: Oxford University Press.

Roper, Burns W. 1985. "Early Election Calls: The Larger Dangers." *Public Opinion Quarterly* 49 (Spring): 5–9.

Rosenbaum, David E. 1997. "Americans Want a Right to Die. Or So They Think." *New York Times,* June 8, E3.

Rosenstiel, Tom. 2005. "Political Polling and the New Media Culture: A Case of More Being Less." *Public Opinion Quarterly* 69 (Special Issue): 698–715.

Rosenthal, Jack. 2006. "Precisely False vs. Approximately Right: A Reader's Guide to Polls." *New York Times,* August 27, 10.

Rothenberg, Stuart, ed. 1983. *Political Report,* vol.6, August 5.

———. 1985. *Political Report,* vol. 8, October 25.

Rowland, Darrel. 1998. "Abortion Poll: Government Should Have No Say in Decision." *Columbus Dispatch,* May 22, 1E–2E.

———. 1999. "Poll Indicates Support for Concealed-Gun Bill." *Columbus Dispatch,* 7 November, 4A.

———. 2010a. "Kasich up by 17 Points in Poll; Fewer Democrats Plan to Vote than in 2006 or 2008." *Columbus Dispatch,* September 17.

———. 2010b. "Quinnipiac Numbers: Poll Has Strickland Gaining on Kasich." *Columbus Dispatch,* October 6.

———. 2010c. "Dueling Polls in Governor's Race: Kasich by 4 vs. Dead Heat." *Columbus Dispatch,* November 1.

Rubin, Alissa J. 2000. "Americans Narrowing Support for Abortion." *Los Angeles Times,* June 18.

Salwen, Michael B. 1985. "Does Poll Coverage Improve as Presidential Vote Nears?" *Journalism Quarterly* 62 (Winter): 887–891.

Schier, Steven E. 2006. "False Justification." *Washington Times,* June 27.

Schneider, William. 1989. "One Poll May Be Worse Than None." *National Journal,* December: 2970.

Schuman, Howard, and Jean M. Converse. 1971. "The Effects of Black and White Interviewers on Black Responses in 1968." *Public Opinion Quarterly* 35 (Spring): 44–68.

Schuman, Howard, Graham Kalton, and Jacob Ludwig. 1983. "Context and Contiguity in Survey Questionnaires." *Public Opinion Quarterly* 47 (Spring): 112–115.

Schuman, Howard, and Stanley Presser. 1977. "Question Wording as an Independent Variable in Survey Analysis." *Sociological Methods and Research* 6 (November): 151–170.

———. 1981. *Questions and Answers in Attitude Surveys: Experiments on Question Form, Wording, and Context.* New York: Academic Press.

Schuman, Howard, Stanley Presser, and Jacob Ludwig. 1981. "Context Effects on Survey Responses to Questions about Abortion." *Public Opinion Quarterly* 45 (Summer): 216–223.

Schwarz, Norbert, and Hans J. Hippler. 1995. "Subsequent Questions May Influence Answers to Preceding Questions in Mail Surveys." *Public Opinion Quarterly* 59 (Spring): 93–97.

Shapiro, Robert Y., and Lawrence R. Jacobs. 2002. "Public Opinion, Foreign Policy, and Democracy: How Presidents Use Public Opinion." In *Navigating Public Opinion: Polls, Policy and the Future of American Democracy,* edited by Jeff Manza, Fay Lomax Cook, and Benjamin Page, 184–200. New York: Oxford University Press.

Shlapentokh, Vladimir. 1994. "The 1993 Russian Election Polls." *Public Opinion Quarterly* 58 (Winter): 579–602.

Sigel, Roberta S. 1996. *Ambition and Accommodation: How Women View Gender Relations.* Chicago: University of Chicago Press.

Silver, Nate. 2008. "Debunking the Bradley Effect." *Newsweek,* October 21. www .newsweek.com/2008/10/20debunking-the-bradley-effect.print.html.

Smith, Andrew E., and Clark Hubbard. 2000. "First in the Nation: Lessons Learned from New Hampshire." *Public Perspective,* May/June, 46–49.

Smith, Ted. J., III, and J. Michael Hogan. 1987. "Public Opinion and the Panama Canal Treaties of 1977." *Public Opinion Quarterly* 51 (Spring): 5–30.

Smith, Tom W. 1984. "Nonattitudes: A Review and Evaluation." In *Surveying Subjective Phenomena,* vol. 2, edited by Charles F. Turner and Elizabeth Martin, 215–255. New York: Russell Sage Foundation.

———. 1987. "How Comics and Cartoons View Public Opinion Surveys." *Journalism Quarterly* 64: 208–211.

———. 1988. "Speaking Out: Hite vs. Abby in Methodological Messes." *AAPOR News,* Spring, 3–4.

———. 1993. "Actual Trends or Measurement Artifacts? A Review of Three Studies of Anti-Semitism." *Public Opinion Quarterly* 57 (Fall): 380–393.

———. 2002. "Reporting Survey Nonresponse in Academic Journals." *International Journal of Public Opinion Research* 14 (4): 469–474.

———. 2003. "An Experimental Comparison of Knowledge Networks and the GSS." *International Journal of Public Opinion Research* 15 (2): 167–178.

Smyth, Jolene D., Leah Melani Christian, and Don A. Dillman. 2008. "Does "Yes or No" on the Telephone Mean the Same as "Check-All-That-Apply" on the Web?" *Public Opinion Quarterly* 72 (Spring): 103–113.

Smyth, Jolene D., Don A. Dillman, Leah Melani Christian, and Mallory McBride. 2009. "Open-Ended Questions in Web Surveys: Can Increasing the Size of Answer Boxes and Providing Extra Verbal Instructions Improve Response Quality?" *Public Opinion Quarterly* 73 (Summer): 325–337.

Smyth, Jolene D., Don A. Dillman, Leah Melani Christian, and Michael J. Stern. 2006. "Comparing Check-All and Forced-Choice Question Formats in Web Surveys." *Public Opinion Quarterly* 70 (Spring): 66–77.

Sniderman, Paul, Edward Carmines, Philip Tetlock, and Anthony Tyler. 1993. In Richard Morin, "Racism Knows No Party Lines." *Washington Post* National Weekly Edition, September 20–26, 37.

Solop, Frederic I., and Kristi K. Hagen. 2002. "War or War?" *Public Perspective* 13 (July/August): 36–37.

Specter, Michael. 1996. "Russian Pollsters Are Seldom Right." *New York Times,* May 15, A1.

Squire, Peverill. 1988. "Why the 1936 *Literary Digest* Poll Failed." *Public Opinion Quarterly* 52 (Spring): 125–133.

Squires, Sally, and Richard Morin. 1987. "What Is This Thing Called Love?" *Washington Post* National Weekly Edition, November 16, 37.

Stephens, Scott, and John Mangels. 2002. "Poll: Teach More Than Evolution." *Cleveland Plain Dealer,* June 9, A1.

Stevenson, Richard W. 2000. "Tuesday's Big Test: How Deep in the Heart of Taxes." *New York Times,* January 30, 3.

Stokes, Bruce. 2009. "Not So Popular Where It Counts." *National Journal* 23 (July 25): 2.

Sturgis, Patrick, Caroline Roberts, and Nick Allum. 2005. "A Different Take on the Deliberative Poll: Information, Deliberation, and Attitude Constraint." *Public Opinion Quarterly* 69 (Spring): 30–65.

Sudman, Seymour. 1986. "Do Exit Polls Influence Voting Behavior?" *Public Opinion Quarterly* 50 (Fall): 331–339.

Survey Sampling Inc. 1997. "Sacramento Is Most Unlisted." *The Frame,* March, 1.

Sussman, Barry. 1984. "Do-It-Yourself Tax Reform: Many Think Cheating Is Okay." *Washington Post* National Weekly Edition, May 28, 36.

———. 1985a. "To Understand These Polls, You Have to Read the Fine Print." *Washington Post* National Weekly Edition, March 4, 37.

———. 1985b. "Americans Prefer Tax Cheating to Being Paid to Inform the IRS." *Washington Post* National Weekly Edition, May 13, 37.

———. 1985c. "Pollsters Cheer Up about Public's Opinions of Polls." *Washington Post* National Weekly Edition, June 3, 37.

———. 1985d. "Do Pre-election Polls Influence People to Switch Their Votes?" *Washington Post* National Weekly Edition, 10 June, 37.

———. 1986. "With Pornography, It All Depends on Who's Doing the Looking." *Washington Post* National Weekly Edition, 24 March, 37.

Taylor, Humphrey, John Brenner, Cary Overmeyer, Jonathan W. Siegel, and George Terhanian. 2001. "Touchdown! Online Polling Scores Big in November 2000." *Public Perspective,* March/April, 38–39.

Taylor, Marylee C. 1983. "The Black-and-White Model of Attitude Stability: A Latent Class Examination of Opinion and Nonopinion in the American Public." *American Journal of Sociology* 89 (September): 373–401.

Teitler, Julien O., Nancy E. Reichman, and Susan Sprachman. 2003. "Costs and Benefits of Improving Response Rates for a Hard-to-Reach Population." *Public Opinion Quarterly* 67 (Spring): 126–138.

Tenpas, Kathryn Dunn. 2003. "Words vs. Deeds: President George W. Bush and Polling." *Brookings Review,* Summer, 32–35.

Torry, Jack. 2002. "Battelle Computer under Fire for Election Flop." *Columbus Dispatch,* November 13, A4.

Tourangeau, Roger, Mick P. Couper, and Frederick Conrad. 2004. "Spacing, Position and Order: Interpretive Heuristics for Visual Features of Survey Questions." *Public Opinion Quarterly* 68 (Fall): 368–393.

Tourangeau, Roger, and Tom W. Smith. 1996. "Asking Sensitive Questions: The Impact of Data Collection Mode, Question Format, and Question Context." *Public Opinion Quarterly* 60 (Summer): 181–227.

Traugott, Michael W. 1987. "The Importance of Persistence in Respondent Selection for Preelection Surveys." *Public Opinion Quarterly* 51 (Spring): 48–57.

———. 1992. "A General Good Showing, but Much Work Remains to Be Done." *Public Perspective* 4 (November/December): 14–16.

———. 2001. "Assessing Poll Performance in the 2000 Campaign." *AAPOR News* 28 (Winter): 4–5.

———. 2005. "The Accuracy of the National Preelection Polls in the 2004 Presidential Election." *Public Opinion Quarterly* 73 (Special Issue): 642–654.

Traugott, Michael W., Benjamin Highton, and Henry E. Brady. 2005. *A Review of Recent Controversies Concerning the 2004 Presidential Election Exit Polls.* New York: National Research Commission on Elections and Voting. A Project of the Social Science Research Council. March 10.

Traugott, Michael W., and Vincent Price. 1992. "Exit Polls in the 1989 Virginia Gubernatorial Race: Where Did They Go Wrong?" *Public Opinion Quarterly* 56 (Summer): 245–253.

Tucker, Clyde, James M. Lepkowski, and Linda Piekarski. 2002. "The Current Efficiency of List-Assisted Telephone Sampling Designs." *Public Opinion Quarterly* 66 (Fall): 321–338.

U.S. Census Bureau. 2009. Current Population Survey, October.

Viser, Matt, and Frank Phillips. 2010. "Senate Poll: Coakley up 15 Points." *Boston Globe,* January 10.

Visser, Penny S., Jon A Krosnick, Jesse Marquette, and Michael Curtin. 1996. "Mail Surveys for Election Forecasting: An Evaluation of the *Columbus Dispatch* Poll." *Public Opinion Quarterly* 59 (Spring): 98–132.

Voss, D. Stephen, Andrew Gelman, and Gary King. 1995. "Preelection Survey Methodology: Details from Eight Polling Organizations, 1988 and 1992." *Public Opinion Quarterly* 59 (Spring): 98–132.

Wagner, James. 2010. "The Fraction of Missing Information as a Tool for Monitoring the Quality of Survey Data." *Public Opinion Quarterly* 74 (Summer): 223–243.

Wanke, Michaela. 1996. "Comparative Judgments as a Function of the Direction of Comparison versus Word Order." *Public Opinion Quarterly* 60 (Fall): 400–409.

Wanke, Michaela, Norbert Schwarz, and Elisabeth Noelle-Neumann. 1995. "Asking Comparative Questions: The Impact of the Direction of the Comparison." *Public Opinion Quarterly* 59 (Fall): 347–352.

Wasserman, Lee. 2010. "Four Ways to Kill a Climate Bill." *New York Times,* July 26, A23.

Weeks, Michael F., and R. Paul Moore. 1981. "Ethnicity-of-Interviewer Effects on Ethnic Respondents." *Public Opinion Quarterly* 45 (Summer): 245–249.

Weisberg, Herbert F. 2005. *The Total Survey Error Approach: A Guide to the New Science of Survey Research*. Chicago and London: University of Chicago Press.

Weissberg, Robert. 2001. *Why Policymakers Should Ignore Public Opinion Polls.* Cato Policy Analysis No. 402, 1–16. Washington, D.C.: Cato Institute.

Weissman, Stephen R., and Ruth A. Hassan. 2005. *Public Opinion Polls Concerning Public Financing of Federal Elections 1972–2000*. Washington, D.C.: Campaign Finance Institute.

Welch, R. L. 2002. "Polls, Polls, and More Polls: An Evaluation of How Public Opinion Polls Are Reported in Newspapers." *Harvard International Journal of Press/ Politics* 7 (1): 102–114.

Wiese, Cheryl J. 1998. "Refusal Conversion: What Is Gained?" *National Network of State Polls Newsletter* 32 (Spring).

Williams, Brian. 2001. "Most Ohioans Back Passenger Trains, OSU Survey Finds." *Columbus Dispatch,* March 12, C5.

Winkler, Karen J. 1996. "Organizer Hails Results of Political-Science Experiment." *Chronicle of Higher Education,* February 2, A13.

Witt, Evans. 2001. "People Who Count." *Public Perspective* 12 (July/August): 25–28.

Woolley, Peter J., and Dan Cassino. 2006. "Bush Withers Republicans in Garden State Senate Races." *Polling Report,* August 28, 1, 7–8.

Wright, Debra L., William S. Aquilino, and Andrew J. Supple. 1998. "A Comparison of Computer-Assisted and Paper-and-Pencil Self-Administered Questionnaires in a Survey on Smoking, Alcohol, and Drug Use." *Public Opinion Quarterly* 62 (Fall): 331–353.

Wright, James D. 1981. "Public Opinion and Gun Control: A Comparison of Results from Two Recent National Surveys." *Annals of the American Academy of Political and Social Science* 455 (May): 24–39.

Zaller, John, and Stanley Feldman. 1992. "A Simple Theory of the Survey Response: Answering Questions versus Revealing Preferences." *American Journal of Political Science* 36 (August): 579–616.

Zinsmeister, Karl. 2003. "Summary and Analysis of the First Iraq Poll." The American Enterprise Online, September 10. www.taemag.com/issues/articleID.17697/ article_detail.asp.

Zogby, John. 2008. "Polling the New Hampshire Primaries: What Happened?" www .huffingtonpost.com, January 9.

Zukin, Cliff. 2004. "Sources of Variation in Published Election Polling: A Primer." www .aapor.org/pdfs/varsource.pdf.

Index